BECOMING BLACK

BECOMING BLACK

Creating Identity in the African Diaspora

MICHELLE M. WRIGHT

DUKE UNIVERSITY PRESS   *Durham and London 2004*

© 2004

Duke University Press

All rights reserved

Printed in the United

States of America on

acid-free paper ∞

Designed by R. Giménez

Typeset in Adobe Minion

with Empire display by

Keystone Typesetting, Inc.

Library of Congress

Cataloging-in-Publication

Data appear on the last

printed page of

this book.

2nd printing, 2005

CONTENTS

ACKNOWLEDGMENTS

First and foremost, my thanks must go to Simon Gikandi and Marlon Ross, who served as cochairs of my dissertation committee and have always provided that genius of mentoring only a few possess. They allowed me to make my own mistakes and, after providing invaluable foundation, let me make my own way with this project and were always available for guidance and suggestions. They are not only intellectual mentors but also role models and precious friends. Alina Clej provided the intellectual roadmap for those heady poststructuralist critiques, sharpening my skills as a discourse analyst, and pushed me when I was ready to settle for merely adequate results. Yopie Prins, whom I have known since I was an undergraduate, spent precious hours not only aiding me in this project but also preparing me as a professional in the field. I must also thank Alan Wald, who was not part of my committee but may as well have been, given the time, advice, and support he has so generously donated without a second thought.

I owe equal gratitude to my editor, Ken Wissoker, whose calmness and ability kept me calm and able, and to his assistant Christine Dahlin, who is simply the ideal when it comes to getting impossible amounts of work done quickly and efficiently, not to mention flawlessly. My anonymous readers at Duke provided me with such detailed and intelligent reports that *Becoming Black* bears their indelible stamp, of which I am quite proud.

I will always be indebted for the intellectual support so generously given by Joe Trotter and Tera Hunter and for the financial support of the Center for Africanamerican Urban Studies and the Economy at Carnegie Mellon University. My former colleagues at CMU, Kathy Newman, Carol Hamilton, David Shumway, Kristina Straub, Jon and Nancy Klancher, Sharon Dilworth, and Susan McElroy were always on hand to swap disappointments and successes, as well as share ideas and offer sugges-tions. I also owe a great deal to my research assistant from my time at CMU, Amy Scerba, who, it seemed, could effortlessly produce reams of rare and undiscovered documents in response to my rather vague re-quests. My assistants here at Macalester, Anne Poduska and Jim Burk-land, possessed equally unflagging energy and resourcefulness, as well as an enviable equanimity in the face of looming deadlines and hundreds of pages of manuscript I have revised yet again. I have found wonderfully warm and supportive colleagues at Macalester and in the community at large: Jim Dawes, Baris Gumus, Stacey Margolis, Tonya Pollard, and Eleanor Courtemanche provided me not only with excellent written critiques on difficult sections of this book but then topped it off with an hours-long discussion session that energized me for the next round of rewrites. Peter Rachleff graciously read the whole manuscript and of-fered invaluable advice in the final stages. David Okamura-Wilson, Mary Trull, Laura Engel, Wang Ping, Duchess Harris, Tere Martinez, Jim Laine, Jim von Geldern, Beth Cleary, Sonita Sarker, Ahmed Samatar, Robert Warde, Tony Pinn, Leola Johnson, Karen Warren, Adrienne Christiansen, Karin Aguilar-San Juan, and my chair, Stuart McDougal, have also provided the kind of professional advice and personal support that is paradoxically both abundant and priceless. I also owe a substan-tial debt of gratitude to John Wright and Rod Ferguson at the University of Minnesota, who have helped sharpen some of the duller edges in my work.

I thank the day I met Mia Bay, with whom I have had many a fruitful and invaluable conversation and who was key, along with Simon Gikandi, in pointing me to Ken Wissoker. Without Tina Campt, my sections on Afro-German and Black British literature would have verged on the dreadful; she was as good as her word in letting me know I could contact her at any time for advice and information, and in the process has become a very dear friend. Great thanks as well to Peggy Pietsche and Annette Wierschke, who were instrumental in my introduction to Afro-German discourse in Germany. It was Ajuan Mance, a longtime friend and col-league, who introduced me to Carolyn Rodgers and shared her consider-able expertise on Black female poets in the United States, whether we were lunching in Bangkok, hiking to the train station in Stockholm, or buzzing around the Bay Area in a convertible. Alan Rice, Sabine Broeck, Dwight McBridge, Claudia Tate, Deborah Gray-White, Frieda Ekotto, Hazel

Carby, Chandan Reddy, George Elliott Clarke, Vera Kutzinksi, Virginia Tilley, and Dunbar Moodie have been wonderful colleagues and mentors, providing me with substantial opportunities to discuss and present drafts of my work both in the United States and abroad.

Research for this project was also supported by a University of Michigan Rackham predoctoral grant, a postdoctoral grant from the Mellon Foundation and Social Sciences and Research Council, as well as a Falk Award in the Humanities and a grant from the Faculty Development Fund at Carnegie Mellon University. Thanks to these granters, I was able to realize the larger comparative focus of this project.

Finally, I must thank my father, Wilbur I. Wright Sr., who taught me early on to defend my ideas and pursue my dreams, and my mother, Elaine Wright, who did not live long enough to see this work completed but never doubted it would be. My siblings, Gretchen Wright and Wilbur Ira Wright Jr., reminded me that I am human and it is okay to make mistakes. Far above everyone else, my partner Virginia Nugent has provided me with a measure of love, guidance, and support I doubt I deserve but will claim regardless.

INTRODUCTION

Being and Becoming Black in the West

In her prose poem "Blackness," from her 1992 collection of short stories *At the Bottom of the River*, Jamaica Kincaid describes the complex series of contradictions that produce Black identity in the West:

> The blackness is visible and yet it is invisible, for I see that I cannot see it. The blackness fills up a small room, a large field, an island, my own being. The blackness cannot bring me joy but often I am made glad in it. The blackness cannot be separated from me but often I can stand outside of it. The blackness is not the air, though I breathe it. The blackness is not the earth, though I drink and eat it. The blackness is not my blood, though it flows through my veins. The blackness enters my many-tiered spaces and soon the significant word and event recede and eventually vanish: in this way I am annihilated and my form becomes formless and I am absorbed into a vastness of free-flowing matter. In the blackness, then, I have been erased, I can no longer say my own name. I can no longer point to myself and say "I." In the blackness my voice is silent. First, then, I have been my individual self, carefully banishing randomness from my existence, then I am swallowed up in the blackness so that I am at one with it.[1]

I say "in the West" because Blackness only became a racial category with the forced removal of West Africans to the Western Hemisphere. From the start, Black identity has been produced in contradiction. Although there is no biological basis for racial categories (there is no such thing as a "black," "white," or "Asian" gene, and the amount of genetic disparity between persons of different races is the same as that between persons in the same racial category), Blacks in the West have nonetheless had their history shaped by the very concrete effects of Western racism. Unlike Black Africans, who ultimately define themselves through shared histories, languages, and cultural values, Blacks in the diaspora possess an intimidating array of different historical, cultural, national, ethnic, religious, and ancestral origins and influences. At the same time, despite this range of differences, they are most often identified in the West as simply "Black" and therefore as largely homogeneous. Given these contradictions, the attempt to offer an overarching definition for Blackness looks to be a losing game.

Yet what Kincaid posits here is less a definition of Blackness and more an examination of the "in between" space that Blackness seems to inhabit: within contradiction ("visible yet invisible"), the material and the abstract ("not the earth, though I walk on it"), and the struggle between Black identity's individual and collective aspects ("I am swallowed up in the blackness"). Above all else, what Kincaid's passage conveys is the inherent fluidity of Blackness and its ability both to harm and heal the Black individual.

For peoples of African descent living in majority-white nations in the West, the harmful and the healing potential of Black self-consciousness, or subjectivity, are both quite clear and quite real. Seeking to determine Black subjectivity in the African diaspora means constantly negotiating between two extremes. On one end stands the "blackness that swallows" (to adapt Kincaid), the hypercollective, essentialist identity, which provides the comfort of absolutist assertions in exchange for the total annihilation of the self. On the other end stands the hyperindividual identity, most commonly found in poststructuralist critiques of racism and colonialism, which grants a wholly individualized (and somewhat fragmented) self in exchange for the annihilation of "Blackness" as a collective term. Any truly accurate definition of an African diasporic identity, then, must somehow simultaneously incorporate the diversity of Black identities in the diaspora yet also link all those identities to show that they indeed constitute a diaspora rather than an unconnected aggregate of different peoples linked only in name.

Recent scholarly attempts to produce a history of Black or African diasporic self-consciousness in the West have tried to negotiate between these two extremes by linking different Black communities through a common historical moment or a shared cultural trope—usually one with West African origins. These efforts, as many critics have pointed out, have been only partially successful because there is no one historical moment or cultural trope to which one can link all of the African diasporic communities now living in the West. While an Afro-German will no doubt find the Middle Passage a significant event, it is not what brought him or her into Germany; in like kind, an Ibo woman or man of Maghrebi or East African origin is automatically located outside a Yoruba cultural trope that is nonetheless directly significant to many contemporary Caribbean and/or African American communities.

Historical moments or cultural tropes function for only a handful of specific communities and hence cannot function as tropes that might produce the African diasporic subject. A truly diasporic approach to Black subjectivity must not be ethnically specific yet must provide some sort of specificity. It must translate across languages and cultures yet not effect so much transformation as to be unrecognizable to other Black communities. Cultural traditions, historical traditions, and political traditions will therefore serve only limited use. An *intellectual* tradition however, is an entirely different matter. While scholars have scratched their heads over how to negotiate these extremes to produce Black self-consciousness, or subjectivity, for some decades now Black writers and thinkers living in the West have been producing their own answers. The first generation of theories, emerging in the first half of the twentieth century, were counterdiscourses that directly opposed nineteenth-century French, German, British, and American discourses, all of which posited the Black as Other to the white subject. The second generation of theories, beginning in the late 1960s, also countered the idea of a Black Other, at the same time dissenting from the inherently masculinist and nationalist constructions of the Black subject produced by the first generation.

In this book I argue that there is a twentieth-century intellectual tradition of African diasporic counterdiscourses of Black subjectivity that is defined not by a common history or a common cultural trope but by a particular theoretical *methodology*. In true diasporic tradition, this methodology moves between a variety of specific Western theoretical formations (specifically Hegelian and Marxist dialectics and Bakhtinian dialogics), but every single counterdiscourse that comprises this tradition understands Black subjectivity *as that which must be negotiated between the abstract and the real* or, in theoretical terms, between the ideal and the material. This tradition is also marked by three theoretical postulates: (1) while all theories of Black subjectivity directly counter those originary discourses that posited the Black as Other to the white subject, they must counter those Black Others in different ways because *not all Black Others are the same*; (2) while a theoretical model that stages subjectivity as a negotiation between *dual* dialectics—one idealist, one materialist—can produce a Black *male* subject that is part of the Western nation, those dual dialectics will produce an antithesis or Other that, when coupled with nationalist discourse, will inevitably produce the Black *female* as Other; (3) only the introduction of dialogic structures can subvert the fallacious arrangement of time and space on which nationalist discourse (and, consequently, the Black male subject) relies to bring the Black female subject into being. Even further, the introduction of a dialogic structure of subjectivity subverts those Black subject formations that rely on discretely bounded Others. This means that Black subjects who come into being through the dialogic cannot come into being through the Western nation, but only through a series of multivalent and intersected historical and cultural formations that I identify as the African diaspora.

In framing this tradition specifically as an African diasporic counter-discourse, my study locates itself within the existing African American and African diasporic scholastic tradition that underscores both the impossibility of ignoring the role of race in eighteenth- and nineteenth-century Western intellectual tradition and the impossibility of attempting to wholly segregate Black and white intellectual traditions in the West from one another. For example, both Henry Louis Gates Jr.'s *Figures in Black* and Paul Gilroy's *The Black Atlantic* show us not only the overriding importance the role of the Black Other played to (white) Western discourses of belonging, but the resulting centrality of Black counterdiscourses to the further exploration of these discourses of belonging as they intersect with questions of subjectivity, culture, modernity, and the nation. Through this particular understanding of Black counterdiscourse in the West, this study shares Gates's and Gilroy's use of counterdiscourse as a means of pointing to the ways in which Western concepts of the subject and the nation are both responding to Black experiences in the West.

Yet I depart from Gates and Gilroy in two important ways because I frame "Blackness" as a concept that cannot be (1) limited to a particular national, cultural, and linguistic border, or (2) produced in isolation from gender and sexuality. In *Figures in Black*, Gates argues that there are dangerous areas of conflation that must be avoided between "literary theory" and "the black idiom":

> I have turned to literary theory as a second circle. I have done this to preserve the integrity of black texts, by trying to avoid confusing my experiences as an Afro-American with the black act of language that defines a text. On the other hand, by learning to read a black text within a black formal cultural matrix and explicating it with the principles of criticism at work in both the Euro-American and the African-American traditions, I believe that we critics can identify and produce richer structures of meaning than are possible otherwise.
>
> This is the challenge of the critic of Afro-American literature: not to shy away from literary theory, but rather to translate it into the black idiom, renaming principles of criticism where appropriate, but especially naming indigenous black principles of criticism and applying these to explicate our own texts.[2]

This analysis of a counterdiscourse on the Black subject that compares subject formation across a range of sociopolitical categories (race, nation, gender, and sexuality) does and does not cohere with what Gates terms "indigenous black principles of criticism." Specifically, within this African diasporic tradition, two main tropes, the mask/veil and the Black mother, operate as theoretical arguments, neither consciously derived from nor deploying either a shared, homogeneous, or indigenous Black cultural form. A trope such as the mask/veil, while pointing to a common strategy, also ends up being deployed differently in different texts, therefore demonstrating that a shared black idiom is not necessarily synonymous with a shared Black identity. Even more striking, the Black mother is deployed by Black feminist writers to directly contravene the way in which this figure was demonized by both white discourse (the recently resurrected Moynihan Report) and Black nationalist discourse. Thus some idioms are deliberately deployed to signal dissent rather than compliance with the originary discourse's use of that trope.

As such, Gates's reliance on the term "black" to signify a homogeneous set of practices and/or experiences elides philosophical, cultural, and historical differences and, in insisting on either absolute difference or none, denies us a framework in which to understand "Blackness" as a unity of diversity. By producing a comparative analysis of how subject formations by African American, Afro-German, Black British, Black French, and Anglophone and Francophone writers countered those discourses that produced Blacks as Other to the (white) Western subject—an analysis that also looks at how gender and sexuality inform the construction of these diasporic subjects—this project seeks to understand how Black theories of subjectivity both differ and remain the same across the African diaspora.

In *The Black Atlantic* Gilroy at once offers a way of understanding "Blackness" across national borders and outside a homogeneous culture or ethnicity. He posits Blackness as something produced by and in opposition to a Western discourse that locates the Black as Other to the Western nation:

> My concern here is . . . exploring some of the special political problems that arise from the fatal junction of the concept of nationality with the concept of culture and the affinities and affiliations which link the blacks of the West to one of their adoptive, parental cultures: the intellectual heritage of the West since Enlightenment. I have become fascinated with how successive black intellectuals have understood this connection and how they have projected it in their writing and speaking in pursuit of freedom, citizenship, and social and political autonomy.[3]

Yet while Gilroy posits his exploration of the Black in the West through a discursive formation that speaks to both the ideal and material conditions of being Black in the West (located as Other yet also part of the Western nation), he limits his survey to mostly African American, heterosexual, and masculine norms, a subject formation that offers little difference from the white subject in the Western nation, with the exception of race. Yet the category of race can never be fully divorced from the related categories of gender and sexuality. The nationalist myth that produces a racial Other also insists on a heteropatriarchal structure wherein men and women who fail to conform to the idealized heterosexual relation of active male and passive female are also produced as Other. Countering Gilroy's claim, I show that the attempt to read one's status as Other to the nation through only *one* of the categories—namely, race—(re)produces the same structure of exclusions with a Black subject reliant on Black Others in order to come into being. As such, this text understands "Blackness" as a social category produced in relation to both gender and sex categories. In line with this critique, it is only when we see Black subjectivities produced through, rather than in exclusion to, these categories do we arrive at theories of the Black subject that successfully negotiate the ideal and material formations that must predicate Black subject formation.

OTHERS FROM WITHIN AND FROM WITHOUT

In his book written with Immanuel Wallerstein, *Race, Class, and Nation*, Etienne Balibar offers the formulation of "internal" and "external" Others to point to the ways in which members of the Jewish and African diasporas in the West face different types of racism and must therefore amass different sets of strategies. Even peoples defined by the *same* racial category can be rendered Other in *different* ways. In looking at Black populations in the West, the first difference we encounter is between those blacks brought into the "home space" of the colonizer—African Americans—and those who were brought to a "third space"—the Caribbean—in which neither blacks nor whites originally understood that space as their "home."[4] Although in this book I focus almost exclusively on the Anglophone, Francophone, and Germanophone populations of the African diaspora, I also hold that the relationship between those populations and their West African colleagues, allies, and comrades means we must also consider a third type of placement, namely Black Africans being colonized within their own home space by European military, political, and economic powers. In addition, this study argues that contemporary Black populations in France, Germany, and Britain all possess different immigrant histories, not only in terms of their chronological history, physical placement, and the racial discourses in each that sought to interpellate them, but also in the ways they have subverted, resisted, or otherwise reacted against those discourses.

I begin by examining those nineteenth-century discourses on the white subject and Black Other that were directly and/or explicitly responded to by the first set of twentieth-century African diasporic theorists. The different spatial relationships perceived by the authors *and* the sociopolitical agendas underlying their originary discourses were central to the development of the different Black Others we see in each text. Thomas Jefferson, whose notion of a "veil" of Blackness is articulated in

Notes on the State of Virginia, posits the "Negro" as a malevolent force that may physically reside within the nation yet remains psychically Other to that nation, not unlike a nasty virus on the national body whose sole aim, as dictated by nature, is to weaken and ultimately destroy that nation.[5] This is one form of the Other-from-within. While mostly specific to the relatively unique American idiom, where Africans were brought into the home space of the colonizer, it is not always used in African American counterdiscourses of the subject. As I will later demonstrate, the Other-from-within was also used in other African diasporic counterdiscourses.

In the introduction to his widely influential work *Philosophie der Geschichte* (Philosophy of History), G. W. F. Hegel famously posits that the "Negro" stands outside analytical history—namely, that history of intellectual, technological, moral, and cultural progress guided by the Absolute of reason. Yet *implicitly*, Hegel deploys that African, or Negro, as the exact antithesis of the white European (or, more specifically, German) subject. I argue that this is the central and ultimately confusing paradox that defines the Other-from-without: that Other's existence is consistently denied any role of importance, and yet its implied inferiority is the crux of Europeans' arguments for their ostensibly self-evident superiority. While Hegel was specifically describing Africans, his comments on the slave trade (that it was most likely the only way Africans would learn to appreciate freedom and thus develop into subjects) strongly suggest that his opinions extended to all members of the African diaspora.[6] Unlike the Other-from-within, whose unbearable proximity posits an immediate and inexcusable danger to resident whites, I argue that the Other-from-without represents a challenge to the European seeking to secure subject status by exercising his will to power. To defeat and colonize Africans and Africa, Hegel holds, in both *Philosophy of History* and *Philosophy of Right*, is the prerogative of the European, who is largely defined by the will to power. The Other-from-without is the European's antithesis, and defeating this Other inevitably leads to synthesis, or the constitution of the European subject par excellence.

LOGICAL FALLACIES

Following Hegel, the foundation for all Western theories of subjectivity is the dialectic, and, more specifically, a dialectic driven by *Aufhebung*, or the dynamic of upheaval in which inferior beings, cultures, and civilizations are overthrown by those that are superior. In the three discourses on (white, male) European subjectivity on which this book focuses—those of Georg Wilhelm Friedrich Hegel, Count Arthur de Gobineau (aka the Father of Modern Racism), and Thomas Jefferson—I posit that the role of the Negro is preordained: he will be Other to the white subject. At the same time, I show how, even though the crucial role of this Negro or African Other (the two often share the same definition in these texts as an inferior species intrinsically foreign to Western culture and civilization) is implicit within the text, he cannot be so forceful or so strong as to potentially challenge the ostensibly superior white subject. In the attempt to use the Negro Other as an anchor *and* deny his centrality to the formation of the white subject, I show how a logical fallacy develops in all of these dialectical discourses on the white subject and Black Other. Dialectically speaking, this fallacy is what Friedrich Engels later defined as the "negation of the negation" for specific types of *Aufhebung*-driven dialectics, where the antithesis is wholly negated by the thesis with the result that the synthesis is, in fact, no different from the thesis. All of these dialectics begin with a Negro Other and the white subject who together compose an interdependent dichotomy, a dichotomy that is then denied so that the white subject can retroactively be posited as wholly independent in his derivation—a seeming corollary that is in fact essential to the Western concept of the subject as a wholly self-actualized individual.

In theorizing these first and subsequent counterdiscourses on the Black subject, I show how Engels is not the only one to notice this logical fallacy: the earliest revisions of Hegel's, Gobineau's, and Jefferson's theories can be found in W. E. B. Du Bois's *Souls of Black Folk*, the Negritudist poetry of Aimé Césaire and Léopold Sédar Senghor, and in Frantz Fanon's *Peau noire, masques blancs* (Black Skin, White Masks). In some cases this negation of the negation is located, identified, and then "corrected" by producing a synthesis composed of *both* thesis *and* antithesis, rather than just the former. I posit that Du Bois produces the "Negro American" subject who, as the term makes clear, is the result of a *synthesis* between Negro and (white) American consciousness, while Césaire's Creole subject achieves consciousness by *recognizing* himself as the *result* of synthesis. At the same time, I show how other counterdiscourses take other paths in their examination of this false dialectic, where the synthesis is nothing more than the thesis. Senghor rejects Hegel's argument that reason is the Absolute, or the ultimate driving force for progress in the world (through which his dialectic of the subject is ultimately derived), instead arguing that the word, or the expression of ideas, is the guiding force for progress. In his masking poems, Senghor holds that the African, not the European, subject is the first and most perfect embodiment of this Absolute. Frantz Fanon moves in the opposite direction, first by asserting that the Antillean *is* the "negation of the negation," a Black skin in a white mask, because he is only able to speak himself through the colonizer's language, a language in which he is always already Other. Fanon, I posit, then points out that there *are* blacks who *have* achieved subject status, and they have done so through this same dialectic by *acting* rather than speaking—through *Aufhebung*, upheaval through revolt, resistance, and revolution. These Blacks, then, become the thesis that wholly overwhelms the colonizer's antithesis, a thesis that wholly negates their negation, and therefore a thesis that *is* synthesis, a wholly Black consciousness, a wholly Black subject status.

LOGICAL PHALLACIES

My project holds that these first counterdiscourses are linked by the common goal of securing subject status for the Black through the same logical processes used by the originary discourses: the dialectic. I argue that by working within the same theoretical idiom of the discourses of Jefferson, Hegel, and Gobineau, Du Bois, Césaire, Fanon—and to a lesser degree Senghor—are able to show that the Black cannot only become a subject, he can be a subject *within* Western civilization—or, more specifically (again with the exception of Senghor), the nation. I argue that because at the time these African diasporic thinkers were writing (the first half of the twentieth century), Blacks in the West were fighting for the full rights of citizenship and/or sovereignty from their colonizers, it was therefore crucial to show that the Black individual deserved to be a full citizen within the Western nation and/or that the Black collective deserved to be recognized as a nation.

Yet the discourse of the modern nation—from its inception in the eighteenth century and in many ways even today—operates on a series of heteropatriarchal assumptions buoyed by an equally heteropatriarchal rhetoric in which the national polity is composed of active (male) and passive (female) members: the former lead, make laws, and otherwise protect the latter, who devote their lives to serving and obeying the former. As a result, I argue, the counterdiscourses of Du Bois, Césaire, Fanon, and Senghor speak of the Black subject only as "he" and allocate to that subject full agency, leaving little room for (and even less discussion of) the Black female subject. It is important to note that Du Bois was a staunch champion for women's rights in his lifetime; even so, the rhetoric he deploys in *Souls of Black Folk* assumes the Black subject as always already male and thus one who, as that active agent, possesses the power to give birth to other subjects. Senghor, no particular champion of female suffrage, goes further by equating the Black feminine with deception. Du Bois, like Césaire and Fanon, also relies on heteropatriarchal metaphors to construct moments at which the Black realizes he is Other within the nation. All three construct this moment, I argue, as one in which the white female, as the nation, rejects the Black male (on the authority of the white male, who frames each anecdote in the form of modernity and/or progress). Black women, when they do appear in these texts, are background objects and therefore are placed even lower than the white female, who is at least granted some agency.

Du Bois, Césaire, Senghor, and Fanon are able to construct counterdiscourses within the same dialectic idiom used by Jefferson, Hegel, and Gobineau because they are able to point to the contradictory role played by the Black male as the negation of the white thesis who is then himself negated. While Jefferson's, Hegel's, and Gobineau's dialectics ignore white women, white women, as symbolic of the white Western nation, exist in Du Bois's, Césaire's, Senghor's, and Fanon's dialectics of the Black subject and thus could produce themselves as subjects much in the same way that these first counterdiscourses move the Black male from antithesis to synthesis. Wholly outside the dialectic, the Black female, I hold, does not have the same options.

In the late 1960s, Black nationalist and Black Arts movement writers such as Larry Neal, Amiri Baraka, and Eldridge Cleaver made explicit associations between the Black feminine and slavery and posited the Black female as helpmate, not equal partner, to the Black male subject. Although many Black female writers in these movements did not explicitly challenge this sociopolitical philosophy, counterdiscourses to it do exist, two of the most striking coming from Audre Lorde, the famed Black lesbian activist, and Carolyn Rodgers, a Black poet who achieved national recognition for her work toward the end of the Black Arts movement. What makes these counterdiscourses so striking is the way in which Lorde and Rodgers introduce another theoretical idiom to contest the dialectic of the Black male subject: Mikhail Bakhtin's dialogic critique of the dialectic in which Michael Holquist identifies as the "simplest chronotope," or the fallacious deployment of time and space by the dialectic. While Bakhtin used the critique of the "simplest time chronotope" to dissent from narrative structures in which the protagonist can control and order time, Rodgers's and Lorde's discourses counter that chronotope's inherently masculinist view. Like many other nationalist narratives in the West, the Black nationalist narrative posits a world in which men possess the power to give birth (to other men, of course!) and therefore to construct a linear progression of time and space that starts and stops when they want. I argue that whether explicitly, as in Du Bois, or implicitly, as in Césaire, Senghor, and Fanon, the first counterdiscourses of subjectivity (re)produce a patriarchal worldview in which men give birth to men, or the one produces the one.

Black feminist theorists such as Mae Gwendolyn Henderson and Madhu Dubey have pointed to the ways in which the negative construction of the Black mother can be at least partially recuperated to produce a Black female subject. I examine how Audre Lorde and Carolyn Rodgers directly deploy the Black mother as a trope that highlights this fallacy of a nation of men giving birth to other men and the necessity of acknowledging the active role of the Black female in both subject construction and the nation so as to bring the Black female into being. As a trope the Black mother can accomplish many things at once: it can subvert the nationalist myth of discretely bounded subjects produced from the one; subvert the nationalist myth of discretely bounded racial groups in which Black subjects only produce Black subjects and white subjects only produce white subjects; and, finally, subvert the nationalist construction of the mother as a heterosexual, passive conduit for active male seed that will (re)produce other heterosexual male subjects.

In the last chapter of this book, I explore how African diasporic male and female writers who follow Lorde and Rodgers also deploy critiques of both white and Black forms of nationalism, moving toward a concept of the Black subject that is neither always already male nor always already understood as part of a national collective. Instead, the diaspora, as a dialogic formation in which many subjectivities exist that cannot be organized into thetical and antithetical categories, becomes the formation par excellence of the subject, bringing us back to (and, chronologically speaking, up to), the cross-cultural collective imagined in Paul Gilroy's *The Black Atlantic*.

The texts I discuss range from dense philosophical treatises to experimental poetry, and I read them through a range of dialectic and dialogic subject formations to show how this tradition of African diasporic counterdiscourses on the subject is not only directly engaged with those European discourses of the white subject and Black Other but in fact subverts and revises some of their most central tenets. Through this methodology, I show how African diasporic theories of subjectivity, although often ignored or misrecognized as works of fiction bereft of theoretical content, are an undeniable part of the nineteenth- and twentieth-century theories of subjectivity.

Thomas Jefferson's *Notes on the State of Virginia*, G. W. F. Hegel's *Philosophy of History*, and Count Arthur de Gobineau's *Essai sur l'inégalité des races humaines* (Essay on the Inequality of the Human Races) deploy a dialectic structure in which the white thesis overcomes the Black antithesis and achieves thesis-as-synthesis subjectivity. All three are also the explicit and/or implicit focus of the counterdiscourses we find in W. E. B. Du Bois, Aimé Césaire, Léopold Sédar Senghor, and Frantz Fanon. The respective constructions by Jefferson, Hegel, and Gobineau of the Black as either an Other-from-within or an Other-from-without produce different variations of Black Others (and white subjects) that are important to understanding the variations in Black subject construction that are ultimately derived from these original discourses.

Chapter 1, "The European and American Invention of the African Other," begins with Hegel's introduction to *The Philosophy of History*, as it offers the most explicit and detailed blueprint of the dialectic of subjectivity. This introduction is famous because it asserts the three main points with which colonialist discourse justified its right to invade the sovereign territories of non-European nations, usurp the rights of non-Europeans, and exploit both specifically Black territory and Black bodies for its own political, material, and social gain. Hegel argues that, of the three different types of history (chronological history, or the simple passing of time; philosophical history, or the examination of the *idea* of history; and analytical history), the last is the one that concerns theories of subjectivity because it is the history of intellectual, technological, and moral progress—and the history that Africa and Africans stand utterly outside. Standing outside this history, Africa remains mired in a primitive past, one lacking an understanding of freedom—that which should ultimately distinguish humans from animals. As "proof" of this exaggerated claim (he himself never traveled to the African continent), Hegel relies on largely undocumented anecdotes, tales of foolishness, ignorance, and mayhem on the part of Africans. Through these anecdotes, I argue, Hegel draws a neat dichotomy between the African and the European: whereas the former is driven by inhuman desires and irrational thought processes, the latter is driven by only the fully human desire for improvement and progress, rational thought processes that prove themselves as rational through their material embodiment in organized forms of government, sophisticated social systems, as well as scientific and technological prowess. Hegel's Negro Other is an Other-from-without: located in Africa and hardly an immediate threat to the German or European polity (indeed, as the anecdotes clearly indicate, the African is in fact only a threat to his fellow African). Instead, this Other serves as an *opportunity* for both German expansion and the initiation of African progress: because the subject is guided by reason, his rational thoughts achieve embodiment through the acquisition of property and wealth. As Tsenay Serequeberhan notes in "The Idea of Colonialism and Hegel's Philosophy of Right," Hegel suggests that Africa, as a land in which irrational beings live but do not progress, serves as the perfect opportunity for both German expansion and African progress.

African progress? Hegel's racist rhetoric posits that the African Other is an empty vessel, devoid of any use value—but it does allow that perhaps one day the African can achieve subject status. The means by which he might achieve this status, Hegel explains, is the dialectic of "freedom" (which is perhaps best understood as "free will" in order to mark it as distinctively human). In order to comprehend and thus achieve free will, the hallmark of the subject, the African must first learn what it means to be deprived of that freedom—and what better opportunity for that than to be enslaved by the (white) subject? This is the hallmark of the Other-from-without: because Hegel's subject is guided by reason, through which he realizes what he desires (also known as the will to power), it logically follows that his antithesis is incapable of harnessing any sort of thought process to a concrete goal. The European subject possesses logos, or the ability to apprehend an abstract concept, enunciate it, and thus bring it into realization. The white German subject's Other, the Other-from-without, lacks this logos and can only hope to achieve it (and thus subject status) by being deprived of his freedom. Only by being enslaved, Hegel argues, will the Black develop an appreciation for freedom, and thus the disciplined ability to think, enunciate that thought, and act on it.

While separated by a continent, Hegel's Other-from-without is nonetheless valuable to the German subject, not only for the lands and their natural resources he has failed to develop but for the cheap labor he offers his white superiors. While Gobineau's Aryan subject in *Essay on the Inequality of the Human Races* is also dialectically determined against a Negro antithesis (in fact, Gobineau explicitly identifies himself as a Hegelian), Gobineau's agenda is quite different from Hegel's. Hegel celebrates the progressive spirit of European civilization; Gobineau laments the decline of "Aryan civilization," which he attributes to the decline of the European aristocracy and the rise to power of the lesser classes. In fact, as Michael Biddiss has pointed out, Gobineau's theorization of the supposed intrinsic nature of racial difference is ultimately intended as a metaphor to explain the supposedly biological roots of class differences. Indeed, Gobineau's willingness to place the "African chieftain" above the French peasant and even perhaps the French bourgeois—in addition to his insistence that the Aryan lacks the artistic temperament that is the sole possession of the Negro—underlines his willingness to posit class as a more accurate signifier for inherent differences of ability than race. As I will demonstrate, this complex and contradictory reading of racial difference makes Gobineau central to the Negritude counterdiscourses of Aimé Césaire and Léopold Senghor. This does not, however, mean that Gobineau's depiction of the Negro is somehow more fair-minded than Hegel's: instead, like Hegel, Gobineau asserts that the African races are the most inferior and, to the artistic temperament with which he accredits those races, he adds the irrational lusts of the savage for violence, blood, and sex—the same lack of reason and civilized feeling that Hegel asserted. Gobineau speaks of the Negro in Africa and in the Caribbean despite the vivid presence of Blacks in nineteenth-century France's major port cities and urban centers, including Nice, Marseilles, and Paris. Nonetheless, his Negro Other is an Other-from-within because its cruel, violent, and oversexed nature poses a direct threat to the relative purity of the Aryan subject and Aryan civilization.

Anticipating Hegel's and Gobineau's formulations by several decades, Thomas Jefferson's Negro Other shares many of the same qualities. Intent on defining an American nation in which whites are subjects (and American Indians a race that might be integrated into the nation with proper education and a firm hand), Jefferson also constructs an Other-from-within. In an attempt to posit America's Black population—a cornerstone to the rapidly expanding American economy whose arrival dates almost as far back as that of the oldest white American families—as nonetheless foreign to the nation, Jefferson argues that nature, rather than white slavers, plantation owners, and legislators, has made the Negro a slave.[7] Jefferson proceeds to construct "blackness" as a *thing* rather than a shade of color, using the metaphor of the veil as nature's marker of inferiority, an ultimately unknown quantity that nonetheless covers the Negro's face and therefore with it the visage of humanity.

While counterdiscourses on the Black subject are an inarguably effective means of negating discourses on the Black Other, their potency is always already partially compromised by the simple fact that they must engage with the parameters set by the latter, regardless of the often fantastic claims made by that originary discourse. Chapter 2, "The Trope of Masking in the Works of W. E. B. Du Bois, Léopold Sédar Senghor, and Aimé Césaire," argues that this first group of counterdiscourses shares a specific set of strategies best understood through the trope of masking. I argue that Du Bois's use of the veil, Césaire's use of ventriloquism, and Senghor's use of the "African mask" are all masking devices that highlight the logical fallacies in Hegel's, Gobineau's, and/or Jefferson's discourses on the dialectic of the white subject and Black Other. More specifically, these first African diasporic counterdiscourses use masking to signal the fallacy of the "negation of the negation" on which racist dialectics rely.

Friedrich Engel's critique of the "negation of the negation" is the defining difference between idealist and materialist dialectics. As Engels points out, idealist dialectics simplify the moment of negation by wholly erasing its presence at the moment of synthesis. Fully fleshed out in Karl Marx's *Eighteenth Brumaire*, Marxist theory has argued that the moment of negation—as evinced in actual social revolutions—is far more complicated. While revolutionaries may succeed in overthrowing a regime, the result of this overthrow cannot wholly erase the power and influence accumulated by the defeated regime: its foreign and domestic allies, administrative expertise, and other effects all remain to some degree or another. Within the specific idiom of discourses and counter-discourses of subjectivity, Du Bois, Césaire, and Senghor all deploy variations of this argument by engaging with *both* idealist and materialist dialectics. In these counterdiscourses, all three men point to how the Black must negotiate between the racist discourse of the idealist dialectic that produces them as Other and the reality of the materialist dialectic in which they are subjects within Western regimes and cultures that view them and act on them as Other. In *The Souls of Black Folk*, Du Bois's famous trope of the veil has many manifestations: an infant's caul, a geographical border, double consciousness, and white racist beliefs, to name a few. Yet, as I demonstrate, these different manifestations all operate in the same way if we understand the veil as symbolic of the negotiation his Negro American subject must make between idealist and materialist dialectics.

Léopold Senghor uses the trope of the African mask to symbolize a similar negotiation, signifying both the existence of an "African" culture and history that predate Western civilization and the fallacy inherent within the idealist dialectic on the Black Other that asserts the originary status of Western civilization *and* its superiority over African civilization due to the supposed primacy of the white over the Black. In like kind, Aimé Césaire's *Cahier d'un retour au pays natal* (Notebook of a Return to My Native Land) uses the act of ventriloquism to symbolize the dizzying paradox of the Creole subject who is so familiar with the discourse of his negation that he can enunciate it better than the white subject—at once signaling the way in which he is viewed as Other even as he performs as a speaking subject.

At the same time, Du Bois, Césaire, and Senghor produce different Black subjects through their use of masking—differences that speak directly to both the particular way in which these Black thinkers understand the relationship of the Black to the West and the specific way in which they are Othered by idealist dialectics. In *Souls*'s dialectic of the Negro American subject, Du Bois replaces one Hegelian dialectic drive—the *Aufhebung*, or upheaval of the Black Other by the white subject—

with the drive of *Sehnsucht*, or longing, in which thesis and antithesis merge to produce synthesis—in this case the Negro and the American sides of the Negro American subject. I show how Du Bois's agenda is explicit from the first pages of *Souls*: he wants to demonstrate that the Negro American is not an intrinsically malevolent and dangerous Other-from-within, as Jefferson had signified through his use of the veil, but a subject who is being Othered by white American racism. In an era where Hegel's theories dominated American philosophical discourse, Du Bois does not reject Hegel but in fact uses Hegelian logic to show that the Negro American *can* attain true self-consciousness (an idea Hegel explicitly entertains in his *Philosophy of History*), but this consciousness is constantly imperiled by a racism that actively seeks to block the dialectic of progress, where synthesis would grant the Black subject status in the West. In short, Du Bois's theory of the Negro American counters Jefferson's discourse of the Other-from-within with the Hegelian dialectic driven by *Sehnsucht*, in this case the longing to become a subject in the West.

Senghor's and Césaire's counterdiscourses use a very different tactic, namely, Gobineau's assertion of the Negro's artistic drive and the Aryan's lack thereof, to counter Hegel's discourse of the Other-from-without. They counter Hegel's assertion that the Negro Other stands outside analytical history, bereft of culture, progress, and civilization, with a significant revision of Gobineau's discourse of the Negro Other. Senghor deploys his trope of the African mask to indicate a signifying chain through Gobineau: if the Negro race is the sole possessor of the artistic drive, then the Negro is the true creator of the word. This is a far greater and more universal Absolute than Hegel's Absolute of reason, he argues, because the word is the expression of *all* ideas, of which reason is an obvious subsidiary, being the expression of only one specific idea. In short, Senghor trumps Hegel's Absolute with the one unwittingly bequeathed to him by Gobineau, reordering the signifying chain of Hegel's discourse to bring the African and African civilization squarely within the realm of analytical history. Césaire also uses Gobineau's assertion of the Negro's artistic ability to negate Hegel's discourse of the Negro as an Other-from-without, but he does so by concentrating on Hegel's assertion that the Negro Other lacks logos. In *Cahier*, Césaire deploys a complex system of language that is at once French and *more* than French—a synthesis or merger of French colonialist discourse and the lived reality of the Martinican Creole. Césaire's protagonist in *Cahier* demonstrates a deft use of logos, able to master French colonialist discourse—and thus to negate its central tenet of the Negro lacking logos. Not unlike Du Bois, Césaire's Creole subject is a merger of the French colonialist culture in which he was raised and his native Martinican culture, which at once incorporates that influence and embraces a painful and triumphant history of domination and resistance. As his neologisms, Creolisms, and complex vocabulary demonstrate, the Creole subject possesses a far more complex logos than that of the white subject, because the former's logos is the complex negotiation between idealist *and* materialist dialectics.

Yet it is important to note that Du Bois's discourse of the Negro American subject is not selfsame with any and all counterdiscourses of African American subjectivity, nor are Senghor's and Césaire's counterdiscourses selfsame with Francophone African counterdiscourses and Francophone Caribbean counterdiscourses respectively. Rather, the nature of these counterdiscourses speaks less to the material circumstances of oppression in which each of the authors found himself than to the individual philosophies espoused by each as to the relationship between the Black and the West. Perhaps the most memorable example of the antistructuralist nature of counterdiscursive formation can be found in Frantz Fanon's theory of the Black subject. Although Fanon, like Césaire, was born and raised in Martinique and educated in France, his theory of the Black subject not only differs radically from that of his compatriot, it inspired a new generation of Black activists throughout the African diaspora who, despite their diverse backgrounds, nonetheless came to embrace Fanon's counterdiscourse as the *only* solution to ending white oppression.

Fanon's theory of the Black subject found in *Black Skin, White Masks*, and its relationship to the Black Power movement is the focus of chapter 3, "Some Women Disappear: Frantz Fanon's Legacy in Black Nationalist Thought and the Black (Male) Subject," where I argue that although Fanon's deployment of the masking trope is noticeably different from that of his predecessors, he nonetheless commits the same critical logical fallacy as his predecessors, from Hegel to Césaire, which assumes national formation within an idealist dialectic. The last half of the chapter focuses on this logical fallacy (again stemming from the negation of the negation) that erases the possibility of a female subject and forces us to look toward dialogic/diasporic subject formations to recuperate the Black female as a subject.

Postcolonial discourses of the subject, whether focused on South Asian and/or African diasporic formations, often cite *Black Skin, White Masks* as an example of the totalizing effects of colonialist discourse in which we are forced to wonder, as Gayatri Spivak so famously put it, if the subaltern can speak. Unlike his predecessors, Fanon does not use the trope of masking to signal the idealist and materialist dialectics that the Black subject must negotiate in order to come into being. While, like Césaire, Fanon focuses on Hegel's question of logos, he diverges from Césaire by arguing that the Black Martinican is *only* able to express himself through colonialist discourse. Fanon goes on to assert that this "speech act" does not signal the Black's mastery of logos but in fact signifies the "white mask" that allows the Black only to speak of himself as Other. In short, the idealist dialectic is not a fallacy but the inevitable conclusion for the colonized Black who seeks subject status through the colonizer's language. Yet Fanon's insistence on the hopelessness of achieving subject status through the idealist dialectic does not, as many critics have assumed, conclude his counterdiscourse on the Black subject. Instead, Fanon uses the trope of the white mask to underscore the need for the Black to reject the idealist dialectic of the colonizer's discourse in favor of the materialist dialectic of *action*. In a fascinating twist, Fanon counters Hegel's discourse on the Negro Other with Marxian *and* Hegelian dialectics. Not all Blacks, Fanon points out, have failed to achieve subject status —only those who did not achieve their freedom through *Aufhebung*, or upheaval against their white oppressors. In other words, the way to achieve subject status is to embrace the materialist dialectic of action. The dialectic drive of upheaval remains the same, but the dialectic itself changes.

Unsurprisingly, Fanon's counterdiscourse of the Black subject realized through the action of *Aufhebung* found great resonance in the 1960s and 1970s American Black nationalist movement, because it offered both an explanation for the "failure" of the civil rights movement and an attractive solution of Black self-reliance. At the same time, Fanon's theory is not so radically different from those of his predecessors if we look at the heteropatriarchal nationalist rhetoric on which it is predicated, best exemplified in the strikingly similar ways Du Bois, Césaire, and Fanon narrate the moment at which the Black comes to realize he is read and acted on as Other in Western discourse. I posit that *Souls, Notebook,* and *Black Skin, White Masks* all structure this moment as one in which a white female rejects the Black male, a deliberate revision of the Western nationalist metaphor that posits the Western patria as the white female who must be protected against the Black male Other by the white male citizen. While the critique these anecdotes make is clear—the Black male is *misrecognized* as an interloper by the racist white female—they fail to question the heteropatriarchal discourse undergirding this nationalist rhetoric, one in which only men may claim a positive agency, white women must remain passive, and Black women do not exist. To use a phrase from a French thriller produced at the time of Fanon's writing, *des femmes disparaissent* (some women disappear).

Yet, just as Du Bois, Césaire, Senghor, and Fanon focus on the negation of the negation in the idealist dialectic to produce counterdiscourses of the Black (male) subject, chapter 4, *"How I Got Ovah*: Masking to Motherhood and the Diasporic Black Female Subject," argues that the counterdiscourses on the Black female subject use the same tack by focusing on the fallacy on which Black nationalist discourse relies. While figures of the Black mother abound in African American women's novels at the time (perhaps most famously in Toni Morrison's *The Bluest Eye* and Gayle Jones's *Corregidora*), it is in Carolyn Rodgers's critically acclaimed collection *How I Got Ovah* and Audre Lorde's famous collections *Coal* and *The Black Unicorn* that the trope of the Black mother is deployed to signal the fallacy inherent in the Black nationalist subject, Bakhtin's "adventure time," or the "simplest time chronotope."

While not explicitly nationalist, Du Bois, Césaire, and Fanon all assume the nation as the collective identity for both white and Black subjects. This is hardly surprising, given that Hegel's, Gobineau's, and Jefferson's theories of the subject implicitly or explicitly posit the nation as a collective subjectivity—hence the need to locate, identify, and expunge those who are "Other" to the national body. Yet, in building on rather than negating this formulation, their subjects are always already gendered as male because nationalist rhetoric explicitly denies agency to the female (or, as we see in these first counterdiscourses, [re]produces the white female as irrational agent). As a result, I argue, counterdiscourses seeking to produce the Black female as a subject are faced with a conundrum: while the fallacy inherent in nationalist thought is clear (one cannot negate the fact that only women can give birth, and thus possess at least *some* agency), there is no "Black female Other" in this dialectic through which one might point to the idealist fallacy and produce a Black female subject. In other words, how do you counter a counterdiscourse in which you are effectively erased, in which you simply do not exist?

Both Rodgers and Lorde answer this question by using the Black mother as a version of Bakhtin's "adventure time" critique on which the Black nationalist subject relies. Both Rodgers and Lorde deploy the trope of the Black mother within the frame of a mother and daughter dyad to show three things: that the Black male subject cannot be the sole possessor of agency because he alone cannot create other subjects; that all subjectivities are therefore "intersubjective" in that they come into being through other subjects, not apart from them; that because all subjects are intersubjective, subjectivity cannot be produced dialectically, as thetical and antithetical relations do not exist. Yet, even as both women share the same agenda of producing Black female subjects, their reading of the subject differs in important ways. Unlike the earlier counterdiscourses, Rodgers's collection of poetry *How I Got Ovah* eschews the dialectical development of the subject and replaces it with a dialogic structure in which the conflated subjectivities of mother and daughter are produced as both distinct and shared, where consciousness is achieved through an encounter between thesis and antithesis but endlessly (re)produced and lost through each intersubjective encounter.

However, my analysis also points out that Rodgers does not question the heterosexist assumption of nationalist discourse, thus implicitly allowing only two possible definitions for intersubjective relations that are always already heterosexualized: through the reproductive metaphor of the mother and daughter, or the heterosexual relationship between men and women. While Rodgers's trope of the Black mother enables Black female subjectivity, it effectively heterosexualizes "intersubjectivity," leaving little space, if any, for the queer Black subject.

As we might expect from one of the most influential Black, Caribbean, and lesbian theorists of the African diaspora, Audre Lorde's trope of the Black mother imagines a different means through which the Black female subject can be realized. I argue that while Rodgers's counterdiscourse focuses on Black nationalism's patriarchal fallacy of a dialectically derived —and therefore discretely bounded—subject who is always already male, in both *Coal* and *The Black Unicorn* Lorde's counterdiscourse engages with the idealist fallacy that undergirds heteropatriarchal discourse. My analysis shows how Lorde's use of the Black mother is similar to Senghor's use of the African mask in that she deploys it to disrupt the *signifying chain* on which heteropatriarchal discourse relies. Just as Senghor's mask symbolizes African culture and civilization that exists before and during (and, as he hints, most likely after) colonialism, Lorde's Black mother symbolizes the idealist fallacy of a masculine thesis, and therefore the fallacy of *any* originary thesis—a "chicken-or-egg?" defense, if you will.

Through this particular deployment, Rodgers, like Lorde, asserts the intersubjective nature of all subjectivities, yet by producing her Black mother outside a heterosexist framework through queer mothers, adoptive mothers, and symbolic mothers, Lorde effectively negates Rodgers's equation between the production of the subject and heterosexual sex. By highlighting the fallacy of Black nationalism's "simplest time chronotope" in favor of a Black mother that signifies a more complex chronotope of the intersubject, in which space and time are not linear but circular, I show how Rodgers and Lorde also move away (implicitly and explicitly respectively) from the construct of the nation as the collective identity of subjectivity. Because *How I Got Ovah, Coal,* and *The Black Unicorn* reject dialectical formations (which in turn ultimately rely on discretely bounded notions of the thesis and antithesis), in favor of the intersubjective chronotope where space and time are always already conflated, the collective identity of the intersubject is also conflated, moving from the discrete boundaries of the nation to the infinitely more complex conflated space and time of the African diaspora.

Rodgers, but more explicitly Lorde, points to the African diaspora as a complex space in which different types of Black intersubjects coexist. In chapter 5, "The Urban Diaspora: Black Subjectivities in Berlin, London, and Paris," I show how contemporary Black writers in Germany, Britain, and France both advance this notion and (re)formulate it. Echoing the way in which the first generation of counterdiscourses deploys the mask to signal the negotiation between the idealist nature of racist discourse and the materialist reality of existing as a subject who is viewed as Other, all the writers discussed in that chapter use the urban setting as a space in which the Black subject must negotiate between the idealist discourse of a discretely bounded nation possessing discretely bounded racial and gender categories, and a "diasporic" reality, if you will, in which time, space, gender, and race conflate in both dizzying and frustrating ways.

While the counterdiscourses emerging from three distinct communities in the form of essays, biographies, poetry, and novels can be understood as sharing a common insight into the complex reality the diasporic Black must negotiate, it would be dangerous to understand these communities as selfsame with one another, or as an aggregate counterpoint to African American counterdiscourses on the Black subject. I organize chapter 5 into three sections—unavoidably reifying the notion of discretely bounded cultural and national identities—so as to prevent the greater error of implicitly assuming a homogeneous, transcendental notion of "Blackness" that is impervious to material conditions and individual interpretations. In the first section, "The Impossible Minority: Afro-Germans," I interpellate my analysis of Afro-German counterdiscourses through the relatively unique historical and cultural conditions that produce, I argue, an Other-from-within who is misread as an Other-from-without. More specifically, I show how Afro-Germans, largely the product of interracial liaisons or marriages and born within all-white German communities that are mostly rural, must engage with a discourse that misrecognizes them as African. As a result, the bulk of Afro-German counterdiscourses come in the form of autobiography, through which they underscore an Afro-German subject who is the complex product of the African diaspora and consequently cannot and should not be understood as wholly produced by—and therefore wholly Other to—the Western nation. These autobiographies reject nation formation in the form of a racist and atavistic (white) German discourse that lacks the ability to understand subject formations that are not dialectically arranged—that is, Blacks who are not African Others but African diasporic subjects who are also German.

In the second section of the chapter, "Inverted Empire: Black Britons and 'Reverse Colonization'," I explore the ways in which four Black British women novelists return to the heteropatriarchal discourse of the nation to make similar critiques, yet toward different ends. In her landmark novel *The Unbelonging*, Joan Riley argues that the Black female body of her protagonist, Hyacinth, effectively serves as the battleground for white male, black male, and white female subjects, all of whom have a stake within a discourse that promises them subject status should they be able to overthrow an Other. Hyacinth's combined gender and racial status, Riley makes clear, render her an irresistible candidate for that role of Other. Hyacinth's status as an Other desperately seeking subject status within this heteropatriarchal discourse is revised in three contemporary Black British novels also written by women. Naomi King's *O.P.P.*, Jo Hodges's *The Girl with Brains in Her Feet*, and Andrea Levy's *Fruit of the Lemon* offer a less bleak reading of the Black female seeking subject status within this discourse, all arguing through various ways that while the Black female can claim agency, this agency is never wholly complete and can only come into being in resistance to this discourse, rather than attempting to find a space in it.

Yet not all discourses that explicitly embrace the Black subject as diasporic produce a subjectivity that is truly diasporic—that is, not produced through the nation's dialectic of self and Other but instead produced by the multivalent histories and cultures of the diaspora. In the final section of the chapter, "Beyond Negritude?: Contemporary Black French Literature and the Afro-Parisian Novel," I use two novels—Simon Njami's *African Gigolo* and Daniel Biyaoula's *Agonies*—as examples of each approach to explain crucial differences between what I term the "nationalist" and "diasporic" Black subject. While Njami's protagonist Moïse (the gigolo of the title) encounters a wide variety of African diasporic subjects—from African nationalists to stateless mulattos to Antillean prostitutes—he nonetheless achieves subject status through nationalist discourse: by overcoming his fear of the Black female Other to claim subject status that can *only* be male. By contrast, Biyaoula's novel offers a truly dialogic structure of several protagonists, all of whom come to ruin through a structure of subjectivity that ignores diasporic differences and unsuccessfully attempts to posit a homogeneous Black subject who is always already male, and an Other that is always already female.

BECOMING BLACK? POSTCOLONIAL THEORY FROM THE AFRICAN DIASPORA?

The title of this manuscript points to three crucial interventions I want to make in the three fields of study with which this book engages: African American and African diasporic studies, postcolonial studies, and poststructuralist theory. In using the phrase "becoming Black" I do not mean to imply that, until the beginning of the twentieth century, peoples of African descent in the West were bereft of either an individual or a collective identity. Instead, I use the term "Black" as a signifier for the complex negotiation between dominant and minority cultures that all peoples of African descent in the West—philosophers or not—must make in order to survive, whether physically or psychologically (and here we might include the rejection of one cultural identity over the other as a negotiation, however unsuccessful). As such "becoming Black" highlights the fluidity of Black identity in the West, and our ever-evolving understanding of it.

While prominent postcolonial scholars such as Gayatri Spivak and Homi Bhabha have offered numerous possibilities for a postcolonial subject, their derivations ignore all but those of South Asian descent, often "reinventing the wheel" by bypassing those African diasporic works of theoretical significance in favor of dialoging with their colleagues in poststructuralism. Like its postcolonial sister, poststructuralist theory is explicitly committed to questioning, subverting, and ultimately replacing oppressive epistemologies of Western European colonialist thought. Yet it unwittingly acts on the very racist assumptions it seeks to overturn by failing to consider that the direct targets of these epistemologies and practices—peoples of African descent in the West—might in fact possess their own body of sophisticated counterdiscourse that is valuable far beyond the ethnographic information it offers.

This study seeks to challenge those assumptions in both poststructuralist and postcolonial discourse even as it seeks to underscore the diversity of Black subjectivities currently at work in the African diaspora. Finally, *Becoming Black* asks us to understand any and all negotiations of the subject—white, Black, or otherwise—as negotiations always already in the making, and not the final word.

CHAPTER ONE

The European and American
Invention of the Black Other

Over two hundred years before Jacques Derrida became celebrated for his theory of deconstruction, Blacks in the Americas were deconstructing white Western nationalist discourses celebrating the dawn of democracy. Texts such as David Walker's *Appeal* and John Marrant's *Sermon* offered counterdiscourses that asked whether the West could indeed claim racial superiority in societies so dependent, in so many ways, on Black slaves. Today, sexual, racial, and ethnic-minority scholars and activists are still deconstructing this discourse that refuses to understand democracy and Black chattel slavery as inherently incompatible with one another. Old habits die hard. Despite a dizzying number of technological, social, and political advancements, Western discourses on the Black (not to mention the woman, the queer, almost any other ethnic and/or racial minority, and the non-Christian, among others) remain as antiquated, fantastical—and central—as ever. By "central" I mean the way in which most Western mainstream (and even some academic) depictions of Africa, Africans, and those of African descent cling to their fantasies of a primitive, homogeneous peoples who are "undeveloped" in more than an economic sense. For the West, the image of the Black Other is as vibrant as ever, reminding us that the belief in Black inferiority is the result not of objective observation but instead the need for self-definition. In order to posit itself as civilized, advanced, and superior, Western discourse must endlessly reify Africa and the Black as its binary opposite.

While there are many Others in Western discourse (the phallicized female, the lecherous homosexual, the inscrutable Asian, the noble savage), it is the Black Other that is used most often in discourses of self-actualized agency, or subjectivity. The modern white subject, some two hundred years old, is exactly as old as the Black Other on which he relies. Although this book is concerned with the theoretical development of Black subjectivities in the African diaspora, we must first begin with the Black Other, that figure from late-eighteenth- and nineteenth-century Western philosophy without whom the white subject could not have come into being.

One cannot divorce the Black Other and Black subject that follows from the specific historical, cultural, and even philosophical discourses through which s/he is interpellated. By intersecting the sociohistorical with a theoretical analysis to fully understand how that Black Other came into being, this chapter will show not only the logical fallacy that allows the production of that Black Other for the white subject but also how *different* Black Others were produced to theorize and/or justify the specific relationship with the Black envisioned by that specific discourse.

The concept of identity is inextricably intertwined with the concept of the nation, a link established toward the end of the eighteenth century, when absolute monarchies collapsed in Europe and the thirteen colonies rebelled against the British crown. Suddenly territories were no longer defined by which ruling family owned them, nor were the inhabitants of the territories identified simply as the subjects of the sovereign. Spurred by and spurring this development was the Enlightenment, in which European philosophers placed man at the center of their philosophical discourses. The nature and notion of man—specifically the *European* man—became a central question.[1] This question was posed not only internally; even as the infrastructure of European countries became increasingly chaotic, the new trade routes established in the latter part of the sixteenth and earlier part of the seventeenth century to Africa and the Americas had also redefined the European continent. Explorers were now discovering that Europe was a relatively small landmass with a relatively small number of people. At the same time, the methods by which precious metals, raw materials, and slaves were enriching countries such as Spain, France, and Britain contradicted (or at least questioned) the humanist tenets developed by the *philosophes*. Therefore, the ontological and epistemological concerns underscoring the question "Who and what was the European man?" were qualified by questions regarding the geographical, political, and moral aspects of the "new" European.

Of course, no concrete answers or agreements were forthcoming. The Enlightenment, although loosely united by its humanist impulse, was composed of diverse spirits, from the royalist, anti-Semitic humanism of Voltaire to Jean-Jacques Rousseau's anticolonialist, antimonarchical humanism. Nonetheless, the Enlightenment did produce discourses that became dominant in European and American theses on progress and civilization: Europe was posited as its center, European man as its highest achievement.[2] More importantly, these assertions were based on the role European and American thinkers had relegated to the lands that lay outside their borders and the inhabitants of those lands. The aggressive and xenophobic biases that produce Black Others to the Western nation and the Western subject are the direct descendant of these early discourses on European and American national identity.

While there are a range of these discourses to choose from and, indeed, one would be hard put to discover an eighteenth- or nineteenth-century European or American philosopher who did *not* talk about Black inferiority relative to the white, some discourses have achieved greater influence than others, both in mainstream discourses and African diasporic counterdiscourses. Of all nineteenth-century figures, Georg Wilhelm Friedrich Hegel ranks as one of, if not the, most prolific, influential, and wide-ranging thinkers of his age. Hegel's theories of the nation state, the citizen, property, rights, history, and phenomenology are still largely operative today, even if we are not always aware that it is Hegel's formulation we are referencing. It is not surprising, then, that Hegel's theory of the white subject and Black Other is also one of his most influential formulations.

All theories of the modern subject in the West are dialectically structured, and Hegel's deployment of various dialectics through which he arranged the Black Other and the white subject is the "granddaddy" of those structures.[3] In the ensuing analysis, I show how Hegel's text on the Black Other, found in the introduction to his *Philosophy of History*, actually has two dialectics at work. One, explicitly defined in the text, famously locates the Black outside analytical history, mired in a developmental stasis from which only Western civilization can rescue him.[4] The other, while not explicitly defined, *implicitly* posits the Black as the antithesis of the white: where the white is civilized, the Black is primitive;

where the white loves freedom, the Black enjoys servitude; whereas the white loves order, the Black embraces chaos, and so on. By placing the Black both within and without his dialectic, ultimately a contradictory position, Hegel's text allowed the Black Other to come into being—an inferior species that "just happened" to be in need of Western influence when the West just happened to need that African's exploited labor, land, and natural resources. While Hegel's introduction makes clear its agenda is not an apologia for colonialism or slavery, the justification for these practices is nonetheless put in place.

Yet this is only one type of Black Other, one who is located outside the West in the Land Analytical History Forgot and, although dialectic in structure, is actually produced by one type of dialectic—that which argues that the West is ever moving forward toward a more enlightened state of being. There is another type of Black Other, as famous as it is confused and contradictory, based on a dialectic structure that argues that the West, in becoming less monarchical and more democratic, is actually moving *backward*. This Black Other belongs to Count Arthur de Gobineau, a nineteenth-century French writer and diplomat who is also known as the "Father of Modern Racism" and whose *Essai sur l'inégalité des races humaines* offered the first extensive secular argument for racial hierarchies that influenced Adolf Hitler, among others. Ironically, Gobineau was more interested in using racial difference as a metaphor for innate class differences, allowing him to argue that without the leadership of those born to rule—the aristocracy—those whom nature had deemed fit only to serve would now lead his beloved France into decay and decline.

Gobineau's use of the Black as an inferior species of human being produces an Other deemed an immediate threat to the nation. Gobineau does not talk about the Black as physically within French borders (although the Black presence was neither rare nor recent), but his obsession with pure bloodlines and the looming threat of miscegenation has him argue that the Black is a direct threat to pure Aryan bloodlines.[5] While Hegel's Other is outside the nation, Gobineau's is, at least metaphorically, in the nation. Yet because Gobineau is more (or at least equally) concerned with class than he is with race, his Black Other cannot speak to the one Western nation that has the dubious distinction of having brought the Black into its "home space," the United States. Although Thomas Jefferson's *Notes on the State of Virginia* predates both

Hegel and Gobineau, its own production of the Black Other serves as a useful and necessary contrast to them, especially when one considers the particular obstacles facing African American counterdiscourses on the Black subject.

Whereas Gobineau is infamous for racist views that he actually undercuts with his polemic against the French peasantry and bourgeoisie, Jefferson embraced his reputation as an antislavery activist—a reputation he still enjoys today—despite being a slave owner who was against emancipation and who legislated harsher measures for both slaves and those whites who treated them as more than animals.[6] Jefferson scholars often point to the section titled "Manners" in *Notes on the State of Virginia* to support their idealized view of this most famous Founding Father. Yet while this section bewails the evils of slavery, its sole focus is on the deleterious effects this system has on whites, not those who were forced to serve as their chattel. A more extensive (and often overlooked) section in the same text produces a Black Other whom nature has made a slave, and yet who nonetheless poses a threat to the nation because he resents this inferior station. While, like Gobineau's Black Other, this Other is also located within the nation, and, like Hegel's Other, understood as primitive, Jefferson goes further in arguing that, as a separate species (prone to mating with apes when in Africa), this Black Other is intrinsically and eternally backward and can never become part of the Western nation.

The ensuing analysis of these discourses and their respective productions of different Others is not a wholly new concept. Etienne Balibar and Immanuel Wallerstein in *Race, Nation, Class* base their analysis of Western nationalism on its troubling dichotomy of the nonwhite Other to the white subject. More specifically, in his chapter "Racism and Nationalism" Etienne Balibar argues that different Others result from different racisms—internal versus external—practiced on different racial groups. While the various Black Others analyzed in this chapter cohere with Balibar's general distinction, I also argue that these Others are conflated rather than discretely defined and, most importantly, that *one* racial group can have different types of alterity placed on it depending on which textual agenda locates it as Other.[7] As this book focuses on theories of subjectivity rather than racisms, Balibar's distinctions can be translated here into two main variations of the Black Other: the Other-from-within and the Other-from-without.[8] The Other-from-without is what we find in Hegel's text: located outside the West yet nonetheless brought in as oppositional and best understood as a void who has the potential to be taught Western values and culture. The Other-from-within is the Other we find in Gobineau and Jefferson in, as we see, two slight variations (which achieve greater importance in the counter-discourses they inspire). Gobineau's Other-from-within, deployed as a target against the peasant, need not be physically located in the nation in order to be an intrinsic threat to the racial integrity of that nation. Yet, as we will also see, Gobineau argues this Black Other occupies a certain position in the Western world and in Western civilization, something Hegel entertains as a future possibility but not a current or past actuality. Gobineau's suggestion that this Other can (with controls) be mixed into the white population to positive effect separates him from Jefferson's Black *American* Other-from-within. Although not used outside the United States, Jefferson's Other is key to understanding African American counterdiscourses on the subject, as this Black American Other is defined as both predestined for servitude under whites and a physical, unwelcome, threatening presence in the nation.

HEGEL AND THE OTHER-FROM-WITHOUT— FROM WITHIN

In his introduction to the *Philosophy of History*, Hegel explains that the world is ruled by reason, which functions as the "Infinite Power," its own "Infinite Material" and consequently the "Substance" and "Infinite Energy" of "the Universe": "It is *the infinite complex of things*, their entire Essence and Truth." Reason, he argues, is the energy and substance that comprises and guides philosophy because the latter is a reflective mode of thought based on inherently logical principles that necessarily produce a clarity and truth of the world that other modes of thought cannot achieve. Locating the origins of philosophical thought in ancient Greece, Hegel determines Europe to be both the birthplace of this eminently reasonable methodology and the only geographical region that is propelled and dominated by reason.[9] In his view, reason alone is the guiding element by which man can come into sentience and thus achieve his full potential, his subjectivity, for it conjoins the material with the spiritual, man's desires with their realization, and consequently makes him free. At the same time, this "free subject" can only be realized within a communal organization—but not *any* communal organization, only the state, because "the subjective will also has a substantial life, a reality which moves itself as an essence, and in which the object of the essential itself is its own being. This essential is itself the union of the subjective and rational will: it is the moral Whole—*the State*, which is that reality where the individual has and enjoys his freedom, albeit only when the individual's knowledge, belief and desire corresponds to the universal."[10]

Without this structure, man remains in or reverts to "his primary animal existence" where he is not in fact free, because freedom "as the *ideal* of that which is original and natural, does not exist *as original and natural*. Rather it must be first sought out and won; and that by an incalculable medial discipline of the intellectual and moral powers." Even further, "the state of Nature is, therefore, predominantly that of injustice and violence, of untamed natural impulses, of inhuman deeds and feelings."[11] The implications of this binary (state/nature) are clear: those who live outside the "moral Whole" of the state are inferior to those who live within (and wholeheartedly support) the state in that the former lack consciousness and therefore all those qualities that would make them subjects. Briefly put, those qualities are morality, intelligence, and, most importantly, the awareness of the transcendental principle that guides and makes the analytical history that, according to Western norms, *alone produces subjects*: reason.

Hegel begins his construction of the subject under reason as the transcendental a priori signifier that he defines within specifically European parameters, attaching subjective values to a supposedly objective (universal) dynamic. Reason is produced as synonymous with European values and standards, and, consequently, that which he determines as irrational is simultaneously determined as non-European. Sentience is also essential to the Hegelian subject, but this sentience is in fact a secondary principle, legitimate only when constructed within the specific parameters of Hegel's "reason"—and, of course, these parameters are distinctly European. Therefore, only Europeans can reach sentience, and only Europeans can be subjects. Hegel makes this clear when he writes that Blacks are wild beings and that "Dieser Zustand ist keiner Entwicklung und Bildung fähig, und wie wir [die Negern] heute sehen, so sind sie immer gewesen" (No development or culture is capable out of this state, and as we see [Negroes] today, so have they always been).[12] And on Africa he writes, "What we actually understand by Africa is that absence of history and unfolding, still wholly in the prejudiced mind of nature, and that here had to be displayed as it is, merely at the threshold of world history."[13] To paraphrase Max Horkheimer and Theodor Adorno's critique of the idealist dialectic, the process has been decided from the start: because Africa is not Europe and, in Hegel's determination, not the least bit European, it is not reasonable, it is irrational. The relation between race and the nation is made clear. The former is in fact the determining factor for the latter, which is in itself synonymous with subjectivity; only Europeans are subjects, because only Europeans are socially organized within the state.

Yet Hegel does not stop at merely determining Africans to be inferior to Europeans by virtue of being "stateless." There is a paradox: even though Hegel posits that Africans show no sign of progressing beyond "the conditions of mere Nature" (that is, they show no signs of becoming Europeans), he argues that enslavement is the only means by which the African might eventually achieve sentience and subjectivity. Hegel states that reason is by nature a progressive dynamic and this progressive dynamic is its primary imperative. In short, in order to maintain itself it must continually expand and, given that reason exists only in Europe, it must expand beyond its European borders in its ultimate manifestation as the state.

Central to Hegel's philosophy of history is, of course, its dialectic structure, driven by an *Aufhebung* that signifies continual progress, an "overcoming" of the antithesis that necessarily leads to a "synthesis"— which, in this case, is actually a subsuming rather than an equalized integration. Traditional understandings of Hegel's dialectic in the *Philosophy of History* have noted that this sublation is justified because it moves toward a becoming. As Michael Forster writes in "Hegel's Dialectic Method," "Having thus reached the negative result that these two categories are self-contradictory, Hegel finally tries to show that there is a positive outcome that unites them but in a manner that avoids their self-contradictoriness, because it not only preserves them but also modifies their senses: the category Becoming."[14] Yet this is not what happens in the dialectic of the Black Other and white self because the contradiction is resolved through the obliteration of the Black: he is enslaved by the white (and rightly so, according to Hegel), for the Africans need to learn how to be free, and the only way to do this is for whites to enslave them.[15] Drawing on outrageous anecdotes of ritual blood baths, markets openly abounding with human flesh for sale, and a silly but cruel Black man lamenting the fact that he has sold his whole family into slavery and is now lonely, Hegel conveniently erases the very real fact of Black sentience to render an Other uniquely unyielding in its antithetical nature.

In *Recognition: Fichte and Hegel on the Other*, Robert R. Williams shows how the relationship between Hegel's self and Other (specifically the self as Other, or self-Othering) is normally intersubjective, based on principle of *Anerkennung* (recognition, or acknowledgment).[16] While admitting that his readings are not categorical, Williams explains that whereas we find deliberate conflation in Hegel between the independent Other and the self-Other, the Hegelian subject, in order to come into being, is reliant not on the subjection but the freedom of the conflated understanding of the two.[17]

This is not what happens in the *Philosophy of History*, where, as we will see, Hegel determines the Negro as all that is Other to the European, the very antithesis to the European subject by lacking consciousness, and then recommends his continued enslavement. Theorists including Tsenay Serequeberhan, Henry Louis Gates, Hazel Carby, and Paul Gilroy, to name a few, critique Hegel's dialectic in order to critique Western subjectivity as a binary disguised as a dialectic. They argue it is crucial to recognize this disguise because it also cloaks a strain of anti-Black prejudice that has been embedded in mainstream Western philosophy since Hegel. According to Serequeberhan and Gates, Hegel's "Other" is not always an abstraction. Serequeberhan notes that Hegel is in fact "stealthily suggesting colonialism as the only viable solution to the fundamental contradictions that emerge from the dialectic internal to civil society and the state."[18]

Hegel's dialectic serves as a colonialist imperative in that the maintenance of the state is contingent on expansion. This argument is supported by his rhetoric in the introduction to *Philosophie der Geschichte* when he expounds on the nature of the African: "In Negro life the characteristic point is the fact that consciousness *has not yet attained* to the realization of any substantial objective existence." Describing the condition of the African as one that has yet to be "attained" points to the assumption that eventually the African will achieve subjectivity. Because Hegel has already made clear that this progression has not occurred in Africa, only one option remains: the African will attain subjectivity through the European.[19] Toward the end of his discussion on Africa,

Hegel suggests that (European) man will take up the sea's invitation to an exploitative commerce, for in commenting on the Negro condition, Hegel opines that Negroes will only come to understand freedom by serving as slaves to Europeans.[20] At the very least, Hegel's process of subjectivity advocates slavery as the most probable means by which Africans might come to achieve subjectivity based on the dialectic of slavery and freedom. Because Africans themselves are unrealized subjects and therefore not free, it is Europeans who must enslave them, for as the quotation makes clear, slavery is justified only within the existence of the state—and the state only exists in Europe. But slavery is not the only process required by Hegel's dialectic; the settlement of lands beyond Europe by Europeans is also an imperative.

In his section on "civil society," Hegel uses his dialectic method to address questions of poverty and wealth, grappling with the dilemma of the latter being a "necessary consequence" in civil society.[21] Recognizing property as the means by which individual agency is achieved in the modern state, he ponders yet another "necessary consequence": the disgruntlement of the have-nots toward the haves. Shlomo Avineri's *Hegel's Theory of the Modern State* focuses on the bind in which the German philosopher found himself. According to his theory of free will, the Hegelian subject has a right to "place his will in any thing. The thing thereby becomes mine and acquires my will as its substantial end (since it has no end within itself), its determination, and its soul—the absolute right of appropriation which human beings have over all things."[22] Herein the bind: the "thing" is subsumed by the thesis of the subject's will; as antithesis, it of course has no end in its own, the synthesis being the "absolute right or appropriation" by the will of that subject. The "thing" thus becomes the means by which the subject asserts his right to property; and yet what is to be done with those subjects who have no access to property, the impoverished? Hegel argues that "the inner dialectic of civil society thus drives it . . . to push beyond its own limits and seek markets and so its necessary means of subsistence, in other lands which are either deficient in the goods it has overproduced, or else generally backward industry."[23] And Serequeberhan then concludes, "Colonialism and colonial expansion are thus viewed by Hegel as the solution to the contradictions of civil society."[24]

Hegel posits these "other lands" as the antithesis of civil society; by virtue of being "deficient" and "backward" they obviously need to be supplied with those essentials they lack and pushed forward. They exist in relation to civil society as a "necessary consequence" of the latter for expansion, sublation, and synthesis. One must also note how Hegel fails to consider the rights of these inhabitants although they also "lack," as Serequeberhan notices, the idea of property. This consequently suggests that Hegel determines these inhabitants as without "free will" and therefore as nonsubjects. As Henry Louis Gates Jr. notes in his introduction to *Figures in Black*, Hegel did in fact view non-Europeans, specifically Africans, as Other to the white subject. In the *Philosophy of History*, Africa is simply the antithesis to the European thesis: it signifies immobility and stagnation, a continent of nonsubjects who are necessarily subject to European free will and the necessary drive toward synthesis. *Aufhebung* is not a passive phenomenon, nor one that exists within; it reaches outward in order to function in devastating and lasting ways.

Hegel's idea of the modern state is still very much alive in Europe and the United States. As argued by Ella Shohat and Robert Stam in *Unthinking Eurocentrism*, Western discourse still uses such grossly inaccurate terms and phrases as the "discovery of the New World."[25] This discourse speaks of needing to keep "aliens" from crossing its "borders"; refers to itself as the "West" and composed of "First World nations"—and all the "others," including nonwhite countries within the Western Hemisphere, as the "Third World." Academic discourse often fails to interrogate its deployment of the category of the "Other" as a synonym for nonwhite; it does not distinguish between a complex abstraction and actual individuals. More specifically, we speak of identity and the various formulations of the subject within the narrow binary of self and Other. It is this category of "Other" that produces nonwhites as non-Western, and therefore always already foreign, always already "Other" to the Euro-American "self." As Homi Bhabha has noted, Hegel's *Aufhebung* plays a critical role in our concept of the modern state, especially in relation to those so-called other lands: "it is precisely this failure to interrogate many of the assumed Absolutes produced by the Enlightenment *philosophes* and their successors (such as Hegel) that leads to the current failures to go beyond notions of the West and the Third World."[26] Bhabha invokes the Hegelian dialectic to demonstrate the way in which the movement from thesis to synthesis erases that which has preceded it: what existed before the thesis or, more specifically, the modern state? According to Bhabha, the nation's past is atemporal, a notion that is "always already there." As he also points out, it is not only the construction of binaries that is problematic. Perhaps even more dangerous is the inherent refusal or failure within the theory to acknowledge this artificial structure, both at the time of its construction and today.

Contemporary constructions of Europe owe much to Hegel's notion of "upheaval," the central force to his dialectic and at the core of his various theories on right, history, and ontology. Central to each theory is the assumption of Europe as united, the thesis that must overcome its diametric opposite—"the West" versus "the Far (or Near) East," "Enlightenment" Europe versus "the dark continent" of Africa—in order to achieve its full potential, a synthesis whose term belies its use as marker of triumph for the thesis in overwhelming and incorporating the antithesis under its own prerogatives and values.[27] The Western construct of the nation operates in the same way, because its structure is derived from a reductive Enlightenment methodology that devolves all relationships into binaries (all of which are versions of the binary of self/Other) and necessarily proposes itself as a defense against the "uncivilized" world outside. Nationality cannot fully accept difference within because nationality is concomitant with "difference without," or without difference. For those who lie within its borders as signifiers of differences—whether racial, ethnic, sexual, gender, or religious differences—they must necessarily be constructed as antithesis to the nationality's thesis. "They" serve as a marker of what the nation is continually attempting to "overcome." Both liberals and conservatives respond to this system: the latter argues that they are not actual members of the nation; the former argues that, despite their differences, they are still part of the nation, that there is "room" to incorporate them. In either case, difference is always already antithetical to the idea of nation. In times of national disintegration, whether it be economic or political, borders are constructed from within (in varying degrees) to prevent infection; a nation may tolerate difference within, but it will not relinquish its view of that "Other" as inherently threatening to the maintenance of that nation's "self."

The notion of the Other, as defined above, is integral to the idea of the self or the nation, the necessary opponent that must be vanquished and sublated. It is unclear if there is an alternative construction available, one that does not rely on binary oppositions. At the very least, we must question the nature of antithesis, in that "difference" is generally assumed to have no life of its own. Difference is rarely able to assert what it is: it must usually contend with what it is not, for that, from the viewpoint of the "thesis," is all that it is. It is the attempt to move out of this binary that is often at the center of postcolonial theory and literature. The latter wants to demonstrate that not only should the methodology of comparison be interrogated but at times comparison is meaningless: instead of thesis and antithesis, we are dealing with apples and oranges.

Hegel's analysis of the modern state proposes colonial expansion as the only solution to *Aufhebung*. Hegel is primarily concerned with maintaining the state although, as Serequeberhan points out, *Aufhebung* knows no limits: once impoverished citizens "develop" other lands, what are they to do when they too reach a state of haves and have-nots? These two formulations—the modern state as dependent on colonial expansion for survival, and the "Other" as a soon-to-be-subsumed antithesis—came to determine how Europeans regarded those who lived beyond their borders but under their control.

This is the fundamental contradiction in Hegel's *Philosophie der Geschichte*: determining the Negro to be outside the dialectic, outside history itself, and simultaneously within that dialectic as the antithesis of the European subject. As Serequeberhan has shown, the gains made from this contradiction allow European expansion into Africa with impunity, as well as the continuation of the highly lucrative slave trade. Theoretically speaking, Hegel has created an Other-from-without who nonetheless functions from within: officially irrelevant to the European nation and the European subject, and yet unofficially *and in praxis* central to the definition of the European nation and subject. As Robert R. Williams has indicated, this is not the relationship between the ideal self and Other Hegel envisioned: nonetheless, it is this antagonistic and aggressive binary between the white self and Black Other that has become the cornerstone for Western theories of subjectivity.

GOBINEAU AND THE OTHER-FROM-WITHIN

Hegel's formulation of the modern state is not the only discourse that responded to this question of subjectivity. Count Arthur de Gobineau's *Essai sur l'inégalité des races humaines*, published in 1853, less than a decade after Hegel's death, also propounds a theory involving the European nation. Unlike Hegel's, Gobineau's ideology found few adherents and many detractors on the Continent. All the same, his construction of the "three races" (Negroid, Caucasoid, and Mongoloid) became central to Europe's and the United States' formulations of the subject, leaving an indelible influence on American racists—and Negritudists. Small wonder, then, that one of his contemporaries referred to the *Essai* as Gobineau's *roman noir du monde*.[28] Whereas Hegel celebrates man's newly awakened capacity to make his own world through self-determination, Gobineau's *Essai* laments a greatness passed and is primarily concerned with the causes of this decline. For Hegel, the subject is actualized within the existence of the state. The subject, by virtue of being realized through the "Divine Wisdom" of transcendental reason, determines his own fate and ensures his own immortality by obeying Hegel's moral imperative of colonization. For Gobineau, such immortality, as constituted by the maintenance of superior bloodlines, is fast becoming nothing more than a memory, polluted by the corrupting influence of lesser bloodlines: "In applying the word *degenerate* to a people, it must and does signify that these people no longer have the intrinsic value they possessed at an earlier time because they no longer have the same blood in their veins . . . definitively speaking, they will die, and their civilization will die with them."[29]

Unlike Hegel's *Philosophy of Right*, Gobineau's *Essai* does not prescribe European colonization or the enslavement of Africans.[30] Although the *Essai* has since been used to justify the oppression of other races, from the system of chattel slavery in the United States to the National Socialists' Final Solution, Gobineau does not in fact advocate slavery or genocide. Hegel's theory begins with the birth of the subject in the form of a citizen of the modern state; Gobineau's *Essai* laments the death of the subject, corrupted by a democratic process and the mixture of bloodlines that pulls the subject down to mediocrity, indistinct from the rest. For Hegel, the modern state constitutes the subject; for Gobineau, the modern state is an inarguable sign of the subject's decline. Although the philosophy is complex and often contradictory, it can in fact be summed up by Gobineau himself: "A man is great, noble, virtuous not by his actions but by his blood."[31]

As his introduction predicts, Gobineau's proposed explanation departs from all previous theories—those mired down by a praiseworthy but misleading tendency toward republicanism and/or morality. Having established that all "true" civilizations are organic in nature and guided by the dialectical principle and that they are furthermore primarily occidental in origin, Gobineau states that they have one thing in common: the shared racial heritage of the dominant group, which is always Aryan. He credits the Aryan race with all the necessary civilizing qualities. In book six of the *Essai*, "La civilisation occidentale," Gobineau observes that the Aryan nations of Europe and Asia have astonished the world with their vigorous drive and their capacity to subjugate other peoples.[32] Morality aside, one cannot ignore how Aryans, and Aryans alone, have founded all true civilizations and consequently are the sole people of historical note; they are the only ones who have made history. Gobineau attributes this remarkable history of achievement to innate qualities:

> The Aryan is thus superior to all other men, principally with regard to his measure of intelligence and his energy; when he conquers his mortal passion and his material desires, he is equally gifted in achieving an infinitely loftier morality because of these two faculties, so much so that in the ordinary course of events, he cannot be reproached for as many reprehensible deeds that one would find committed by the two lesser species.[33]

These innate qualities are also reflected externally through physical characteristics: "Cet Arian se présente maintenant à notre observation dans le rameau occidental de sa famille, et là il nous apparaît aussi vigoureusement bâti, aussi beau d'aspect." (This Aryan calls himself to our attention through the occidental branch of his family, and there he also appears to us as designed with vigor and quite beautiful in aspect.)[34]

This harmony of superior qualities and aspect proves a powerful combination: "Thus placed upon a sort of pedestal and disengaged from the foundation upon which he acts, the 'Aryan German' is a powerful creature. . . . All that this man believes, all that he says, all that he does, acquires a sense of great import."[35] Hegel's influence is obvious here: like Hegel's citizen, Gobineau's Aryan is the only subject, given that he alone determines history. In like kind, the Hegelian citizen's will to power mirrors Gobineau's comments on the Aryan's godlike ability to transform thought into action or, rather, to exercise such power over others and his environment that his thought *is* action. Yet whereas Hegel's subject is a product of a new age of self-determination embodied within the modern state, Gobineau's subject has always already existed; he is not the product of external forces such as government. On the contrary, civilization is the footprint he has left on history, a product of his superiority rather than the other way around. Gobineau's insistence on physical beauty also marks an important divergence from Hegel's citizen. In Gobineau, the inherent, organic nature of the subject is further stressed, deliberately recalling the rhetorical structure of ancient European and Near Eastern mythology.[36] In this structure, a deity is recognized by his or her inferior through his or her striking beauty, thus combining the internal and external and effectively producing a being who transcends the limits of environment. Not unlike the God of the Old Testament, Gobineau's Aryan does not rule over the world; the Aryan creates the world and therefore *is* the world.

Gobineau's subject is dialectical because civilization and the nature of the Aryan, the cornerstones of his subject, are also dialectical. Like Hegel's citizen, the superiority of the Aryan is manifested in his ability to subjugate the two weaker races: the Negroid and Mongoloid. However, Gobineau's definition of synthesis is quite different from Hegel's and is ultimately what distinguishes the *Essai* from the Hegelian worldview. For Hegel, synthesis is the moment at which the subject achieves completeness by overcoming the Other. The subject's guiding principle is invoked through the Spirit: "Der Geist ist wesentlich Resultat seiner Tätigkeit: seine Tätigkeit ist Hinsausgehen über die Unmittelbarkeit, das Negieren derselben und Rückkehr in sich." (Spirit is the essential result of its own activity: its activity is the transcending of immediacy of existence, the negation of the same and the return into itself.)[37] For Gobineau, synthesis is more literal: it signals miscegenation between the Aryan and the lesser races. In fact, Gobineau notes that if the Aryan has one failing, it is his propensity toward racial intermixture, and it is this drive (one shared by all races) that ultimately causes the decline of civilizations: "Masters also encounter thousands of ways to tolerate—and sometimes to enable—this tendency [to intermix]. In the end, the bloods intermingle and two men of different origins, no longer linked to distinct groupings, are further conflated."[38]

THE NEGRO AND THE DIALECTIC OF RACE

Gobineau has already contended that no civilization can remain racially pure (which he equates with stagnation). It is the nature of all great civilizations, he argues, to incorporate other peoples, either through territorial expansion or mass emigration. Lesser races flock from the uncivilized margins to the civilized center in search of a better life. Intermixture is even necessary (within limits), for it is Gobineau's belief that variety is the spice of civilized life. A civilization is dynamic and as such requires different influences on its body in order to continue functioning. Yet there is a caveat: too much intermixture with a lesser race will bring the dominant group into decline, its masculine vigor corrupted by the more feminine and thus passive qualities of inferior blood:

> It is when the regulating elements of society and the elements developed by aspects of ethnicity reach multiplicity that it becomes impossible for them to live in harmony with one another; to submit to, in a sensible manner, a necessary homogenization and, consequently, to obtain, through communal logic, these instincts—and instincts of the community—the *raisons d'être* for societal ties. There is no greater pestilence than disorder because, as bad as it makes the present time, it prepares the way for a future that is far worse.[39]

The relationship between self and Other is more complicated in Gobineau's schema. According to Hegel, the self overcomes the Other, the latter nothing more than a mere shadow, helpless against the natural force of *Aufhebung*. *Aufhebung*, as determined by Hegel, consists of subjugation, not intermixture. For Gobineau, *Aufhebung* is both subjugation and miscegenation. Hegel's definition of the Other is the Negro, that exact antithesis of the citizen, inactive as opposed to active, barren as opposed to fecund, and clearly the basis for the psychoanalytic definition of Other as a projection of the self; for Gobineau, the Other does not completely lack dynamism.[40] Although the Negro lacks the Aryan's discipline, determination, and drive, he nonetheless possesses a certain creative vitality—although his inability to motivate himself in any constructive way prevents him from producing anything of note with that energy. In one of the most famous passages of the *Essai*, Gobineau describes the Negro:

> The Negro is the most humble and lags at the bottom of the scale. The animal character imprinted on his brow marks his destiny from the moment of conception. He will never evolve beyond his limited circle of intelligence. He is not, however, a pure and simple brute, for within the narrow confines of his cranium there exist indications of

grossly powerful energies. If these mental faculties are mediocre or even non-existent, he nonetheless possesses desire, and consequently a will of terrible intensity. Many of his senses are developed with a vigor unknown to the two other races, principally taste and smell. . . . These principal traits are combined with an instability of mood, a variability of sentiment that cannot be determined and that annuls, for him, virtue along with vice. One could say that the very way in which he pursues his object in such a fit of passion, putting his sensitivity in flux and inflaming his longing, renders the first promptly appeased and rapidly casts the second into a forgotten oblivion. Lastly, he has as little respect for his own life as he does for those of others; he kills for the sake of killing, and this automaton that is so easily moved is, in the face of suffering, either a coward who seeks refuge in death or is else monstrously indifferent.[41]

Unlike Hegel's passive Other, Gobineau's Negro seems to possess, if anything, too much energy, which he cannot discipline. Whereas Gobineau's subject is quintessentially human, the description of his Negro suggests animal instincts and drives. (Indeed, Gobineau was not beyond classifying the Negro as ranking below certain species of animals!)

There is an irony in the comparison between Hegel's and Gobineau's theories of the relationship between the self and Other. Hegel, by positing the subject within a political and social definition and not a racial one, ends up with an Other, a Negro who is deprived of any humanity, serving as a mere shadow of the European.[42] In contrast, by using a racial determinant despite his claims of his subhuman nature, Gobineau's Negro is relatively more substantial, an actual being with drives and desires and capable of having an effect on civilization, however limited. In this instance, Gobineau's Negro possesses more energy and drive than his Aryan, paradoxically rendering the Aryan a mere shadow of the more animated and dynamic Negro. This relatively slight distinction (with regard to the amount of time Gobineau devotes to analyzing Negro inferiority) is not merely an interesting factoid but will prove an important touchstone for Negritudist counterdiscourses.

Yet Gobineau's Negro and Hegel's both share the inability to progress, measured against European accomplishment. Both Gobineau and Hegel depict Africa as a dark continent populated with savage tribes that have failed to move beyond the initial stages of human development, rooted in manners and mores any European would consider retrograde.[43] However, Hegel's Other possesses far fewer threatening aspects than does Gobineau's depiction. Because Hegel's subject is rooted in the state, military and political domination is at the heart of his *Aufhebung*; because Gobineau's subject is determined by miscegenation, not metaphysics, synthesis takes on the biological definition of racial intermixture. Whereas Hegel's self is necessarily drawn to the Other in its drive toward subject status, Gobineau's self (in the form of the Aryan), while also drawn to the Other, ultimately cannot control this contact. Gobineau's Other, unlike Hegel's, is capable of causing the decline of even the greatest of civilizations. Strictly in terms of the relation between synthesis and subjectivity, the theories of the two men are distinct from one another because Gobineau's subject is not brought about by a process: he is already constituted. The subject becomes imperiled by the dialectic, by the very nature of his thesis, that is, the drive toward intermixture.

Unlike Hegel, Gobineau was not interested in determining the nature of the new European nation. It is important to note that for Gobineau, "nation" is explicitly a racial group rather than a sociopolitical construct, and his use of the term "civilization" instead of "nation" or "state," as used by Hegel, points to a focus on historical patterns and trends rather than a specific means toward an end, such as a blueprint and/or apologia for European colonialism. Given this, Hegel's depiction of the Negro/Other is understandably shadowy and disdainful: the Negro merely represents a creature who happens to inhabit those lands earmarked for European expansion; he serves no real purpose and plays no meaningful role in the development of the modern state except perhaps as a source of cheap labor.[44] Hegel's Negro is an animal in that his existence cannot be denied but metaphysically can be determined as inconsequential.

The justifications given by England, France, and Germany for the political and economic exploitation of Africa are reflected in Hegel's defense of colonization. The enduring European image of the African as a barbarous but ultimately helpless child reverberates in the *Philosophy*'s deployment of this African Other as proof of the European civilization's dynamic rather than destructive presence. The development of the late European Romantic version of the Negro, as noted by Leon-François Hoffman, follows in the same vein, producing an image (with some variation) that dovetails with the Romantic longing for a return to a preindustrial past.[45] The Negro becomes the noble savage, representative of the nature of man before the Enlightenment, when rational thought severed man's ties to his natural environment.[46]

Hegel's and Gobineau's Black Others underscore how the production of identity is first and foremost contingent on one's political (and of course philosophical) agenda.[47] This contrast parallels the difference between their respective discourses. The former posited the Negro as "outside" the state, another raw material, one might say, for Europe to refine and develop. In Gobineau, however, the Negro is evoked as a threat from within that has contributed to the degeneration of the Aryan race and consequently the decline of civilization.

Because the arrival of the Negro predates the formation of the American nation,[48] Gobineau's discourse on the Negro as a "pestilence" (*fléaux*) already located within the body *but not originally of it* allowed his American translators Josiah Nott and Henry Hotz to justify the need to either keep the Negro permanently segregated from the white populace and/or advocate the wholesale "recolonization" of the Negro to another country or colony. Because most Black Americans predate most white Americans, American racists cannot argue (within strict chronological parameters) that the Negro, because he was a newcomer to the nation, cannot and does not belong as a member of the nation.[49] However, by reducing the Negro to an inferior bloodline as Gobineau does, Hotz and Nott could ignore this anachronism and posit the Negro as, one could say, biologically foreign—and, therefore, always already foreign to the American body of the nation.[50] Cassirer argues that although ancestral pride predates Gobineau, it is Gobineau who first introduced the notion of ancestral superiority as a value that seeks "to destroy all other values."[51] The majority of scholars on racism agree that the exact origins of European racism cannot be determined, especially given that "race" signified a variety of characteristics and/or groups before scientific categorization proceeded to define what in fact constituted race—although the primary marker was visual difference, forcing race scientists to concoct a range of outrageously suspect experiments that predetermined Negro and/or Asian inferiority.[52]

As Michael Biddiss has argued, Gobineau's theory of racial hierarchy first appeared in the *Essai* and then slowly disintegrated in his later works as he came to encounter a range and diversity of peoples who defied his already complicated racial categories.[53] Biddiss attributes the *Essai*'s race theory to Gobineau's growing pessimism about emerging democratic reforms in Western Europe that, to his mind, erased necessary class distinctions. Although the *Essai* does contain vitriolic passages on the inferiority of the "Negroid" and "Mongoloid" races, it also makes statements, such as the following, that fly in the face of the other pronouncements:

> I admit, yet I admit, before one proves it to me, all the marvels one will be able to relate within this genre of the boorish savage. I have denied that there is any sort of excessive stupidity or chronic ineptitude, even amongst the most degraded tribes. I will go even further than my adversaries in that I do not doubt there are a good many African chieftains who surpass, through the force and abundance of their ideas, by the intensity of their active faculties, the common level of our peasants or even the level that our bourgeoisie, satisfactorily instructed and reasonably gifted, can attain. Once more, one hundred times more, it is not upon the narrow terrain of individuality that I posit myself. . . . Let us then leave these puerilities and compare not men, but groups.[54]

As Cassirer notes, Gobineau's Aryan is not remarkable in his individual achievements, since all achievements are the domain of his superior racial strain. Yet what Cassirer does not comment on is that Gobineau's race worship cannot be extricated from his aristocratic prejudice, and that the *Essai* uses racial classification as a means to an end, not as an end in itself. The fact that Gobineau readily concedes the superiority of the African chieftain over a French peasant (and even an educated member of the bourgeoisie) says less about his disinterest in the nature of the individual and more about his belief that class (in this case bloodlines, further confusing the issue) is more important than race.[55] The *Essai* in fact contains passages wherein Gobineau rails against the French peasantry, declaring them French only in that they occupy French soil: they in no way reflect the achievements of French civilization. Not only is the peasantry an inferior breed (as opposed to the nobility, whom Gobineau traces to the Teutonic line) who have trouble incorporating even the slightest aspect of an education but they also reject the opportunity when it is offered to them. In one of the many anecdotes Gobineau draws on to prove his point, he details how the peasant conscript, after returning from service, proudly dispenses with the education he has received in the military, emptying his mind of facts, figures, and even the alphabet. Relative to this stubbornly stagnant French peasant, Gobineau's Negro possesses some talents and intelligence.[56]

In like kind, Gobineau's views on miscegenation also fail to be uniform. As stated above, intermixture is a good thing only when it comes in a small package. Yet at the same time, Gobineau states quite clearly that the Aryan is incapable of artistic achievement, since such activity has no place in his practical, materially oriented mind. According to the *Essai*, all artistic achievements within a civilization can only be traced to the Negro:

> Most certainly the Black element is indispensable in developing a race's artistic genius, for we have seen what a profusion of fire, of flames, of sparks, flights of fancy and lack of reflection reside in its essence, and how much the imagination, this reflex of sensuality, as well as all material appetites enslave themselves to the impressions that create the arts, indeed to a degree of intensity wholly unknown to the other families of humans. This is my point of departure, and if there is nothing more to add, certainly the Negro would appear as the lyric poet, the musician, the sculptor *par excellence*. . . . Yes, again, the Negro is a human creature who is seized by the most energetic sort of artistic mood—but at this indispensable condition rather than what his intelligence will have penetrated and understood with regard to the actual undertaking.[57]

Although this pronouncement of the Negro's artistic abilities could hardly be considered "freeing," it proved far more popular in counterdiscourse than Hegel's Negro-as-void. Of course, as Gobineau made clear in previous and proceeding passages, art, with regard to the creation and development of civilizations, is quite frivolous. Further, it is not the Negro but rather the intermixture between the Negro and the Aryan that produces the artist, given that the former is in need of the discipline as well as the ability of the latter to combine thought and action. The Other thus serves as a source of energy for the self to harness, and the synthesis achieved produces the great artist. Because miscegenation can result in a beauty that conforms to European standards, the delineation between mixture and purity is further confused.

There are more significant ramifications: contrary to Gobineau's observation that one cannot help but notice the resemblance between a Negro and a baboon (as opposed to the Aryan's unrivaled beauty), the

Essai declares that there is no woman so beautiful as the "mulattress." Again, this statement does not elevate the Negro, and given that miscegenation was most likely effected through rape rather than consent, we can hardly celebrate Gobineau's attitude as progressive. At the same time, these and other pronouncements on synthesis inevitably impart to the Other a form of identity, albeit limited and limiting. Furthermore, Gobineau's insistence that his theory be read with regard to groups and not individuals disallows the Aryan subject the means toward asserting individual greatness; to a certain degree, his superiority is not of his own making, and Gobineau's subjectivity becomes one in which the subject is merely representative of the many. In the same vein, the allowance for the Negro chieftain to surpass the white peasant or even the white bourgeois in refinement and intellectual achievement produces a subjectivity with fluid lines in which the individual is not restrained or even enabled by the inferior or superior traits of his race but his class.[58]

Gobineau's aristocratic and antidemocratic leanings complicate his racial theory and at times undermine it. For Gobineau, race is a multivalent and at times a floating signifier; underneath the rubric of the Caucasoid, he produces divisions within divisions. In his treatment of the "lower" classes, he distinguishes between the peasant and the aristocrat with the same rhetorical weapons he deploys to discuss the difference between the Negro and the Aryan. The divisions within the Negro also become complicated and contradictory: the "pure" Negro is assigned a set of concrete characteristics, but other passages discuss the majority of African cultures as racially mixed, with some cultures meeting his standards of a "true" civilization. Gobineau "solves" this conundrum by stating that these superior African cultures were obviously founded by earlier Aryan peoples, but this in turn defies his categorization of the Negro, in that it leaves few "pure" Negroes, and therefore a minimum of individuals, let alone groups, who actually conform to his stereotype.[59] The Negro becomes more of an abstract idea than an actual individual, just as the "idea" of the Aryan, with regard to the French peasant and working class, bears as little resemblance as an infant to an adult with regard to developmental capacity. This, above all else, is what distinguishes Gobineau's Negro from the stereotypes deployed by Hegel and Jefferson: Gobineau is not interested in justifying colonization, brutality, and enslavement and therefore does not link this supposed racial inferiority to the exploitative imperatives known as the "civilizing mission."[60]

The *Essai*'s treatment of miscegenation also undermines his racial determinants. On one hand, Gobineau's subject is constituted by refusing synthesis with the Other; on the other hand, synthesis, as miscegenation, is inevitable and to a certain degree necessary for a civilization to achieve greatness. One could argue that Gobineau's treatise is advocating social integration through racial miscegenation. One could also argue that Gobineau is proposing that Blacks should be enslaved and/or colonized and forcibly "mated" with whites in order to improve their race. Yet, because the *Essai* produces itself as philosophical treatise in which the nature and ways of man are described and not prescribed, a responsible textual reading provides little justification for the colonialist project and/or slavery.[61] By attending to the question of miscegenation (something Hegel avoids or has failed to consider and which in fact became a significant dilemma in European and American colonialism), the *Essai* both addresses and becomes confused by the inherent paradox: if the Aryan is superior to the Negro, does intermixture raise or lower status? On the surface, this question becomes a matter of perspective; that is, whether the determination is relative to Aryan or Negro status. Yet one must still debate which is the greater force: whether the Aryan's superiority outweighs the Negro's inferiority, or vice-versa. As we have seen, Gobineau has answered this question with regard to opinions on artistic capacity; the Negro provides the ink, but the Aryan guides the hand. Miscegenation allows for the harnessing of raw energy that would otherwise remain undirected. Gobineau also posits opinions on the colonial site with regard to miscegenation:

> The state is divided into two factions that do not remain separate because of incompatible doctrines, but because of skin: the mulattos take one side, the Negroes the other. To the mulattos being, without a doubt, more intelligence and a spirit that is more open to cognition. I have said it already with regard to the Dominicans: the blood of the European modifies the African nature and it is possible for these men, founded within a mass of whiteness and under the constant supervision of good role models, to become useful citizens besides.[62]

This is because, unlike the French peasant, who mates only within his own group, the mulatto will in fact take on some of the superior traits of the Aryan, although he will of course never be more than a faint reflection of the latter.[63] In contradistinction to Gobineau's vociferous opposition to the French peasant ever being considered a citizen, the mulatto, given this superior infusion of blood, is almost welcomed into the fold and encouraged to become an active participant. Further, as Francesca Castradori notes in *Le radici dell'odio* (Roots of Evil), Gobineau's hierarchy of races further collapses with his positive reading of those who possess both Aryan *and* African ancestry.[64]

Because Hegel's discussion of the subject, unlike Gobineau's, does not allude to race, one might assume that the German philosopher disallowed race as a category in determining subjectivity. After all, Hegel's theory on the modern state elides racial determination in that his theory of subjectivity is produced within the culturally and politically based notion of the subject as citizen. However, Hegel's categories are clearly racially based in that the European is always already a citizen and therefore a subject, just as the African is always already Other. Unlike Gobineau's, Hegel's categories of self and Other are static, despite the absence of racist pronouncements. At the same time, Gobineau is predicating the mulatto as citizen only within the colonial space. However, in this case it is Gobineau's trope of blood and the concurrent rhetorical metaphor of fluidity that result in a wider definition of citizenship; in Gobineau, racial determinants prove far less static than those of class. Of course, it must be remembered that Gobineau's Negro is still denied access to citizenship, exactly as Hegel's Negro remains Other. At the same time, by determining "Negro blood" as the sole possessor of positive qualities, Gobineau leaves many doors open—rhetorical opportunities that the founders of Negritude use to revolutionary effect.

After revealing his allowance for the mulatto within civil society, Gobineau moves along dialectically: if an Aryan *Aufhebung* can produce a superior breed of Negro, what if synthesis is endlessly repeated?

> The mulattos would live by the shore, with the purpose of maintaining constant contact with the Europeans, in a rapport that they seek. Under the direction of the latter, one would see merchants, courtiers above all, lawyers and doctors squeezing even closer those ties that caress them, mixing more and more, gradually ameliorating, losing, in measured proportions, their character, along with their African blood.[65]

In one of the few chapters that actually prescribes the arrangement of peoples within colonial society, Gobineau's vision runs contrary to the social pessimism that is the guiding principle in the *Essai*. Colonial expansion and the inevitable intermixture between races are produced as a means of uplifting and developing the Negro in a harmonious, multiracial—but monocultural—setting.[66]

It is impossible to draw a strict comparison between Hegel's and Gobineau's theories of subjectivity. Hegel's theory is embedded within a political doctrine that is geared toward asserting the right of the European citizen-as-subject to expand into other continents. By positing sovereignty as a universal law and then determining Europe as the only space within which sovereignty may be properly located, the theory of the modern state produces a subject specifically geared toward the colonialist project. In contrast, the so-called biological determinants for Gobineau's subjectivity lacks a specific aim. The fact that the *Essai*, unlike Hegel's discourse, focuses on racial degeneration makes it far more compelling for American racists who were intent on "proving" the Negro as an inferior presence that was detrimental to the nation as a whole. In the same vein, Gobineau's production of the peasantry as an inherently inferior breed (useful only in that they cultivated the land) would be transplanted onto the American scene to justify the enslavement of Blacks: Gobineau's aristocratic bias would be reformatted into American racism.[67]

As a treatise that asserts the impending death of the subject and yet at the same time wanders into the possibilities of subjectivity through racial intermixture, Gobineau's *Essai* contains a series of contradictions that belie the prevailing argument and concurrently produce a relation between self and Other that is far more fluid, more complex than Hegel's, but ultimately incoherent. Moreover, the *Essai*'s strident royalist views prevent just any European from assuming or asserting subject status; as this argument has shown, racial divisions often serve as a metaphor for class, perhaps most boldly revealed in Gobineau's refusal to grant the European "lower" classes subject status, or even entertain the possibility. In contrast, the Negro, when acknowledged as having an aristocratic and/or Aryan background, is granted the possibility of subject status.

Within the specific contexts of race and class, one can in fact posit

Gobineau and Hegel as opposite sides of a coin: Hegel's aim (hypothetically speaking) is to grant every European man subject status, whereas Gobineau, if anything, is intent on denying large sectors of the European population any status whatsoever—again, an intent far more compatible with the American scene. For Hegel, the production of the subject is contingent on the Other, in that the subject cannot come into being or be maintained without the Other remaining within an antithetical relationship to the self and being barred from ever achieving subject status. In short, the superiority of the self relies directly on the inferiority of the Other. In like kind, the superiority of Gobineau's Aryan, as Cassirer has noted, is achieved in comparison with the lowliness of the Negro. Yet there is a blurring of lines, for neither the Aryan, nor the Negro, nor the so-called Mongoloid are ever contained within one category alone. Unlike Hegel, Gobineau's subject always teeters on the brink of advancement or decline, depending on which way the bloodlines are flowing or where class lines are being drawn. For Gobineau, the dynamic inherent within the dialectic is taken quite seriously and becomes the prevailing determinant in subjectivity. Contrary to Hegel, the process of subjectivity is not a predetermined one; quite often, it proves a crapshoot. This instability (or fluidity, depending on which way one looks at it) is located within the fatal flaw of the Aryan self and his predilection for intermixture. This flaw is also located within Gobineau's refusal to adhere to abstractions: synthesis often appears as the product of miscegenation, as opposed to Hegel's synthesis as the product of violence against the Other in the form of warfare and economic exploitation.

This is not to argue that Gobineau's *Essai* is not racist, or that it is superior to Hegel's; both theories are hopelessly Eurocentric in their views and intrinsically flawed. Rather, it is important to determine how both theories had an impact on the European and American colonialist practice as well as to locate the gap between what those theories actually argued and how they were deployed, specifically with regard to Gobineau and the American "Gobineauists." Furthermore, it is important to identify those moments in both Gobineau's and Hegel's discourses that are paradoxical, reiterating once again that these discourses were produced from specific political and/or economic aims on the part of each author. Here, I have attempted to render as dry an account of these discourses as possible, to maintain a structural line between discourse and counterdiscourse.

Several decades before Hegel and Gobineau developed their respective doctrines on nation and nationality, America was asking similar questions. No longer defined as a colony of Britain, and possessing an "immigrant" population with ancestries ranging from Nigeria to France to North America itself, revolutionary leaders were faced with the task of defining who was and who was not "American." Lacking a shared history, ancestry, religion, and in some cases even a common language, America nonetheless was viewed as having a unique aspect that excited many Enlightenment philosophers. The fledgling nation was the first step in a political experiment attempting to *form a nation*—not just annex other territories—based on shared political beliefs rather than cultural or historical ties. The idea of creating a nation was revolutionary: hitherto, nations were defined as the territories of the sovereign, and nationality often amounted to no more than an indication as to which monarch you "belonged." Several decades later, Hegel's discourse on subjectivity would outline a schema in which a person came into being through his role in the state; Gobineau would produce a polemic that produced an exclusionary version of nationality.[68] At its inception, America struggled with both issues: if America and its people are defined by a common love of freedom, how can it justify the enslavement of Negroes or the genocide of Native Americans?

Many prominent American statesmen such as Alexander Hamilton and Benjamin Franklin contended that slavery was in fact contrary to the ideals on which the nation had been founded. Slavery, they argued, was not only antithetical to being American, it would eventually prove a threat to America's unity if allowed to continue.[69] Thomas Jefferson, a wealthy Virginia plantation owner and a powerful ideologue, countered by rephrasing the dilemma: how do we prevent the "Negro problem" from destroying the nation? Slavery, Jefferson would suggest in his many letters and statements to abolitionists and other antislavery factions, was not in itself antithetical to the American ideal; it was *Negroes* who were antithetical to the American ideal, and it was Negroes who were the true threat to this young democracy.[70] Studying Jefferson is crucial to understanding the American invention of the Negro because Jefferson was the principal author of the Declaration of Independence and its idealist rhetoric excluding those who are not white. Declaring "all men are created equal" in a nation that held hundreds of thousands in bondage, and then arguing in *Notes on the State of Virginia* (1784–1785) that the freedom of American citizens could only be ensured through the enslavement and/or the wholesale removal of Negroes, Jefferson not only laid the groundwork for this paradoxical discourse on the (white) American subject and the (Negro) Other but used the law to maintain the schism between Black and white, creating a vision of America in which the Negro played no part.

Given its concurrence with the popularity of political discourses on representative government, the American Revolution was celebrated by many Enlightenment philosophers as the dawn of a new age they had helped create. No longer, it seemed, would democratic ideologies remain mere philosophies but instead would manifest themselves as nations. The very *idea* of a thought becoming reality, a notion becoming a nation, proved even more seductive, for if nothing else the Enlightenment was a movement that stressed man's ability to change his world and develop anew: not just customs, ideas, and values, but actual *nations*. Jefferson capitalized on this notion of thought becoming action: the Declaration of Independence represents the idealism of a logocentric thinker who takes the prerogative of logos in its classical sense as law and, as law, the will to be.[71] The word is everything. There was an added benefit in declaring this nation a democracy irrespective of its actual conditions: America was wholly and totally "new." America had no past: previous to this Declaration (and long before independence had been won) there had existed a British colony that sanctioned slavery and the slave trade. Therefore, the newly democratic republic shared no relation to these previous practices; it was as if one template had been removed and another set down on the same geographical region—and Negro slaves had somehow been left behind. Logos, therefore, directed and represented the *reality* of the American nation, further suggesting that only those who had access to this logos—those who were literate—could direct and represent the nation. Although the literacy level among the white population was low, the *idea* of a literate Negro was itself fantastical, as only the former were associated with the spoken and written language, and it was language that composed the nation.[72]

All the same, ignoring the fact of slavery did not make it go away, especially for a slave owner of Jefferson's magnitude. In reviewing Jefferson's letters and writings on the Negro and slavery, it is important to note that he never actually engaged in a debate over the matter with his audience or correspondent; rather, he made his pronouncements and considered the matter finished, as if the conclusion of the word signaled the conclusion of the matter entirely. As Winthrop Jordan has noted, Jefferson grew increasingly irritable on the question of slavery, as if surprised and upset that the matter persisted in spite of the finality of his words.

Part of the Enlightenment's logocentric philosophy is the relationship between man and nature; although the two were not necessarily opposed to one another, the former was viewed as dynamic, and the latter static. Although human ability as well as moral and intellectual comprehension had changed greatly from the time of ancient Greece up to the eighteenth century, a common argument ran, nature had remained unchanged: trees had not changed their shape, the seasons, with little variance, performed in order and on time. Most importantly, animals displayed no signs of progress, typically indicated as a failure to develop language.[73] Logos came to represent man's inherent superiority to nature and, during the Enlightenment, achieved a status that overwhelmed all other modes of being: a thing could not exist if it could not be expressed or if it could not express itself through language.[74] Not surprisingly, eighteenth-century tracts describing nonwhites often repeated and underscored terms such as "indescribable," "wordless," and "beyond description/words," stressing how language and the savage were antithetical to one another.

Jefferson also deployed this binary in his descriptions and commentary on those of African descent. In *Notes,* he constantly compares Blacks to horses, dogs, domestic animals, and the "Oran-Ootan." He writes that Negroes have failed to learn anything despite constant exposure to "the conversation of their masters." Within this rhetoric he urges his audience not to confuse Negroes with whites: "Will not a lover of natural history then, one who views the gradations in all the races of animals with the eye of philosophy, excuse an effort to keep those in the department of man as distinct as nature has formed them?"[75]

When addressing the subject of Blacks who had in fact mastered logos—such as Phillis Wheatley for her translations of classical Greek verse and her poetry, Banneker for his almanac, Ignatius Sancho for his novel—Jefferson could not ignore the actual production of the written word. In response, he likened Banneker's almanac to "a good imitation," suggesting that, like a parrot, Negroes may *mimic* human actions, but mimicry does not a man make. In the case of Phillis Wheatley, Jefferson attributed her writing to another faculty altogether—not her mind, but her heart. In stating that "Religion has produced a Phyllis Whately [*sic*]; but it could not produce a poet," Jefferson divides the act from intentionality. Wheatley's translations and works are reduced to a series of transcriptions of sensations—her words lack meaning in that they kindle "the senses only, not the imagination."[76] Jefferson's deployment and definition of language is based on the idea that the appearance of a word in itself signifies nothing more than a series of marks on the page, the way a chicken might scratch the dirt in agitation or in search of seed. Animals, by virtue of their physical attributes, can mimic and leave traces, but these actions are merely that. Negroes, possessing the same physical characteristics as whites, are more likely to confuse the kind-hearted who wish to believe them to be the equal of whites. Whites, by contrast, do not produce mere "scratchings"; their words *precede* their actions and therefore will them into being, hence the significance of the Declaration. Within Jefferson's schema, Negroes are neither absent nor ignored in the Declaration; they simply do not belong within the realm of language.[77]

In line with this thinking, we can return to Jefferson's defense of slavery. As mentioned earlier, Jefferson viewed Negroes as a remnant from colonialist times, an anachronism within the modern state. Because slavery is never mentioned in the Declaration or preamble of the Constitution, it does not, as such, exist. Negroes, however, *do* exist (like livestock) and it is not slavery but the natural condition of the Negro—his dependency, his lack of intellect, his infantile disposition—that has misled those who believe him to be treated unfairly.[78] It is the Negro, and his inability to progress, that has produced the slave system and furthermore perversely prolonged it even within the American democracy. As the following passage from the *Notes* argues, slavery in itself has nothing to do with the present condition of the Negro:

> The improvement of the blacks in body and mind, in the first instance of their mixture with whites, has been observed by every one, and proves that their inferiority is not the effect merely of their condition of life. We know that among the Romans, about the Au-

gustan age especially, the condition of their slaves was much more deplorable than that of the blacks on the continent of America. . . . The American slaves cannot enumerate [the selling of old and sick slaves] among the injuries and insults they receive. . . . When a [Roman] master was murdered, all his slaves, in the same house, or within hearing, were condemned to death. Here punishment falls on the guilty only, and as precise proof is required against him as against a freeman. Yet notwithstanding these and other discouraging circumstances among the Romans, their slaves were often the rarest artists. They excelled too in science, insomuch as to be usually employed as tutors to their masters' children. Epictectus, Terence, and Phaedrus, were slaves. But they were of the race of whites. *It is not their condition, then, but nature, which has produced the distinction* [my emphasis].[79]

Jefferson begins by observing that "Blackness" can be altered when mixed with white blood. His rhetoric already assumes Black inertia and white activity, for this intermixture and the resultant change is accredited to the white blood; yet the fact that the issue is considered Black, not white or even half-white, points to the impossibility of trying to change or transform this inert Blackness. On this level, Blackness functions in the manner of nature, in that one can alter but not wholly transform natural conditions. Within a structure of binary oppositions, Blackness serves as the stagnant "negativity" that the dynamic "positivity" of whiteness can change partially through intermixture but cannot affect the original state of the former.[80] If this Black negativity is further considered as nonlingual, the inability to change within itself or even alter significantly from an infusion of white blood becomes easier to understand. Logos, after all, is the will to be; lacking words equals lacking the ability (synonymous with the will, in this structure) to produce oneself. Because the will to be is absolute, the *difference* between the mixed offspring and its Negro parent is the indication of its *whiteness*. The *sameness*, that which locates the issue as nonetheless Negro, is the indicator of *Blackness*, or simply what has not changed.

When we move on to Jefferson's discussion of slavery in ancient Rome, we are already reading with regard to his previous statement: whiteness indicates difference, and Blackness "sameness." According to Jefferson, slavery in ancient Rome was *different*: it was far more cruel and oppressive.[81] Nonetheless, as he notes, many slaves excelled in the arts and sciences—both disciplines, it must be remembered, defined through their relationship with language.[82] Because Jefferson ends his brief history on slavery in ancient Rome with the slaves excelling and tutoring their masters' children, he suggests that the dynamism of whiteness eventually leads to incorporation within the masters' family and, through the act of teaching, progressing and making a *difference*. By choosing such an ancient example, Jefferson implies that his European ancestors had passed out of such ill-fitting employ centuries ago, further underscoring the retrograde nature of enslaved Blacks. Lacking this will to be, Negroes will remain the *same*.

The passage that follows the one on slavery goes on to state more explicitly the nature of the Negro with regard to logos-as-law. Adding that whatever nature denied them in the head "in . . . the heart she will be found to have done them justice," Jefferson writes that Negroes may pilfer, but they cannot be held responsible for this act because, "That disposition to theft with which they have been branded, must be ascribed to their situation, and not to any depravity of the moral sense. The man, in whose favor no laws of property exist, probably feels himself less bound to respect those made in favour of others."[83] The most misleading and damaging section of this passage is the statement at the end that there is not a single law in the nation that is *not* arbitrary, founded in force, and devoid of conscience. Because the passage is discussing Negroes, the rather vague use of "laws" is actually specifying those sanctioning slavery. Under the laws that Jefferson himself played a large role in creating, Negroes are considered property and not men (despite Jefferson's use of "man" in this passage); therefore, only the laws sanctioning slavery actually apply. More specifically, it is the *criminal* slave codes to which Jefferson is referring—codes that he made more draconian while abolishing and/or lessening harsher punishments for white criminals.[84]

Through a double negation, Jefferson is arguing that the slave laws are in fact just, obey points of order, and were conscientiously designed, which of course can only mean that Negroes are enslaved because that is right, just, and the decision of moral men. However, it would be *unjust* to prosecute a Negro for petty theft because the laws of property—to put it mildly—are not in his favor. Jefferson describes the relation between the law and the citizen as one of reciprocity. In America, all literate men have a relationship with the logos: this relationship is the basis for the nation and the engagement of such reciprocity is what confirms one as an American, a subject. The Negro, as the nonlingual Other, has no relationship with the law; outside this relationship, the act of petty theft has no inherent meaning. As Jefferson writes, pilfering by Negroes should not be construed as a reflective act of retaliation but should be "ascribed to their situation" which is, quite literally, outside logos.

Within Jefferson's schema, the Negro does not merely exhibit but *is* a retrograde influence that ultimately threatens the progressive dynamic of the American subject. It is the nature of the Negro's stagnant negativity that would infect the American body should incorporation be attempted:

> It will probably be asked, Why not retain and incorporate the blacks into the state, and thus save the expence of supplying, by importation of white settlers, the vacancies they will leave? Deep rooted prejudices entertained by the whites; ten thousand recollections, by the blacks, of the injuries they have sustained; new provocations; the real distinctions which nature has made; and many other circumstances, will divide us into parties, and produce convulsions which will probably never end but in the extermination of the one or the other race. To these objections, which may be political, may be added others, which are physical and moral.[85]

The passage begins with a vague reference to the "deep rooted" white prejudice that would disallow replacing immigrant workers with Negroes. Yet the statements that follow undercut any notion that this prejudice is counterproductive or even questionable. The Negro is described as vengeful, prone to violent actions, and naturally different from whites. The prediction that any attempt at replacement would cause divisions and produce "convulsions" strongly suggests those natural divisions should be respected in that they cannot be overcome. White prejudice is thus (re)produced as a natural revulsion, further underscored by "deep rooted," a metaphor that corresponds to nature.[86] By forecasting that these divisions between Black and white are eternally irreconcilable, Jefferson is suggesting that the differences are inherent and conjunction is therefore "unnatural." Because the American subject is seen as the possessor of logos, the will to be, and therefore dynamic, integration of the races is unthinkable because of Negro negativity: whites are not adverse to change, but Blacks are incapable of it.[87]

The unchanging "sameness" of the Negro is, paradoxically, a difference. Yet it is a difference because whites *are able to recognize*—even instinctively, Jefferson suggests—a natural division between themselves and Blacks. This aspect of the analysis may appear to the reader as mere hairsplitting, but in the following passage the use of the word "difference" with regard to whites and Blacks respectively is modified by two very different adjectives, the former suggesting dynamism, the latter stagnation: "The first *difference* which *strikes us* is that of color. Whether the black of the Negro resides in the reticular membrane between the skin and the scarf-skin . . . the *difference is fixed in nature*, and is as real as if its seat and cause were better known to us."[88] Although in this passage the dynamism of the subject is accorded primacy over the stagnation of the Other, it also paradoxically points to the need to respect the laws of nature over an unnatural attempt to ignore such differences. Knowledge, it seems, is subsumed by natural law. Yet on closer investigation we see that it is in fact the *dynamic* difference, the province of the subject, that reveals the *static* difference of the Other. Man and nature do not exist in a hostile relation to one another, man simply cannot change that which is fixed, and he is alerted to this impossibility by virtue of his own progressive tendencies. In short, the subject's dynamic difference strikes him to reveal the fixed difference of the Other. It is as if one is asked to compare the life of a human being to that of a rock and explain the differences of their respective biographies. One would explain that the man is different because he has grown and progressed; the rock retains difference because it has remained the same.

Various debates have emerged regarding W. E. B. Du Bois's famous use of the veil in *The Souls of Black Folk* and subsequent essays and writings. One possibility that has not been fully explored, however, is its use originating with Jefferson. In the following passage, Jefferson uses the opposition between the stagnant and the dynamic to assert the inferiority of the Negro: "And is this difference of no importance? Are not the fine mixtures of red and white, the expressions of every passion by greater or less suffusions of colour in the one, preferable to that eternal monotony, which reigns in the countenances, that immovable veil of black which covers all the emotions of the other race?"[89] In advocating intermixture between Native Americans and whites, the rhetoric of the passage adds a sense of aesthetics, suggesting that, even from without, miscegenation between Black and white must strike one as horrific, given that "immovable veil" of the former.[90] Reliance on the nature of color to produce guidelines as to which races should mix and which should not transforms Blackness from a color to a barrier. More specifically, one can in fact see the outlines of the face through a veil, but the immovability of the veil points to an unattainable humanity on the part of Negroes, even though they are part of the human family. Using the veil as a metaphor for Blackness also prevents it from being seen as a color. As the passage preceding this one indicates, although referred to as a color, "the black of the Negro" is described as a separate entity, residing just below the skin and not within it. Blackness is either above or below the skin, never simply a color. This rhetoric denies Negroes status as human beings with a different color of skin and distances them from the human family.

As the passage reveals, Jefferson reserves the deployment of coloring as part and parcel of the skin for Native Americans and whites. By producing coloring as a component of the skin, racial bodies preserve their integrity. Whereas the Negro bears an eternal veil, whites and "reds" are produced as naturally inclined to a range of passions and expressions. Without a veil they are also free, literally, to interact with one another on the same level, much in keeping with Jefferson's proposed agenda of miscegenation between the two races.[91] Bereft of an actual physical anomaly that would differentiate Blacks from whites, Jefferson attempts to define the ethereal quality of color as a physical characteristic that nature has produced to segregate the Negro from non-Black peoples. Because the "Indian" is also "colored" it is incumbent on Jefferson to demonstrate when a color is just a color and when it is the marker of inferiority.

The use of the veil also allows Jefferson to conflate the behavior and physicality of the Negro, rendering him incapable of progress. The veil literally "covers" the emotions of Jefferson's Negro; this lack of vivacity is not only caused by an external impediment but is also impeded from within:

In general their existence appears to participate more of sensation than reflection. To this must be ascribed their disposition to sleep when abstracted from their diversions, and unemployed in labour. An animal whose body is at rest, and who does not reflect, must be disposed to sleep of course. Comparing them by their faculties of memory, reason, and imagination, it appears to me, that in memory they are equal to the whites; in reason much inferior, as I think one could scarcely be found capable of tracing and comprehending the investigations of Euclid; and that in imagination they are dull, tasteless, and anomalous.[92]

Jefferson's Negro is overwhelming in his physicality, or, rather, possesses a physicality that overwhelms everything else. The Negro may have a veil as an external obstacle, but he is also bounded within by an inability to will himself to action. Jefferson writes that the Negro body is incapable of movement unless prodded from without and the Negro mind shares this aspect, being incapable of reflection. The Negro capacity for memory, the only sense that is admitted to be equal to that of whites, gains no distinction, for memory is a faculty of retention, functioning the same way as sensation: it is acted upon, not acting.

Jefferson attempted to convince his prodemocratic but antislavery critics of Negro inferiority by presenting the preservation of the fledgling democracy as more crucial than any other concern. His strategy was unique in that he did not attempt to present slavery as an issue wholly independent of democracy but rather linked to it. In describing the American nation as a product of man's immense will to be harnessed through logos, Jefferson tried to provide irrefutable proof of white superiority and thus the democracy of one group in abeyance to another. According to his argument, the presence of Negroes in America did not mean they were *part* of the nation, for America was a nation produced by democratic ideals, not geographical or historical boundaries. Contrasted with this ephemeral construct was the inert body of the Negro, and although human, he lacked any of the properties possessed by whites, the most important being the will to be. Jefferson's idea of the subject is based on a distinction between the intellectual and the physical. The subject is produced in the moment at which thought becomes action, living within a nation that operates on the very same guidelines. In the same vein, America is a nation based on and maintained by her ideology; linked by little else, Americans, in order to preserve their nation, must ensure that the spirit of democracy remains as logos. The Negro, Jefferson argues in *Notes*, is incapable of producing that spirit. Bounded from within and without, the Negro is made external by his static physicality; it is almost as if he is composed of a different element

The Invention of the Black Other | 63

altogether—flesh as opposed to spirit. He does not even possess a face—the synecdoche of humanity par excellence—he possesses a veil. Given the inability to move beyond his veil, the Negro would never be able to mix with the rest of the population. Skin color, rapidly becoming an absolute signifier in the European and American imagination, came to represent not a color but an object in and of itself impeding any progressive potential. In (re)producing Blackness as a physical aberration and whiteness as a coloring that signifies an ability to transform words into deeds, Jefferson hoped to sidestep a point made over and over again by antislavery factions: the fact that the Negro possesses all the characteristics ascribed to humans and therefore could be confused with no other species. Jefferson allows for the Negro's humanity in the vaguest sense but would never allow for his ability to become an American. Although he failed to convince others of the need for wholesale expatriation of Negroes, Jefferson was able to print indelibly on the white American mind this idea of the Negro as antithetical to the American nation.[93]

Others-from-within and Others-from-without are not radically different from one another; they are best understood as variations on the theme of alterity rather than two discrete categories. Recognizing these two forms of Others is valuable in three ways: (1) it underscores the lack of cohesion in Western racist discourses; (2) it underscores the way in which theories of Black inferiority are based on personal agendas and beliefs rather than any sort of objective criteria; and, most importantly for this book, (3) these differences help explain the different types of counterdiscourses that emerge in their wake. This is not to say that one can therefore understand discourses on the subject through a structuralist reading. While racist discourse seems firmly tied to personal agenda—Hegel seeking to establish Germany as the most superior nation in the world; Gobineau seeking to restore the aristocracy in France; Jefferson seeking to keep his slaves (and thus his riches) without taking responsibility for his actions—the reasons for the differences between contemporaneous antiracist counterdiscourses are not so easily divined. This is because the white subject is wholly contingent on a Black Other, but the reverse is not true. Posited as oppositional to Blackness, whiteness assumes a reassuring homogeneity that reifies the concept of a Western civilization that is wholly white and acting in concert. In the counterdiscourses that follow, Blackness achieves a variety of definitions and meanings, some of which are directly at odds with one another, because none of the counterdiscourses prescribe a simplistic inversion of the binary set before them (white subject and Black Other). The simple dialectics produced by the discourses of Hegel, Gobineau, and Jefferson are not replicated in the counterdiscourses that follow. Instead, we see a variety of theoretical structures offered: versions of Hegel's dialectic, idealist and materialist dialectics, and even dialogics emerge in different African diasporic counterdiscourses. At the same time, the counter-discourses that follow, while responding to the specific and different ways in which they are Othered, are also united in their goal: to force the West to recognize that it is not Black Others they must reckon with, but Black subjects.

CHAPTER TWO

The Trope of Masking in the
Works of W. E. B. Du Bois, Léopold
Sédar Senghor, and Aimé Césaire

MASKING AND LOGOS

From the late eighteenth through the nineteenth century, a number of African diasporic writers, including Olaudah Equiano, Mary Prince, David Walker, Martin Delaney, and Alexander Crummel, offered texts that disputed both the quotidian and scholarly anti-Black discourses increasingly embraced by Western populations. By the beginning of the twentieth century, a specific response began to emerge from the African diasporic tradition, a response that directly engaged with the theories and theoretical structures used to support (white) Western claims of superiority. These counterdiscourses, which are the focus of this chapter, constitute the basis for the theories of the Black subject that we see across the African diaspora today, helping us to understand not only the wide variety of options available for theories of the Black subject but also the common theoretical concerns these counterdiscourses share. I show how the trope of the mask (or, in the case of Césaire, the act of ventriloquism) functions as an important component for the texts that are the focus of this chapter, both in terms of theorizing "Blackness" in relationship to the West and as a strategy for evading one of the primary traps of counterdiscourse. I have chosen these texts because all of them have withstood the test of time, albeit not unscathed. In the past two decades, many scholars and writers have come to reject the theories on the Black subject that are examined in this chapter. As David Levering-Lewis and others have argued, Du Bois's theory of double consciousness was abandoned by him quite early in his career and has since been rejected by many Black American academics as indequate to a much more complex problem. Léopold Sédar Senghor's and Aimé Césaire's Negritude movement has also greatly waned in its influence, albeit more in the Anglophone rather than the Francophone diaspora.[1] As I will show in chapter 3, Frantz Fanon's theory of the "masked" Black Other from *Peau noire, masques blancs* (Black Skin, White Masks) has been under sustained attack by both Black and white feminists for its essentialist and therefore limiting view of white, Black, and specifically Algerian women.

Scholars who work in postcolonial theory, African American studies, and/or related minority studies are familiar with the ambivalent status of counterdiscourse. Although counterdiscourse provides a voice for the marginalized and has often proved successful in forcing the terms of the debate (in this case the racial subject) to become more equitable, it nonetheless contains a crucial weakness. Because counterdiscourse only comes into being through discourse, it is always fundamentally subsidiary to the latter. Because Hegel, Gobineau, and Jefferson built their case for the white subject on assertions of black inferiority, Du Bois, Senghor, Césaire, and (in the next chapter) Fanon must respond to these assertions, regardless of their often ridiculous content. At the same time, the *descriptive* limits that counterdiscourse is bound to respect are not synonymous with its *prescriptive* limits. More simply put, having to respond to assertions of Black inferiority does not mean one cannot use that response to move the terms of the debate beyond the binary of inferiority/superiority and Black/white. Masking, as it is deployed in the texts examined here, enables the narrator and/or protagonist to be "double-mouthed." Because Jefferson, Gobineau, and Hegel all insist that the Black is incapable of logos, the act of responding becomes the Black logos—negating the idealist negation of the Black Other through the speech act. The result of this negation of the negation, ultimately Marxist in its sensibilities, is a synthesis that renders the idealist dialectic of the white subject and Black Other as a *descriptive* limit. It can no longer be prescriptive, of course, because the act of response negates the assertion that the Black is incapable of response. In these Black counterdiscourses, the prescriptive limits are thus noticeably different from the original, providing a space for the exploration and/or analysis of the Black subject in the West. By using the materialist dialectic's negation of the negation, in which the Black Other is neither wholly discarded nor wholly annihilated, these counterdiscourses all produce a synthesis that simultaneously speaks to the idealist construction of the Black Other *and* the existence of (or possibility of) the Black subject. Masking signals the enabling of this Black logos, one that differs from its white counterparts because it is "double-mouthed," responding to colonialist discourse while speaking its counterclaim of a Black subject.

Masking is often theorized as a complex performance of subversion and deception that enables a Black subject within the pathologically hostile environment of white racism. My own reading focuses on the trope of masking as a point of comparison in the varying theoretical strategies located in some of the most prominent early- to mid-twentieth-century African diasporic counterdiscourses. Here the philosophical configuration of the speech act, as logos, replaces the concept of performance, and the nature of subversion, as counterdiscourse, becomes slightly different. Du Bois, Senghor, Césaire, and Fanon all deploy the concept of masking to critique the paradoxes inherent within the Western binary of white subject/Black Other, and they examine that paradox within the context of the speech act, or logos. The mask does not so much signal Black performance here as mark the moment at which the idealist dialectic of the white subject and Black Other breaks down. Equally important, it also marks the simultaneous emergence of the Black subject denied by that first idealist dialectic. Although their productions of the Black subject at times vary greatly, this chapter argues that Du Bois, Senghor, and Césaire (as well as Fanon, as the following chapter will show) nonetheless share a common theoretical sensibility. For them, masking is a strategy both to deconstruct Western logos and to assert their own specific understanding of the Black logos, allowing them to analyze the relationship of Black consciousness within the context of the Western racist discourse that refuses to acknowledge this consciousness.

MASKING AS NEGOTIATION

W. E. B. Du Bois's *Souls of Black Folk* has been analyzed and discussed to such a degree that it is nearly impossible to offer a reading that has not already been covered. Indeed, Shamoon Zamir's *Dark Voices* offers one of the most definitive readings of Du Boisian double consciousness by linking it closely and convincingly to Hegel's *Phenomenology of the Spirit*. In the reading below, I argue that *Souls*'s emphasis on history, culture, politics, and economics suggests that Du Bois is using both idealist and materialist structures to construct the Black and address his contradictory status as an Other-from-within. I also propose (especially in light of my later reading of Fanon) that Du Bois is responding to Hegel's discourse on the African in the introduction to the *Philosophy of History*, borrowing Hegel's concept of *Sehnsucht* to drive his dialectic, rather than Fanon's focus on *Aufhebung* in applying the master-slave dialectic to his reading of the Black colonial. In applying this reading to *Souls* I suggest that double consciousness is not in fact the state of the Du Boisian subject but that the veil, produced by a materialist—rather than an idealist—"negation of the negation" is used in *Souls* to both critique the limits of the idealist dialectic and demonstrate that the Black operates both within and without the discourse of the white subject and Black Other.

At first glance it is difficult to understand why Negritudists Aimé Césaire's and Léopold Senghor's theories of the Black subject draw on Gobineau's assertion that the artistic accomplishments of any civilization is fundamentally derived from "Negro blood," especially when one considers that Gobineau argued that the Negro's lack of intellectual ability meant that he was simply the ink pen that needed to be guided by the Aryan hand. Both Senghor's and Césaire's counterdiscourses respond to the Black as an Other-from-without. Senghor's mask at once recalls Gobineau's pronouncement on "Negro art" and the useful Black monopoly on it that Gobineau's bizarre racist logic accords. Césaire's counterdiscourse also uses masking (in this case as ventriloquism) as the means by which the Black can confront and reject his figuration as an Other-from-without and thus achieve subject status. These three counterdiscourses provide new models for the subject that combine the theoretical specificity that the idealist dialectic of the subject allows with the historically grounded concerns of Marx's materialist dialectic. By engaging these two models and placing them in tension with one another, these theories construct a Black subject who, although in part bounded by the racism of the originary Western discourses, draws on materialist structures to point to the fallacies of the former and the freeing possibilities of the latter. At the same time, all these counterdiscourses, regardless of the degree to which they deploy materialist dialectics in favor of idealist ones, assume an essentially idealist formation of the nation: the Black is either citizen or interloper, and the female either passive landscape or, for all intents and purposes, nonexistent. As such, they are best understood as the first in a series of counterdiscourses rather than the finite canon on African diasporic subjectivity.

In philosophy, the dialectic is often hailed as the step that moves us beyond binary oppositions.[2] Yet the dialectic Hegel deploys when writing on the enslavement of Africans and the colonizing of Africa clearly serves an agenda meant to ensure and propagate hierarchical distinctions and binary oppositions between the races. Looking at the quotation below from Du Bois on double consciousness, we can see this "dialogue" between Hegel and Du Bois on the dialectic of the Black and the Western nation quite profoundly:

> This history of the American Negro is the history of this strife,—this longing to attain self-conscious manhood, to merge his double self into a better and truer self. In this merging he wishes neither of the older selves to be lost. He would not Africanize America, for America has much to teach the world and Africa. He would not bleach his Negro soul in a flood of white Americanism, for he knows that Negro blood has a message for the world. He simply wishes to make it possible for a man to be both a Negro and an American, without being cursed and spit upon by his fellows, without having the doors of Opportunity closed roughly in his face.[3]

Du Bois posits the relationship between the American Negro and the white American as Hegel's idealist dialectic. Just as Hegel posits the subject as moving toward synthesis in order to achieve self-consciousness, Du Bois states that the American Negro is also moving toward synthesis— or "merging" as he puts it—to achieve self-consciousness. Du Bois attempts to underscore Hegel's ideal of synthesis as a mutual and equal joining by writing that neither "Africanizing" America nor "bleaching" the Negro soul is an acceptable move toward synthesis.[4] Rather, as he reiterates at the end of the passage, the American Negro is authentically moving toward synthesis because he is striving to be *both* a Negro and an American. White racism, characterized here as spitting, cursing, and the denial of entry, is deemed antidialectical (and therefore antiprogressive) because it attempts to block this move toward synthesis.[5] Finally, just as Hegel's ideal dialectic functions as an inexorable force continually moving toward synthesis, Du Bois's use of the term "American Negro" in this passage suggests that even as the Black strives to be both a Negro and American, he already *is*. Du Bois's "Negro American" points to a synthesis that exists even as it moves toward it.

Du Bois begins by placing the African American in history, a space denied to him by Hegel, who posited analytical history (the only truly meaningful history) as produced and controlled by reason, the force that separates Europe from all other nations (with the occasional and fleeting exceptions of Japan and China). By locating the Negro outside history, Hegel also located him as the antithesis to European reason, and thus inferior in intellect and moot in the history of the world as a history of civilizations. Du Bois reverses this process with his first statement and the term "American Negro"—which immediately invokes a historical (temporal and geographical) context. Du Bois's American Negro is now "inside" the dialectic, but the process does not stop there. He claims the American Negro is defined by a longing to merge his "double self into a better and truer self," aligning the African American subject with the dialectic but producing him as thesis *and* antithesis, not simply the latter. On a rhetorical level, Du Bois has removed the Black from his position as antithesis and, rather than simply switching him over, *expands* the concept of the Black to incorporate the entire dialectic. The Black is no longer simply a function; he is an ongoing process, he is a subject. According to Du Bois, this subject's longing functions dialectically in his search for synthesis. More importantly, synthesis is defined as a merging of thesis and antithesis as opposed to Hegel's equating *Aufhebung* with colonization, wherein the thesis subsumes its antithesis in its inexorable drive toward synthesis. Synthesis as *Aufhebung* is then rejected in the final sentences of the passage, where Du Bois points out that subsuming synthesis only leads to missed opportunities—for both Blacks and whites. To "Africanize America" is to reject and ignore the value of white American culture, just as "bleaching" the Negro soul disallows the contributions of African Americans to be recognized and appreciated. Tellingly, Du Bois uses a rhetoric that emphasizes the idea of the synthesis as an expansion of knowledge, reinforcing the "Du Boisian dialectic" as an impetus toward education rather than mastery, perhaps a less tangible but philosophically more useful telos. Du Bois's modification is important because it responds to one of the most important frames for Hegel's dialectic when he writes on the European's—or even more specifically the German's—relationship to the "exterior" world. *Aufhebung*, upheaval, becomes *Sehnsucht*, or longing, restructuring the impetus without corrupting the dynamic that ultimately drives the dialectic. This is not to say that Du Bois's use of the idealist dialectic is radically different from all of Hegel's dialectic structures, only that *Souls* deploys a dialectic we see more often in Hegel's *Philosophy of History* or his *Philosophy of Right*.[6] Finally, Du Bois produces his dialectic as the means toward the eradication of discrimination and segregation. This indicates the paradox of Du Bois' Negro American: he is not the American antithesis but the progressive aspect of the nation in that he seeks merger and self-consciousness toward states that, according to Hegel, are almost self-explanatory as progressive goals.

There are two important disruptions here. Recalling Derrida's famous argument from *On Grammatology* on the limitations of the "unilinear" text to effect dialogic discussion, Du Bois's "Negro American" clearly privileges the first term over the second—but this first term, as underscored throughout *Souls*, is multivalent, composed of striving, disruption, and synthesis. The term "Negro American," then, only functions as a binary opposition within racist discourse. In *Souls*, "Negro American" achieves a different opposition, one in which the dialectic of the Negro encounters the opposition of the same term already incorporated within American. Du Bois's paradox of the Negro American in *Souls* moves beyond Hegel's idealist structure of the dialectic to incorporate the materialist concerns: racism, political disenfranchisement, and economic exploitation. Du Bois's Negro, then, defies Hegel's simplistic rendering of him as an ahistorical antithesis, an Other-from-without. The American invention of the Negro had produced him as an Other-from-within. Within the realm of philosophical oppositions, the Negro slave, as the antithesis of all that was progressive, democratic, and civilized, was therefore the antithesis of the American nation and its citizens-as-representatives.[7] In the American discourse, the Negro had agency, but a very specific one: as antithesis, he was inherently opposed to the democratic order. The "Negro problem," then, was not a problem of white racism but a problem of Black antithesis: the *Negro* could not be incorporated into the American landscape because he *was a Negro*. This is the primary illusion of which Du Bois attempts to disabuse his readers.[8] In the first and perhaps most famous chapter of *Souls*, Du Bois confronts the American rhetoric of the "Negro problem" to argue that this act of exclusion is not the Negro's:

> Between me and the other world there is ever an unasked question: unasked by some through feelings of delicacy; by others through the difficulty of rightly framing it. All, nevertheless, flutter round it. They approach me in a half-hesitant sort of way, eye me curiously or compassionately, and then, instead of saying directly, How does it feel to be a problem? they say, I know an excellent colored man in my town; or, I fought at Mechanicsville; or, Do not these Southern outrages make your blood boil? At these I smile or am interested, or reduce the boiling to a simmer, as the occasion may require. To the real question, How does it feel to be a problem? I answer seldom a word. And yet, being a problem is a strange experience,—peculiar even for one who has never been anything else, save perhaps in babyhood and in Europe.[9]

Du Bois points to the "Negro problem" as a product of the logos that has been produced by white Americans, even those who are sympathetic to the cause of Negro suffrage. He first produces himself as estranged from the "other world" and indicates the source of this estrangement as the "unasked question." The question, more poignantly, is not one that is posed in an aggressive or derogatory manner, yet it nonetheless has that effect because it is logos—the collective speech act that the speaker is constantly bombarded with and, through it, categorized as "a problem." The act of deploying logos belies its overarching power: it is simply a rather vague question produced as an informal comment. It comes from a number of white individuals—and Du Bois posits their individuality by briefly describing the different means by which the question comes to be posed and the variety of forms it takes. Its power is irrational and unmistakable in its effect, capable of casting the Negro quest for inclusion into the Negro-as-problem.

In this first chapter of *Souls*, the epistemological homogeneity of whites with regard to Blacks is underscored, producing a racist discourse that is perpetuated by ignorance. Further, Du Bois reveals the double consciousness of the Black subject, pointing to the monological limitations of anti-Black discourse and its idealist dialectical structure, further revealing these limitations as that which divides him from the "other world." The divide is of course not the question, for the question is not a question at all, it is an assertion of Black antithesis, revealing the thesis, this monological discourse of the Negro-as-problem, as an impediment in the Black subject's drive toward synthesis. Du Bois attacks the idea of the Negro as "a problem," revealing its dehumanizing impulse, and points to another reality, one where the white interlocutor is actively attempting to dehumanize the Negro.

Although the white discourse-as-thesis asserts Blackness as antithesis (the "problem" that prevents national synthesis), it is clear that Du Bois rejects the legitimacy of this production of the dialectic because he simultaneously produces a counterdialectic, one that rejects the accuracy of the thesis and deconstructs its role in the dialectic (that is, reducing the Negro to a problem). The passage following this one explores the pain, frustration, and humiliation of the African American in finding himself posited as the American antithesis: "it dawned on me that I was different from the others; or like, mayhap, in heart and life and longing, but shut out from the world by a vast veil."[10] The American thesis is a false one, because it desynthesizes through the deployment of the veil; it is an antidialectic and therefore nonprogressive. Because the antidialectic actively rejects synthesis, it resembles a binary opposition in which whiteness rejects Blackness because that is the nature of the former. We might also note that this whiteness produces Blackness *in order to reject it* because that is the nature of "whiteness" within this specific context. *Souls* makes a bold critique of the American dialectic of the subject, accusing its entire structure (and not just the thesis) of being antidialectical, antiprogressive, and, therefore, anti-American, opposed as it is to the Black subject.

In "On Being Crazy," a 1926 article from the *Crisis*, Du Bois uses an anecdote from the quotidian to demonstrate the fallacies of the American idealist dialectic on race through a materialist critique:

It was one o'clock and I was hungry. I walked into a restaurant, seated myself and reached for the bill-of-fare. My table companion rose.

"Sir," said he, "do you wish to force your company on those who do not want you?"

No, said I, I wish to eat.

"Are you aware, sir, that this is social equality?"

Nothing of the sort, sir, it is hunger—and I ate.

The day's work done, I sought the theatre. As I sank into my seat, the lady shrank and squirmed.

I beg pardon, I said.

"Do you enjoy being where you are not wanted?" she asked coldly. Oh no, I said.

"Well, you are not wanted here."

I was surprised. I fear you are mistaken, I said. I certainly want the music and I like to think the music wants me to listen to it.

"Usher," said the lady, "this is social equality."

No, madam, said the usher, it is the second movement of Beethoven's Fifth Symphony.[11]

Yet not all whites have the same relationship to the logos that insists upon a Black/white binary. The narrative follows the same format, from a theater to a hotel, until it ends with a longer scene between the narrator and a white "wayfarer." The latter makes a point of walking through the mud so as to avoid touching the former because "Niggers is dirty," to which Du Bois responds, "So is mud." The ensuing conversation juxtaposes race and class as the educated Du Bois argues disingenuously with the white interlocutor who, based on his speech and statements, is a poor and uneducated Southerner. In attempting to explain why he does not want Blacks to vote, the latter becomes confused when Du Bois points out that he is in fact better educated than the Southerner. " 'Well then!' he returned, with that curiously inconsequential note of triumph. 'Moreover,' he said, 'I don't want my sister to marry a nigger.' " Du Bois's famous response, one which he deploys in a variety of formats in several of his writings, is (1) that the white man's sister is free to say no to a proposal from a Negro suitor, and (2) that the wayfarer is presupposing that Du Bois *wants* to marry his sister, an assumption now rendered laughable given the differences in education and station between the "nigger" and the wayfarer. The passage ends with the two unable to reach an understanding: "Go on, I said, either you are crazy or I am. 'We both are,' he said as he trotted along in the mud."[12]

The central point of "On Being Crazy" is to show that the Black is not a static force: rather, he is a dynamic, intelligent being who is the target of hostile whites who do not first look for his humanity and find none there but instead assume that he is not human, not an equal. This suggests that the supposed lack of progress on the part of Blacks is not due to their static nature but to active racist white opposition and racist perception that continually attempts to push them back. Syntactically speaking, Du Bois places his white interlocutors in the spotlight by enclosing their dialogue in quotation marks, automatically differentiating it from the narrative and thus presenting it as an opposing force to the "dialectical narrative." The dynamic of the narrative reinforces this dialectical structure of a white antidialectic because each action committed by the narrator is met with an antithetical reaction that attempts to unseat him—quite literally in the first two instances—at the restaurant and the theater. The simplicity, regularity, and acceptability of these actions, from basic human needs such as eating and sleeping to the supposedly bourgeois activity of attending a concert, further posits this antidialectic as unnatural and intrusive. The reader is shown how Du Bois is constantly and aggressively confronted throughout the day through both speech and act.

The specific wording of the interlocutors is also key: Du Bois's narrator is absolutely literal about each action he is committing, refusing to legitimate the opposing discourse that attempts to read him as the always already malevolent Other-from-within. By maintaining this literal discourse, the opposing one, dependent on logos to assert his or her whiteness in this narrative, becomes "crazy" in that he or she cannot identify a simple action and must instead imbue it with devious intent. The conversation reaches a ridiculous climax every time the accusation of "social equality" is leveled. Although equality is the central tenet of American democracy, these white subjects explicitly protest the narrator's attempt to claim this supposedly God-given right, and therefore can only be read as opposed to synthesis and the dialectic as a whole.[13] Their speech act has an illogical derivation and therefore becomes moot when met with a less idealist and more materialist speech act—even from the abject Black. It is unclear at this point whether being crazy indicates an impotent logos or an illogical logos.

In the final encounter with the white wayfarer "Blackness" is discussed and deconstructed in a more complex and irresolute manner. As stated earlier, the juxtaposition between race and class serves to deconstruct the idea of the American "Negro" as an inferior "species." Although the narrator is Black and the wayfarer is white, it is the former and not the latter who symbolizes erudition and reflection. Here Du Bois is pointing out that intellect is not biologically determined. Even so, as his final comment shows (which, significantly, invokes the title of the piece, suggesting that it is not always the educated who can provide insight to a complex situation), the wayfarer is not reduced to a stereotype of the "ignorant white." Unlike the whites in Du Bois's previous encounters, the wayfarer does not ask Du Bois to remove himself—*he* removes *him*self, from the clean side of the road to the muddy side. In that moment we see Black and white reduced to the same circumstances in spite of race and class categorizations because of racism and poverty. Although traveling the same road, these two men do not find common ground. The wayfarer, the only white character who is willing to discuss his racism, and the only white whom the narrator approaches for such a discussion, is unable to produce a coherent explanation for his beliefs. The two vague justifications he does produce, ignorance and lasciviousness, fail to fit the narrator, who is educated and married to a Black woman.[14] The historical construct of race is also critiqued when the narrator, asked if he is a "nigger," responds that his grandfather "was called that." The wayfarer concurs, missing the point, but, for the reader, the point has been made: that the term possesses only constructed meanings contingent on history, economics, culture, and politics—not biology. Exasperated by the wayfarer's refusal to question his own racism, the narrator tells him to "go on," stating that one of them must be crazy. The wayfarer then reveals a flash of ironic brilliance in pronouncing *both* of them "crazy" as he "trotted along in the mud."

Before this final encounter, it is clear to whom the title "On Being Crazy" is referring: the reader cannot ignore how ridiculous the other characters sound in their attempt to remove and denigrate the protagonist. Yet this same snobbery is reversed when the narrator encounters the wayfarer and decides to quiz him on his strange behavior (suddenly walking on the muddy side of the road). This snobbery becomes apparent in the narrative when one contrasts it against the previous scenarios because, in this final scene, the narrator offers withering commentary on his interlocutor, noting that he has "a curiously inconsequential note of triumph" and that he is "oddly illogical." Although this rather staid and formal structure of rhetoric is a constant throughout the anecdote, it is cast into relief in this last scene, given the wayfarer's background. Consequently, the reader is forced to see how the narrator himself is involved in a game of one-upmanship based on stigmatizing certain sectors of society, in this case working-class whites.[15] Just as the wayfarer is unwilling to relinquish his racism, the narrator is unwilling to forgo his bourgeois bias against the working class. Considering his three previous experiences, the reader can understand his motivation for first approaching and then ridiculing the wayfarer. In the end, they are both "crazy," for both insist on maintaining the separateness of their social identities even when the moment points to obvious conflations, highlighted by the rather obvious metaphorical setting of the road. The wayfarer is confronted with a man who "looks" Black, but quite obviously does not act that way, resulting in the paradoxical moment of (re)producing the inferiority of the latter in the hope that it will become visible. The narrator, in turn, projects and maintains a nonlingual image of his interlocutor in order to reinforce a class division that the latter will not acknowledge. In Du Bois's dialectic, thesis and antithesis are not race specific, but they are interchangeable. Simply speaking, any thesis that attempts to prevent or that resists synthesis is an antidialectic.[16]

Du Bois's reading of the speech act is instructive here. In a departure from his dealings with the other white interlocutors, the narrator does not dispute the wayfarer's statement that "niggers is dirty." In fact, he implicitly agrees while offering a literal statement ("so is mud"), indicating that the wayfarer's act betrays a double meaning: anyone can be a nigger if "niggers is dirty." The wayfarer's discourse is even more literal than that of the narrator, literal to the point that it is purely metaphorical. Having already deconstructed racial categories, the wayfarer's discourse on the "nigger" only reveals a series of base beliefs that have no bearing on actual human beings. "Nigger" and all that the term signifies has become metaphorical, a transformation the narrator acknowledges when he states that he is certain of what the wayfarer means by "nigger"; indeed, he has just experienced the empirical underpinnings of that term. The wayfarer is desperately trying to deploy the logos that white American culture claims to be his—indeed, it is what links him to those whites whose economic and political strength bar him from extended or intimate contact with them. Yet his epithets and subsequent confused claims are like a sputtering car one is trying to revive: without the material clout of income and position, the idealist logos that pronounces the white subject and the Black Other simply fails to materialize here.

This does not mean, however, that the narrator has the upper hand.

The inability of either man to subject the other to his own logos, or speech act, underscores the ambivalent nature of the speech act and how it requires not just discourse but praxis in order to function. The narrator tries the same disingenuous literalism to underscore the wayfarer's diminished means; the wayfarer, clinging to the discourse that insists all Blacks are inferior, responds both directly and indirectly by trotting out racist arguments in a confused form. Clearly, this is not a discourse he can master. Yet neither man wins this battle of words, each attempting to assert this subject status (the narrator as an educated bourgeois, the wayfarer simply as white) at the expense of the other. When the wayfarer pronounces both of them to be crazy, we again see impotence and illogic as the key to their failure and so-called insanity. According to Du Bois, when the idealist dialectic deploys race, it forfeits logic to do so, and the resulting logos can only be understood as "crazy"—making its oppressive presence all the more noxious and unbearable.

Although *The Souls of Black Folk* begins with those famous passages on the Negro as a split subject, it also produces this Negro as a conscious subject—one who functions in spite of white racism. This is a complex state of affairs because the Negro American is simultaneously doubly conscious and unrealized. Dialectically speaking, we are beginning with the "third term" (the Negro American realized) *and* a synthesis that refuses to merge his two dialectics. While one could frame this within rather elaborate Hegelian terms, this dissonance can also be explained as the primary difference between Marxist and Hegelian dialectics. While I cannot argue that Du Bois's argument is Marxist, I would suggest that the idealist dialectic, while certainly a cornerstone of his thought in this era, cannot fully explain a subject who is both split and whole. In *The Algebra of Revolution*, John Rees explains that the most significant difference between Hegel's and Marx's dialectics is how each treats the "negation of the negation": that moment where thesis encounters antithesis. "In Hegel," Rees writes, "it was the mechanism for reconciling thought with existing reality, for restoring reality unchanged at the end of the dialectic process." In Marx, however, the function is quite different: "Marx's dialectic opens up the possibility of real material change, a real alteration in the mode of production. And although a crisis in society and the emergence of a class that can resolve it may arise 'with the inexorability of a natural law,' the successful resolution of that crisis is not predetermined."[17]

In critiquing the ways in which America's racist practices have denied its Black citizens the equality it promises them both in spirit and in the law, and submitting an idealist dialectical structure to that critique, Du Bois's *Souls* moves beyond that structure as well. As a diversity of scholars have observed, *Souls* bears a wealth of styles and disciplines, from philosophical to sociological to cultural to musical to literary. There is another important multiplicity here: while opening this seminal work with the blanket statement that the Negro has been denied his "true self-consciousness" by racism, Du Bois also argues that the Negro possesses double consciousness. In other words, there are two forms of consciousness operating: the idealist dialectic's "synthesis," denied to the Black, and a split consciousness, part Negro, part American, through which the "American world" is the mediating influence that "lets him see himself through the revelation of the other world." These two factors, the multiplicity of genres and the two forms of consciousness, can help us to understand how Du Bois's veil serves as a key strategy in the counterdiscourse of the Black subject in that it both responds to Hegel and moves beyond him, largely avoiding the tendency of counterdiscourse to be subsumed, ultimately, by the originary discourse.

Marx's famous critique of Hegel's master-slave dialectic observes that, although on the surface it seems as if Hegel is implying an equality of relations—the consciousness of the master relies on recognition by the slave—Hegel actually uses the negation of the negation (the moment at which thesis encounters antithesis) to reconcile the slave to the existing order. Hegel suggests that once the slave performs work for the master and thus disciplines his fear, the process will lead to a new consciousness that will move him beyond the alienation of working for another—in other words, he will no longer be a slave. *The Souls of Black Folk* also speaks to this situation, but Du Bois locates the slave within a historical context through which freedom has been gained (a prerequisite for becoming a subject, in Hegel's *Philosophy of History*), but the consciousness that emerges is split and in fact is still alienated by seeing himself through another's eyes. Briefly put, the idealist dialectic has partially reneged on its promise of consciousness to the slave although the terms have been met.[18] While *Souls* makes clear that part of this failure belongs to America's racist practices, Du Bois's less orthodox use of multiple genres to discuss this double consciousness suggests that Hegel alone cannot explain the status of the Negro American.

In *The Philosophy of History,* Hegel argues that the Negro is an Other-from-without. In the United States, the African American is an Other-from-within, not seen as African and, although mostly reviled by white Americans and considered inferior, nonetheless viewed as an American "Problem."[19] In *The Souls of Black Folk,* Du Bois does produce Africa as a site of origin and an essence ("he would not Africanize America"), but he places more emphasis on the degree to which Black Americans are from *within* and, culturally, historically, politically, and economically so deeply embedded within the American fabric that their contribution is central and obvious. In the final chapter, "The Sorrow Songs," Du Bois rhetorically asks, "Is not this work and striving? Would America have been America without her Negro people?"[20]

Du Bois had several options in responding to the Western construction of the Negro, and just as much if not more reason to respond only to Jefferson as opposed to Jefferson and Hegel. In *Souls* Du Bois answers both men, and the construction of the veil operates as a sort of Möbius strip in this response.[21] Du Bois had good reason to respond to both: when he was a philosophy student at Harvard, the question of the subject was prominent and, as Gates, Shamoon Zamir, and Levering-Lewis have shown, both the Young Hegelians and idealist dialectics were influential in the late nineteenth and early twentieth centuries. In *Souls,* as we have seen, philosophical questions are directly linked to social, political, and economic status. These questions, though perhaps at times heady and abstract, were far from irrelevant to everyday life and praxis. At the same time, Jefferson's view, and the versions that followed it, of the Black as an inferior of nature whose lowly position in the United States was essentially biological were also part of the American imagination. Both white fantasy and lived reality were part of the Negro American subject, hence Du Bois's concern with both material and ideal aspects of the dialectic as well as his understanding of how the white American logos operates.

The veil is at once composed of idealist and materialist dialectics. Quite in line with both these formations, *Souls,* as a counterdiscourse to the dialectic of the European and African, takes up where Hegel leaves off, namely, with the resulting synthesis. As the first chapter argues, Hegel's negation of the negation simply reifies the thesis because Hegel's Negro is an Other-from-without, a ghost in the dialectic, one might say, present but without material impact. In Marx's materialist dialectic,

John Rees explains, "mediation is no longer a peaceful process of reconciliation but the elaboration of the different forms in which the central contradiction of the age is played out in every aspect of social development."[22] Rees goes on to write that this mediation is "the embodiment of a contradiction." In *Souls*, although the Negro American is not reconciled, split, he is not contradictory: his desire, according to Du Bois, is perfectly logical. Instead, the (racist) white American is being contradictory. The dialectic emerging in "Of Our Spiritual Strivings," then, begins with the split Negro American whose antithesis, or process of mediation, is the racist white American. And what is the result? As many Marxist scholars have pointed out, critics (and even some supposed practitioners) of Marxism have often misread this definition of dialectical materialism as containing an inevitable synthesis (which is most often discussed in terms of social revolution). While in an idealist dialectic this type of mediation could lead to this result (there are times when it does in Hegel), a strictly materialist dialectic must allow the mediation to remain a wild card, in that the contradiction is not quietly reconciled somewhere before it achieves synthesis. Simply put, because Marx and Engels's materialist dialectics must respond to historical contexts, "different historical periods" Rees explains, "produce different dialectics." What sort of synthesis is being produced at the time of *Souls*, many of whose chapters explicitly discuss or frame themselves in Reconstruction, specifically as the dismal end to an era that held so much promise?

The resulting synthesis is the veil, I would argue, which allows Du Bois a strategic array of multivalent effects. The veil is the effect of a dialectic that is both idealist and materialist in its nature. The American discourse that posits the Negro as inferior to the white, as Other to the white, explains the material existence of the American who is Black. This Black American is *not* the inferior of whites but is nonetheless treated as such, which explains why he has not fared as well as his white compatriot. A veil signifies a performance, but it also signifies the limits of that performance in order to define it: even if you choose to acknowledge the impact of the mask, you must also see the actor behind it—a version, one could argue, of the famous psychoanalytic dictum "*I know very well, but all the same*," or the failure that Marx points to in Hegel's use of the negation of the negation.

In all of the discourses of the (white) subject that we have looked at so far, the assumption of a racially determined logos is in place. By writing that the Black is inferior and they are superior, Hegel, Gobineau, and Jefferson erase the historical past and replace it with the current ideology—one of the famous shortcomings Engels apprehends in Hegel's idealist dialectic. With the veil, Du Bois points to the fallacy of this logos but also argues that fallacious ideas can nonetheless have an effect, and it is the veil that signifies both the *Sein* (being) and *Schein* (seeming) aspects of the Negro American subject's existence because it points both to the guise and the face that lies behind it. The veil also signifies the blindness of whites: throughout *Souls* and the essay "On Being Crazy," whites are depicted as acting on fantasy and preconceived notions on encountering the Black. In the narrator's first few encounters, the accusation of "social equality" is both true and not true. So tied to the ideal are whites that simply seeing a Black occupying an adjacent space leads them to assume that equality has actually been reached. The narrator, however, who understands that he operates in both the material and the ideal, sees that this equality is ephemeral and inferior to the material reality of simply eating lunch or attending a concert, and he realizes this fallacy and doubling for all involved by *speaking the material*. This is the double talk of the veil: by speaking the material, he simultaneously rejects the ideal fallacy and asserts another reality—existing in both the fallacy and the reality, as that is the essence of the Negro American subject. Whites may possess some power over the ideal of logos, but no one can be denied the material, and when speaking the material it points to the monological fallacy that defines the ideal. Even self-consciousness is not a requisite to this "material" power, as evidenced by the scene with the wayfarer, who demands respect and consideration even when he is unclear exactly what is being said to him (and by whom—this nigger who is not a nigger).

As the final anecdote in "On Being Crazy" makes clear, not all whites possess logos: it is *not* racially determined. For the poor white wayfarer, the belief that "niggers is dirty" does not lead to the narrator walking in the mud, rather, the wayfarer becomes dirty. In not denying "niggers is dirty," but simply adding that mud is dirty as well, Du Bois enunciates both dialectics, the ideal and the material, now operating simultaneously. In his reading of logos and its vicissitudes, calling someone else dirty does not mean that he or she is; this is true for both the poor and bourgeois whites Du Bois encounters in the anecdotes. Class also makes a difference in logos: if you are a poor white, you may be unconscious that, materially speaking, you occupy much the same abject position racist practice accords to the Black. The wayfarer is not Other in the idealist binary of self and Other, but this difference is without distinction in terms of political and economic clout. According to Du Bois, logos is not meant to unite whites, it is meant to unite wealthy, land-owning whites and their economic and political allies, hence Gobineau's, Jefferson's, and Hegel's similar understanding of logos. In the *Schein* of their discourse, it seems as if they are speaking to all whites, but a materialist critique reveals the *Sein* of class (that is, the owning of property) as marking the true distinction.[23]

Du Bois's Black subject is not just the Negro American but the result of the Negro American and the paradox of the white American logos, which the veil best signifies. This is not to say that the subject and the veil are synonymous, but that the veil sums up the complex construction of the Black subject, simultaneously pointing to the effects of racism and poverty and his being shunned by his own nation. This does not mean that Du Bois reads all Black Americans as alike: one's position with regard to the veil and the choices one makes (especially with regard to logos) will determine one's individual character, one's personality—but the veil links us all. As readers of *Souls* and other works by Du Bois know, the veil has many manifestations: sometimes it is the rough equivalent of the Mason-Dixon line, between the South's pathologically murderous racism and the North's supposedly greater restraint; it is the moment of consciousness when the Black American first experiences exclusion and realizes his/her paradoxical status as an Other-from-within; it is also the infant's caul and cause of "second sight." If we read the veil as simply the Black signifier, that second moment of the dialectic with the materialist negation of the negation, all these definitions fit. Most importantly, the veil does not signify the split Black subject, as many have claimed, but rather the subject fully realized who is simultaneously excluded as Other; such is the paradox of an Other-from-within.

THE NEGRITUDISTS AND THE MASK

In the middle of Du Bois's long career (roughly in the 1930s), the trope of masking also would be deployed to combat the discourse of Other-from-without, speaking as it still did to the heart of this profound contradiction in the Western discourse of the white subject and Black Other. Subsumed by a discourse that posited the Negro slave as a retrograde, stagnant species that might in time come to achieve some level of "whiteness" and thus subjectivity, two notable Negritude artists responded by borrowing from Gobineau and his discourse on the Negro. In an interview with Mbwil a Mpaang Ngal, Aimé Césaire (who coined the term "Negritude") explained his attraction to Gobineau:

> But out of all influences, the most determining seems to have been that of the ethnologists and their predecessors: Gobineau, Lévy-Bruhl, Delavignette, G. Hardy, and above all the romanticism of Leo Frobenius. In the preceding analyses, we underlined the ambiguity of our adhesion to the theses of these "savants." "Yes," says Césaire, "we read Gobineau, Senghor and I. Above all else to refute him, but also because he was the grand theoretician of French racism. At the same time, I have to say Senghor really loved him. That is to say, he loved him because [Gobineau] had the good taste to have said: "art is the Negro." Even those in the Occident have a few drops of black blood. Consequently, our attitude towards Gobineau is highly ambivalent.[24]

To the African American (and even to the African American artist), Gobineau's pronouncement falls squarely in the realm of racist stereotype and consequently would be a problematic ally in a counterdiscourse. Within the American invention of the Negro, the ascription of racial characteristics originates from an idea of the Negro as static. Regardless of the attributes accorded, the move is viewed as dangerous because it reifies the dominant discourse that justifies the suppression and extinction of Blacks on the basis of their permanently retrograde abilities. However, Gobineau's dictum is manipulated into a useful strategy by Césaire and Senghor. While Du Bois responded to an American discourse of the Other-from-within, French and British racist discourses most often mirrored their relationship to the Black in the West: he was not a threat to the interior of a nation but the savage forcibly tamed and trained for productive labor in the faraway Caribbean plantation or the African colony (which in turn are also distinct from one another in key ways). In this discourse, Blacks were encouraged to emulate whites. Of course, they could never achieve the superior intellect and civilized disposition of their masters, but they should nonetheless imitate the example set by them. As Christopher Miller has elaborated, colonizers held that Africa was a "blank darkness" and its peoples equally void of any history, civilization, or culture.[25] This system was in no way radically different from the American concept of the Other-from-within, but the difference between the Negro-as-malignant (or, to use the Du Boisian term, "problem") and the Negro-as-empty are distinctions useful to analyzing both the differences and unities in these counterdiscourses. Du Bois's writings constantly counter a discourse that posits Negroes as violent (albeit stupid and lazy) subhumans. The discourse of the Negritudists, as the rest of this chapter will demonstrate, counters a discourse that simply but devastatingly posited the Negro as nothing.

As exemplified in Hegel's discourse on the Negro-as-Other, the Other-from-without is defined as a void. Within Hegel's binary-cum-dialectic, the corresponding "completeness" of the subject justifies the colonization and exploitation of the Other because the latter will never progress nor contribute to the world unless shown a better example, in this case the colonizer. Hegel's writings on the modern state in his *Philosophy of Right* posit that the invasion and exploitation of Africa and Africans by Germany is a progressive move for all involved. In Hegel's view, Africa and Africans are "barren" and inconsequential, thus providing the critical excuse for the idealist negation of the negation that justifies slavery as well as the political and economic exploitation of Africa and Africans. In his *Philosophy of History,* Hegel argues that only enslavement by the European allows for the possibility of the Black achieving subject status. In the French Caribbean, the discourse on the relationship between colonizer and colonized was similar: the Negro is nothing without European instruction.[26] From Césaire's standpoint, ascribing certain characteristics to this Other that the white subject lacks defies Hegel's "theory" of the African. Gobineau provides a useful (if limited) counterdiscourse to Hegel because he posits the Negro as possessing something the white lacks and can never possess.[27] For the Negritude movement, Gobineau's specific belief that this quality is a clearly dynamic and energetic artistic talent provides an even more useful response to the colonizer's discourse on the colonized as empty and static.

Because racist discourse is always irrational, changing the nature of its assertions (often into polar opposites, depending on the context), the response to Othering differs greatly at different times. In addition, given the ways in which the Other-from-within and from-without overlap with one another, there are often times when one can just as effectively respond to one as to the (pardon the pun) other. Du Bois's strategy of deconstructing the Other-from-within to reveal a paradox—that he is both within and without (excluded, segregated) the nation—works well to discredit aspects of a philosophical discourse that denigrate the Black. That which is at stake in a philosophical argument, however, is not necessarily the same as in other arguments. In the Harlem Renaissance, for example, Black American and Caribbean writers had to combat American stereotypes of their being historically and culturally vacant, lacking logos, and thus only able to mimic. In the context of literary and artistic production, they were an Other-from-without and, in strategies similar to Léopold Senghor's, they deployed the trope of the mask to construct a signifying chain linking them to African, Black Caribbean, and Black American history, culture—and literature. In this context, Gobineau could operate as a more useful (although temporary) ally than Hegel.

Hegel's discourse stated that slavery is a means by which the Negro might eventually *become* a subject; the Negro is "prelinguistic" as opposed to remaining beyond the capacity of speech. Under this logic, the Negro requires white instruction in order to achieve subject status. The language of the colonizer is presented as the language of the subject, whereas the language of the colonized is disallowed because it is not a "real" language—that is, it is non-Western. There is a signifying chain: the Negro has no language of his/her own because he or she has no culture, therefore no civilization, and therefore no history. This chain becomes the basis for the colonizer's argument that the Negro should be grateful for the chance to achieve subject status under the tutelage of the former. The colonized is disallowed from claiming a homeland, much less pining for one. Arguments demanding that the colonized be returned to Africa and/or liberated and accorded sovereignty are annulled through this rhetoric that ultimately posits Negroes as lacking both a history and a homeland that precede the colonizer.[28]

By according the Negro a monopoly on artistry à la Gobineau, the Negritudists can present the Black as the possessor of language within the context of artistic expression, and this expression is not delineated or confined.[29] Gobineau's pronouncement allows them to construct a Black subject, and the statement of artistic ability provides them with a discourse. Contrary to the colonizer's dictum that the Negro stood outside of discourse (and therefore civilization), the Negritudists could claim that the Black possessed both his own discourse and his own civilization.

Given this, the counterdiscourse can then deploy all the things the discourse disallowed. It can accuse the colonizer of an illegal and immoral act, seriously question the colonizer's claim to sovereignty, and demand an equal share in the governance of the "space"—whether Africa or the Caribbean. Using Gobineau, the discourse of the Negritudists claims subjectivity for the Black. Like Du Bois, Senghor and Césaire deployed the trope of masking and ventriloquism, respectively, to pinpoint the failure of Western logos as well as to posit a Black logos.

Senghor and the African Absolute. Because Gobineau's Negro excels in the arts, Negritude is not another artistic movement: it is the *superior* artistic movement. In a neat inversion, the Aryan, within the realm of artistry, becomes a mere shadow of the Negro and can never equal the Negro's artistic achievements. This hierarchy can also be deployed from another angle: if the Negro is essentially superior to all other races in the arts, then it stands to reason that this artistic expression must be taken seriously. One does not ignore the natural genius. Even further, the vague term "art" allows for all different types of expression. In the introduction to a chapter titled "De la Négritude," Senghor, whom Césaire indicated as the most amenable to Gobineau's discourse, explicitly links this artistic sense to language: "I would have titled this third chapter 'The Word, Poetry and African Art' if I had kept to the logical discourse of the European. If I haven't done this, it is to remain faithful to my thought: to put the accent on Negritude, which sustains all of African civilization, even in its Arab/Berber aspect. But the accent must also be placed on the Word which is, at the same time, poetry and art, that is to say Creation."[30] By linking art to language, Senghor is able to posit a more universal role for Africa and its cultural (artistic) influence, for "La Parole" ("The Word") is clearly a transcendental signifier.[31] Even further, Senghor groups language, poetry, and African art under Negritude, then links the latter to "Creation" itself. Whereas Hegel posits reason as the transcendental signifier that is almost synonymous with European achievement, "De la Négritude" posits "Creation," pointing only to Africa as one of its primary contributors.[32] In doing this, Senghor has upended the centrality of Enlightenment precepts, specifically (European) man as the center of the thinking world. It is important to note that Senghor does not posit a structure of binary oppositions. Such a structure would collapse into Hegel's dialectic, merely reversing the European as thesis and the African as antithesis. By decentralizing (European) man's position in the world and producing humankind as an aspect, but not the end-all and be-all of the universe, Senghor is also precluding the right of any Western philosopher (such as Hegel) to determine superior and inferior civilizations and peoples. At the same time, by positing Africa as both the original and continuing possessor of the creative impulse, he relegates Europe to an abject position. Yet this inequality only arises within certain contexts: by invoking "Creation" Senghor posits all humankind (and quite possibly the animal kingdom) on equal footing. Divisions of knowledge are also placed on equal footing: the African and his arts is not to be denigrated next to the European and his claim to science—after all, "the Word" takes precedence above all else. As opposed to reason, creation suggests itself as wholly inclusive, an important aspect of Negritude that is often overlooked. European colonization is condemned, but Europe is not rejected or barred from the counterdiscourse, a fact made evident by the deployment of Gobineau and others.[33]

Western life-science still holds that man is distinct from all other mammals because he possesses a complex language to communicate abstract ideas, and he can act on them; the importance of logos in determining subjectivity within contemporary Western disciplines should not be underestimated.[34] The fact that colonialist discourses also made a point of denigrating the linguistic ability of the colonized indicates that the West has long held an idea of language as a primary marker of subject status. Senghor argues that respect and consideration for language is not exclusively Western: "Therefore we will begin—because we have begun— with the word, with Poetry which, in nearly all civilizations, is the principal art. Principal in Africa more than anywhere else because in poetry the word is proffered, acted upon in the form that is the most charming because it is the most active."[35] Senghor responds to the discourse of the Black as mimic when he posits human beings as part of the universe but not its center. Human beings are *part* of creation, not the *creators* themselves; therefore, some human beings cannot claim themselves distinct from other human beings.[36] From the viewpoint of creation, we are all the same; we *all* speak a language. By making this assertion, Senghor is dismissing whatever claims and reams of evidence whites might submit regarding the Negro as alingual. By extending the gift of language to *all* races, his counterdiscourse holds any claim of the Negro as nonlingual as patently false; whoever has made such a claim is simply mistaken. This counterdiscourse, in short, seeks to discredit the discourse that attempts to posit a racial hierarchy.

Artistic ability, however, is constructed as a hierarchy. Colonialist discourse accorded Caucasians linguistic ability within a power structure in which the concept is the most highly valued. Intellectuality (and therefore subject status) was based on an idea of the abstract, or—when directly contrasted with the Negro—the degree to which one was less physical in communication.[37] Although their claim to logos links speech with action, it is the first term, not the second, that dominates nearly all Western discourses that assert Black inferiority.[38] In Senghor's passage, a perceptive variation of Hegel's will to power and Gobineau's Aryan is performed. As discussed in the first chapter, Hegel and Gobineau credited the Aryan with the superhuman ability of the speech act, or logos. That is to say, as the center of the universe, the Aryan need only speak and his will is performed. In response, Senghor takes the stereotype of the Negro as a primarily physical being and argues that this physicality is logos, the speech act, par excellence. Compared to Europe, which prides itself on its long history and wealth of abstract concepts, Senghor's Africa is a land where the word has achieved its pinnacle, where it is "most charming" and "active."[39] Although Senghor ostensibly refuses to replace Eurocentrism with an African-centered philosophy, he nonetheless invokes European values and points to Africa as the site in which those values find their true expression.

Art is not limited by its forms or expressions, nor by which civilizations are determined as artistic. However, Senghor makes clear that African art fits his definition of creation above all others, suggesting there are, in fact, elements of European civilization that lack the creative impetus. Senghor believes that art as manifested by the African man is a declaration of life in that it *only* takes on the expressions of song, poetry, music, dance, painting, and sculpture.[40] Art is a language of life, and life, in relation to reason, functions as a larger rubric under which reason could be categorized.

Both Hegel and Gobineau stated that the Negro was prelinguistic, arguing that he had shown no signs of writing. In Senghor's formulation, language is stretched to a broader definition that certainly incorporates writing but is not limited by it.[41] Because Senghor has (re)defined "la Poésie" as an active dynamic, writing is simply one manifestation of a multifaceted dynamic. The intellectual (and subject) status the European has claimed for the act of writing is, for Senghor, too narrow a definition. While Europe lies still, Africa *acts* on its language. European discourse claims that the African shows no sign of writing; Senghor's counterdiscourse claims that the African is continually manifesting signs of writing but in an active form, such as dancing—an example also used by Césaire.[42] Simply put, when European discourse claims it can find no signs of civilization in Africa, Senghor retorts that it does not know where to look; after all, Europe does not have a monopoly on intellectual pursuits. In the Senghor passage quoted above, poetry is central to almost all civilizations because it is an active dynamic. In the final sentence, Senghor makes a statement that refutes Hegel and uses Gobineau: poetry is a principal force in Africa because Africa is a dynamic not a static civilization.[43] In the same vein, Gobineau's model of racial classification links the colonized Blacks to their African origin. In short, the very performance of art on the part of the colonized Negro links him to Africa, according him or her the right to deploy African artistic tropes within the performance.

As a trope for the Negritudists, the mask links to two aspects in the Western discourse on the Negro. First, the African mask is part of a chain of signifiers in the Western imagination in which savages dance around in a jungle wearing terrifying oversized masks.[44] Although the mask is ostensibly *not* a body part, quite often the "savages" are only shown with masks on, suggesting that the mask is in fact their face.[45] This leads to the second link: even without a mask, the African is not seen as actually possessing a face. In chapter 2 I indicated how Jefferson had determined that the Negro existed under a "veil." In European discourses that assert the black as inferior (savage, primitive), including Gobineau and Hegel, the description of the Negro underscores his "unnatural" pigment and facial features. In short, regardless of what the Negro is or is not actually wearing, some racist discourses reduce the question of Black subjectivity to the mask, signifying savagery, backwardness, and absence of culture.[46] Most importantly, the predominant European depiction of the savage with the mask renders the black performer silent, possessing a disembodied voice (as if he is channeling) or a voice reduced to the grunts and screams of an animal. According to the European stereotype, the mask signifies the African as one who can only act, but to act without speech is to act without intelligence.

Gobineau's pronouncements on the Negro as a dynamic, vital artistic force work as the basis for a signifying chain that eventuates as a repudiation of the colonial discourse that structures the Black Other as a void. What distinguishes Gobineau's Negro from Jefferson's and Hegel's is cast into relief. According to Jefferson, the Negro is a sad offshoot of nature that is unable to achieve humanity. According to Hegel, the Negro is a void with no history, no civilization—in short, no meaning. Gobineau, by contrast, after lambasting the Negro as a wild, destructive, and inferior being, nonetheless assumes that the Negro has *some* meaning, some role in the world. Of course, the nature and scope of that role, like most of Gobineau's *Essai*, is unclear and contradictory. However, Gobineau accords the Negro the artistic impulse and simultaneously points to the Aryan as deficient in this aspect, to the latter's detriment. Gobineau's description of the artistic impulse is also so vague that it is possible to present it as a legitimate manifestation of the speech act, proof that the Black possesses logos. Yet in using Gobineau's obviously problematic assertion, Senghor does not wholly predicate Black subjectivity because he has the blessing of the "Father of Modern Racism"; instead, Senghor develops his own model by deriving principles Gobineau would have clearly forbidden.

Senghor's mask, while a signifier for Black logos, also points to what the Aryan lacks: an artistic means of expression. Art is language is Africa is history is subject, bringing down Hegel's justification of the colonial project, which rests almost wholly on the Other outside of the signifying chain by virtue of having no culture. Furthermore, Gobineau provides a model in which European culture owes a debt to the influence of the colonized, once again reversing a European colonial discourse that posits the colonized as wholly indebted to the colonizer for whatever attributes the former might evince. At the same time, the colonizer, as described by Gobineau, is always too rational, too objective, and devoid of the artistic instinct, a "fact" that Negritudists link to the colonialist project and its inhumanity. Senghor underscores the idea of the inhumanity of European civilization in the following poem, but does not discredit Europe for this reason. Invoking masks at the very beginning of the poem, he uses them as an umbrella for an examination of the death and deadliness of two civilizations that are oppositions only within Eurocentric discourses. Just as a mask conflates performance and performer, the line between Europe and Africa cannot be drawn so clearly. In "Prière aux masques" (Prayer to the Masks), Senghor deploys the trope of the mask as a signifying chain to examine the relation between—not the opposition of—African art and European reason:

Masks! O Masks!
Black mask, red mask, you white-and-black masks
Masks of the four cardinal points where the Spirit blows
I greet you in silence!
And you, not least of all, Ancestor with the lion head.
You keep this place safe from women's laughter
Any any wry, profane smiles
You exude the immortal air where I inhale
The breath of my Fathers.
Masks without faces without masks, stripped of every dimple
And every wrinkle
You created this portrait, my face leaning
On an altar of blank paper
And in your image, listen to me!
The Africa of empires is dying—it is the agony
Of a sorrowful princess
And Europe, too, tied to us at the navel.
Fix your steady eyes on your oppressed children
Who give their lives like the poor man his last garment.
Let us answer "present" at the rebirth of the World
As white flour cannot rise without the leaven.
Who else will teach rhythm to the world
Deadened by machines and cannons?
Who will sound the shout of joy at daybreak to wake orphans and
     the dead?
Tell me, who will bring back the memory of life
To the man of gutted hopes?
They call us men of cotton, coffee, and oil
They call us men of death.
But we are men of dance, whose feet get stronger
As we pound upon firm ground.[47]

Originally written in French, the language of the colonizer, the poem, ironically, is rendered partially inaccessible through its refusal to posit a Black/white binary opposition ("Black mask" as well as "white-and-black masks"). The masks clearly take on a universal aspect as the narrator uses a local reference ("Ancestor with the lion head") and a global reference ("Masks of the four cardinal points"). The image and function of the masks are obscured by the tenth line, which removes the only two referents of a mask, namely, a face and the mask itself. The masks do not specifically refer to people, although they are clearly linked to Africa, which in turn affirms Africa as the possessor of a universal spirit that extends to the world as a whole. Through these invocations, the narrator identifies himself as a subject: he has a history ("Ancestor of the lion head," "The breath of my Fathers"), a culture, a civilization ("The Africa of empires"). The relation to Europe is obscured: in the line "And Europe, too, tied to us at the navel," exactly who is birthing and whom is birthed is unclear, suggesting, simultaneously, Africa as the mother of the world and Europe as the mother of the colonies.

The crisis that forms the basis for this plea to the masks is global: the world is dying, and the culprit is obvious: "machines and cannons." By positing Europe as a culture of the inorganic derogates, European images of the colonized are revealed as little more than the product of Europe's tendency to look upon the rest of the world as inhuman objects. "They call us men of cotton, coffee, and oil," and its tendency toward projection à la Freud: "They call us men of death." Europe is also characterized as inherently bound up with non-European peoples, "As white flour cannot rise without leaven," and reliant on the African tradition to bring life back from the fatal influence of a reason-induced civilization. Gobineau's *Essai* bemoans the impending collapse of European civilization and also the Aryan's too-rational temperament that bars sentiment. Senghor combines these two ideas to create causality: lack of feeling on the part of the European and an obsession with machines and destruction bode ill not just for Europe but the entire world. Hegel claims the European is a complete subject *because* he is rational rather than emotional; Senghor indicates almost the opposite. Reason, as embodied in the European "civilizing" impulse, is not the driving dynamic of the world; on the contrary, it is what destroys the world.

The transcendental aspect of the masks that the speaker invokes precludes linking them directly and wholly to African culture. In lines 10–17, the masks are described as no more than artifice ("Masks without faces without masks") without human aspect and ageless ("stripped of every dimple/And every wrinkle"), linked to the process of colonization

> You created this portrait, my face leaning
> On an altar of blank paper
> And in your image

that in turn is linked to an empty worship of the written word. "Portrait," of course, whether rendered in the visual arts or writing, is nonetheless only a two-dimensional genre. Masks, then, can be or become reduced, deprived of the human instinct, and engaged in blind idolatry. European colonization is not condemned simply in and of itself but for what it has wreaked on the colonized. All the same, African art, defined as that which is composed of and produces life, can and will provide (given the final line of the poem) a rebirth—an artistic renaissance à la Negritude—in a world that has been obliterated by the European rational impulse and all its attendants. According to this poem, contrary to the Enlightenment belief that reason provides the key to a better world, reason, when it departs from the total celebration of life in its manifest forms, becomes inhumane and thus fatal. One need only look at the effects of colonization, the disfigured masks, to see the proof—or, rather, one need only look at the effects of *French* colonization to see the proof.

Senghor begins his poem with an invocation of the masks, immediately establishing his subject position through the speech act. The first set of masks begins as thesis, or origin: "You exude the immortal air where I inhale/The breath of my fathers"; these masks sustain him from the polluting influence of women or any other profane presence. The second set of masks he calls to he also speaks to; these are the "masks without faces without masks," the ones that have created the portrait of an Other-from-without—the ones that, as he points out, lack substance. This does not mean they lack power: the narrator locates the cause of imminent cataclysm in the European penchant to deploy its logos against the Black, and the hypocrisy and paradox of this deployment is made clear. First European logos attempts, through naming, to turn men into objects, the void of the Other-from-without, "they call us men of cotton, coffee and oil," and then, believing it has accomplished this transformation, European logos tries to suggest that this objectification is in fact the nature of the African himself: "they call us men of death." Again, although there is no substance, no proof to this naming, that does not mean it lacks destructive force; indeed, the poem seems to suggest that voids are powerful by their very nature of defying the life impulse.

However, the very impulse that makes the masks so powerful will also be the source of its own unmaking—if not stopped. Although the European logos posits itself as opposed to Africa, Senghor argues this logos is one of Africa's offspring, "tied to us at the navel." In Senghor's reading, the masks speak to the dangers of European logos: misnaming people as objects, refusing to acknowledge the life force, and understanding the masks as no more than objects without substance. Here, masks signify origin, according the Black subject status by anchoring him to his African roots. Yet these masks can be distorted, and in their antitheses manifest themselves as the empty signifiers of destruction. For Senghor, the negation of the negation is a life-or-death moment: should the antithesis fail to recognize its thesis, synthesis may never be achieved for either party, and the world will be swallowed by the destructive nature of the antithesis. The European masks lack regenerative power because they have mistaken the one-sidedness of naming for the speech act (speaking the truth of a thing because you recognize it for what it is). The technological might of the European does *not* transform his false and destructive logos into an actual speech act: the European may name, and may use force, but these two combined cannot change the identity of the African man: "but we are men of dance, whose feet grow stronger." Senghor's masks emphasize the material aspect of the logos, its roots in culture and traditions—as well as the cost when that aspect is omitted from the equation, when might is mistaken for right.

Aimé Césaire and the Creole Synthesis. Of course, not all the Negritudists constructed the same subject in response to the European discourse of the Negro-as-void, as their responses were not predetermined by colonialist discourse, culture, or ideology; rather, their own philosophies of the meaning of Blackness within the contexts they had experienced and observed were the bases for their responses. Senghor targets the epistemology through which the Enlightenment and its attendant colonialist discourse posit European superiority. He invokes a precolonialist past and places the Enlightenment in a historical moment rather than a transcendental genesis. Consequently, Senghor moves away from a discourse/counterdiscourse of the subject, holding "Creation" as the transcendental signifier and, in an unsurprising move, locating Africa as closest to that center.[48] Aimé Césaire deploys language to move within a dialectical relationship between Europe, Africa, and the Creole tradition to produce a postcolonial subject. His Creole subject reflects the geographical, cultural, linguistic, and historical triangulation between Africa, France, and Martinique that informs his colonial status:

> I don't deny French influences myself. Whether I want to or not, as a poet I express myself in French, and clearly French literature has influenced me. But I want to emphasize very strongly that—while using as a point of departure the elements that French literature gave me—at the same time I have always striven to create a new language, one capable of communicating the African heritage. In other words, for me French was a tool that I wanted to use in developing a new means of expression. I wanted to create an Antillean French, a black French that, while still being French, had a black character.[49]

Césaire does not view language in the same way as Senghor (or, for that matter, the discourse to which Senghor responds). Whereas Senghor understands subject status as created through epistemology, Césaire is far more empirical. Senghor posits language at the center of almost all cultures, the dynamic that is central to the subject. Césaire refers to the French language as "a tool" that would help him to *create* an Antillean French that would serve to express the Creole experience. Language, then, is a means to an end, a way of expressing an experience. Further, language is not (at least not wholly) organic: it can be created. Césaire's rhetoric also asserts a certain hierarchy: the French language is subordinated to Antillean French because it is merely a tool to create the latter. In addition, *all* languages are tools, meant to serve as a way to express experiences. Because Césaire makes clear that he must create an Antillean French for an experience that already exists, experience clearly precedes language—and does not necessarily engender it. Here is a critical difference between the subjectivities of Césaire and Senghor. For Senghor, language is central to the subject: it is a dynamic, active force that constitutes him and creates his culture. Césaire, by contrast, works through language to express a subject already constituted by experience.

Césaire deconstructs the idea of "French" identity to theorize what already exists in praxis: a Creole tradition that blends African and French influences. More importantly, Creole is not half French and half African but something different altogether, a third term in the dialectic. Césaire returns, like Senghor, to an African heritage but produces this heritage as one component of his discourse rather than claim it as a universal element that subsumes European forms. The canonical reading of *Cahier d'un retour au pays natal* (Notebook of a Return to a Native Land) sees it as a dialectical exploration of the author's identity through the lens of Negritude. I agree with this reading but find it too vague. Du Bois's "American Negro" and Senghor's dialectic of the masks can also be read as dialectical explorations of Black identity, and yet these subjects bear little resemblance to Césaire's.

Césaire posits his Creole subject as the experiential synthesis of the dialectic of colonization. For Césaire, synthesis does not signal an ideal state to be achieved—it *has* been achieved. And, although achieved, the situation of the Creole-as-synthesis as it is (re)produced in *Cahier* is not always ideal. The fourth paragraph of *Cahier* affirms the colonized Antilles as synthesis in decay: "At the end of the wee hours, on this very fragile earth thickness exceeded in a humiliating way by its grandiose future—the volcanoes will explode, the naked water will bear away the ripe sun stains and nothing will be left but a tepid bubbling pecked at by sea birds—the beach of dreams and insane awakenings."[50] In a style reminiscent of the nineteenth-century German Sturm und Drang movement, Césaire uses natural imagery (volcanoes, water, and sea birds) to evoke both a physical and psychological atmosphere of decay. Although the reasons for this awful death may be manmade, it is important to note that Césaire uses metaphors of naturally occurring phenomena. Although the force is natural, it is in decay, and composed of two dialectics. The structure of the paragraph produces dialectic within dialectic, the former delineated by em dashes. The "internal" dialectic is the one I have just described. The "external" relies on surrealist phrasing in which adjectives are juxtaposed against unlikely nouns; the "beach of dreams" and "insane awakening" points to a deliberate invocation of surrealism and its Freudian underpinnings. Synthesis is also located in the most abstract of realms: the human unconscious, which here is embedded in the Antillean landscape. Here synthesis is not decay, it is the future thesis retroactively usurping its past, and it embodies promises that will have fallen short. At the same time, this "thickness exceeded in a humiliating way by its grandiose future" could also indicate a future that is coming into being—and far exceeding its humble beginning. Contrary to the European discourse of colonization, "progress" does not always have positive manifestations.

Senghor characterized European progress as an illusion: a mindless march toward obliteration accomplished by machines of "death and destruction." Césaire also sees progress in a negative way, but not in terms of machines, and not culminating in obliteration. Instead, progress is "grandiose," simultaneously ostentatious and ephemeral (dreams), and "insane," rendering within it (the internal dialectic) a barren landscape picked clean by nature. This structure is not unique to this particular paragraph. Césaire begins his piece with the phrase "Au bout de petit matin" (At the end of the wee hours), which is repeated several times for several pages, continuously, determinedly, reproducing a simultaneously lurid and sympathetic description of organic decay and suffering. In its beginning, the *Cahier* poses not one synthesis but several; they can move both forward and backward, even simultaneously—a complex structure of dialectics crucial to understanding Césaire's Creole subject.

Cahier's narrator moves from despair to renewal in his "Native Land." Returning to Martinique from Paris, the narrator relates observations and personal incidents in a deliberately evocative, organic rhetoric. Césaire invents his own words ("alexins" and "hypoglosse"), pairs together unlikely ones ("poussis surnuméraires"), and conjures obscure or highly technical vocabulary that a native speaker would be forced to look up in a dictionary ("tératique").[51] One is confronted with a language obviously linked to French but nonetheless different, and therefore new. The old order is assailed: Césaire begins the *Cahier* with an unforgettable invective against authority, attacking the (white) French speaker with his own language:

> Au bout du petit matin . . . Va-t'en, lui disais-je, gueule de flic, gueule de vache, va-t'en, je déteste les larbins de l'ordre et les hannetons de l'espérance. Va t'en, mauvais gri-gri, punaise de moinillon. Puis je me

tournais vers des paradis pour lui et les siens perdus, plus calme que la
face d'une femme qui ment. . . .

(At the end of the wee hours . . . Beat it, I said to him, you cop, you
lousy pig, beat it, I detest the flunkies of order and the cockchafers of
hope. Beat it, evil grigri, you bedbug of a petty monk. Then I turned
toward paradises lost for him and his kin, calmer than the face of a
woman telling lies. . . .)[52]

Césaire greets the reader with a curse of dismissal, supposedly aimed at a
policeman, but it is the reader who receives the insults first. At the same
time, through the string of curses that identify the speaker as squarely
antiauthoritarian, a strong aesthetic is put into place through repetition
("va-t'en") and certain vowel sounds (the short "a") and the invocation
of another famous epic ("des paradis pour lui et les siens perdus") that
recounts (Western) man's fall from grace.

The speaker identifies himself and the Martinicans he encounters as
the antithesis of both Western aesthetics and so-called Western morals,
but in a form that challenges both the moral superiority of Western
civilization and its victims ("Nous vomissure de négrier"—We the vomit
of slave ships). The collision of this civilization and its victims produces
no easy answers:

I am of no nationality recognized by the chancelleries.
I defy the craniometer. Homo sum etc.
Let them serve and betray and die.
So be it. So be it. It was written in the shape of their pelvis.[53]

Here Césaire's Creole subject defies categorization and/or stereotype, at
least by the West, and defies as well two hallmarks of civilization, government ("chancelleries") and science ("craniometer"). As the last two lines
indicate, though, this is not because the Creole subject is an oddity but
because the Western subject is ultimately a paradox, and therefore limited. The Western subject—and possibly the Creole—serve, and betray,
and die, a mindless service that lacks both soul and subjectivity. In a
sarcastic reversal, the narrator states that such depressingly meaningless
behavior is situated within the chain of human reproduction ("written
in the shape of their pelvis")—but this reproduction is controlled by the
colonizer, suggesting a false reality created by the West that the Black, as
abject, must endure.

Like Senghor, Césaire posits the Western subject as impaired, but, most importantly, this inability is revealed by the Western subject's active racism. Both Césaire and Senghor juxtapose Western discourses of knowledge and/or superiority with Negritude discourses of Western ignorance and/or inferiority. In this sense, at least, the counterdiscourse is not a simple reversal. Whereas European discourses on the Negro denigrated even as they actively enslaved the Negro (that is, as the Negro was not only passive but in forced abeyance), the Negritude discourse denigrates as a counterattack: a counterdiscourse on stand-by, one might say. Now, however, Césaire splits from Senghor because he brings his own subject under critique. In a constantly (re)occurring series of dialectics, there is no static line between critic and the object of critique. Césaire accomplishes these constant transformations through a variety of devices. For example, in the passage that follows the one quoted above, it is important to note that the verse shifts from the first-person singular to the third-person plural. This distancing effect leads into the scene, now famous, of Césaire in a streetcar in Fort-de-France, watching some white passengers make fun of a Black man sitting in the same car. It is in this moment of ventriloquism, also a form of double-talk, that Césaire reveals the nature of his subject:

You must know the extent of my cowardice. One evening on the streetcar, facing me, a nigger.

A nigger big as a pongo trying to make himself small on the streetcar bench. He was trying to leave behind, on this grimy bench, his gigantic legs and his trembling famished boxer hands. And everything had left him, was leaving him. His nose which looked like a drifting peninsula and even his negritude discolored as a result of untiring tawing. And the tawer was Poverty. A big unexpected lop-eared bat whose claw marks in his face had scabbed over into crusty islands. Or rather, it was a tireless worker, Poverty was, working on some hideous cartouche. One could easily see how that industrious and malevolent thumb had kneaded bumps into his brow, bored two bizarre parallel tunnels in his nose, overexaggerated his lips, and in a masterpiece of caricature, planed, polished and varnished the tiniest cutest little ear in all creation.

. . . A comical and ugly nigger, with some women behind me sneering at him.

He was COMICAL AND UGLY,
COMICAL AND UGLY for sure.
I displayed a complicitous smile. . . .
My cowardice rediscovered![54]

The Negro Césaire describes is a poverty-stricken landscape, large but famished. Man and homeland are inextricably intertwined. Through this link Césaire argues that the sneers from the women passengers are not simply toward this one Black man and his supposedly unnatural appearance. The laughter is also aimed at Martinique and its inhabitants.[55] "Blackness" as a concept is also derided, a Blackness trying and failing (from the women and narrator's point of view) to perform subjectivity. The man is described in ways that point to aspects of Western discourse outlined earlier in this section: the conflation between the Black face and the "African" mask.[56] The facial features and the body are described in ways that render them disjointed and fantastic pieces of art, but in the racist reading of "primitive art": exotic and Other.

Of course, Césaire's narrator is also Black, and therefore, technically speaking, he is masked, and Other. In line with Césaire's Creole subject, the masking is complicated and changing. The women who are jeering the "nigger" never actually speak in this passage—the narrator speaks for them, anticipating their derision and disgust, and possibly wholly imagining it, as the women are situated *behind* him. In ventriloquizing these two women, the narrator deploys a devastating command of colonialist language—that is, language embedded in colonialist history. Terms such as "pongo" and "cartouche" point to the peculiar and derogatory cartography of the European colonizer, where an impressive array of cultures and peoples is turned into objects, where everything and everyone is easily objectified and coolly Othered. And yet the narrator is not just a translator: his ability to anticipate and give full voice to racist discourse, combined with his acknowledged complicity, marks him as someone who is also masked against himself and his homeland of Martinique.

The "nigger" is masked by the white women and the narrator on the tram; his humanity is ignored and he is taken apart, blown out of proportion, and misrecognized as Other. The narrator, in turn, has become so painfully aware of his own discourse that he no longer ventriloquizes but actively participates with his whole body. Despite the deforming and racist rhetoric, Césaire's description of the "nigger" also reproduces a human being, a Black subject who may be ravaged by poverty and racism but is nonetheless very much an individual with a history. He is significant in and of himself. For Césaire, therefore, masking is a dynamic of objectification that renders subjects as objects even as the subject remains: one can be simultaneously subject and Other. Indeed, not unlike his contemporary Jacques Lacan, Césaire suggests that *all* subjects are also Others. The women who are "Othering" the Black man are themselves rendered Other by the rhetoric of the passage. They are only "some women" qualified by a sneer; they too have been disjointed: they are faceless, except for that floating pair of sneering lips. Most importantly, they, like all Others, have been ventriloquized. At the same time, they are not wholly Other, unmistakably belonging to that discourse that asserts them as subjects. And, of course, the narrator is also subject and Other.

But this scene does not mean that, for Césaire, all Black subjects are constantly and painfully moving between subject and Other. As he joins in with the jeering laughter he imagines, Césaire recognizes that in that moment he is mimicking racist discourse, a moment of double-talk where he both enables and disables himself. The narrator's ventriloquism is so effortless that the thoughts of the white women flow right through him toward the object of their disgust. The narrator has sacrificed the substance of his body, (re)producing himself as a void that is the Other-from-without, and in that moment is truly the spectral projection that is the Other.

The series of dialectics moves on. The rest of the poem moves toward synthesis, as Césaire searches for and finds his "Negritude." Rather than compare Africans and Martinicans against Europeans and promote the former over the latter, the speaker rejects those points of comparison that are based on traditional European values: industry, conquest, material luxuries, and so forth. Instead, the speaker questions the worth of such inventions and acquisitions and invokes his African and Martinican ancestors to produce a subject that is not notable for colonialist conquest nor the technological inventions that have defined the century. Instead, Césaire celebrates a people who have managed to endure enslavement and who link themselves closely to nature's overpowering forces:

those who have invented neither powder nor compass
those who could harness neither steam nor electricity
those who explored neither the seas nor the sky but those
without whom the earth would not be earth
. . . for those who never explored anything
for those who never conquered anything
but yield, captivated, to the essence of all things
ignorant of surfaces but captivated by the motion of all things
indifferent to conquering, but playing the game of the world
truly the eldest sons of the world
porous to all the breathing of the world
fraternal locus for all the breathing of the world.[57]

Césaire replaces Europe at the center of the world with his Black ancestors, arguing that they are the oldest people, people who transcend "surfaces" and instead respond to the "essence" of the world ("le mouvement de toute chose," "jouant le jeu du monde").[58] There is an interesting moment in these passages that begins with an almost celebratory description of, specifically, the Other-from-without. This is the second aspect to ventriloquism, in which the narrator mimics the European concept of the Other-from-without but shows that, by being able to name in detail all that he supposedly does not know, knowledge must precede this ignorance. This Other is excluded but able to speak his exclusion and is so intimately tied to those who oppress him that, one could joke, he no longer needs them: he can insult himself! Césaire's logos for the Creole subject is born from the contradiction of being an Other-from-without. Being Black, he does have access to the word, which, when used even within a colonialist dialectic where he is Other, can nonetheless be accessed to speak himself and, in doing so, realize his subject status through this contradiction. The process begins with Senghor's absolute signifier of the word, but the act of masking is not the original (syn)thesis; it is, like Du Bois's subject, the *second* synthesis.

The poem also ends similarly to Senghor's, where the latter concludes "Prière aux masques" with dancing. Yet, whereas Senghor intends dancing as a celebration of life, Césaire is more specific and complex. Dancing is the ambivalent celebration of Negritude:

Rally to my side dances
you bad nigger dances
the carcan-cracker dance
the prison-break dance
the it-is-beautiful-good-and-legitimate-to-be-a-nigger-dance
Rally to my side my dances and let the sun bounce on the
racket of my hands.[59]

As in the streetcar scene, the language is energetic and evocative, but with a significant difference: the tone is giddy, jubilant. The Creole celebrates his subjecthood in a very specific way. He is not solemn or deploying a Western discourse of abstract pondering and rumination over the meaning of the individual; the materiality of the speech act is clearly more important. Yet the tone is not a simple joy in which there is blanket reverence for and/or romanticization of Blackness. Here, Blackness at once evokes ecstasy and a hard, humiliating history in which the Black was not always stoic or strictly honorable. Césaire's dialectics move synchronously, suggesting a totality of "Blackness." Negritude, as synthesis, embodies this totality: everything is acknowledged and included, not barring a history of subjugation under a European colonizer. The narrator is a "bad nigger," a jailbird, and part of the earth as he summons all his dialectics, his dances, to his side.

For the Creole subject, the individual is conflated with the Black collective, and an appreciation for one's subjectivity is reached when one can accept and celebrate these disparate histories that stretch across the African diaspora. It is important to note that at the beginning of *Cahier*, the Creole subject is, in fact, a synthesis of colonizer and colonized, but these parts function disparately for him. For Césaire, synthesis is the reconciliation that is the natural cycle of the earth, produced in many forms. It is the volcano destroying the surrounding landscape; it is a devastated Caribbean island suffering under racism and poverty; it is both progress and decay. The Creole subject, then, does not *achieve* synthesis in *Cahier*; he comes to understand it and, in reconciliation, comprehends his own inevitable role in the natural cycles of creation. In the final paragraph of *Cahier*, the narrator welcomes the amalgamation:

to you I surrender my conscience and its fleshy rhythm
to you I surrender the fire in which my weakness smolders

to you I surrender the "chain-gang"
to you the swamps
to you the nontourist of the triangular circuit
devour wind
. . . so then embrace
like a field of even filagos
at dusk
our multicolored purities
and bind, bind me without remorse
bind me with your vast arms to the luminous clay
bind my black vibration to the very navel of the world
bind, bind me, bitter brotherhood
then, strangling me with your lasso of stars
rise,
Dove
rise
rise
rise
I follow you who are imprinted on my ancestral
white cornea
rise sky licker
And the great black hole where a moon ago I wanted
to drown it is there
I will now fish the malevolent tongue of the night
in its motionless veerition![60]

The subject is seeking unification, but this unity is complex. Although he obviously welcomes it, he has no illusions: he will be bound to the entire universe, and therefore all its negative and positive drives—all its dialectics. The subject is already part of creation, but his epiphany means he will no longer feel degraded by his Blackness, nor will he deny his Black brother, even in "fraternité âpre" (bitter brotherhood). The Creole subject will be bound, he might be strangled, but now he finds something where he once thought was nothing. Hegel's void has been converted into a powerful and complex essence. As the last line states, the "great black hole" where he wished to find death he will now "fish" to find the malevolent energy of the night.

The dialectic is spurred by the necessary contrasting dynamics of creation: everything *must* live and die, but one should never deny. Césaire's subject is only able to acknowledge and welcome his oneness with the earth when he pursues the colonizer's discourse to the bitter end, ventriloquizes, and finds himself at the moment of the negation of the negation, a moment that is also a self-negation as an Other-from-without. A risk is entailed here, the same one that Senghor asserts, namely, that when the Black approaches this moment, there is the threat of being overwhelmed by the colonizer's discourse and submitting to it without realizing its fallacies. If the Black realizes the power of his logos in his ventriloquism, however, and embraces both the negative and positive qualities that come with mastering the discourse of being Othered, then he may come to realize his subject status as one who encompasses the whole of the colonial experience.

Césaire, like Senghor, begins and ends with the Absolute of the word and also emphasizes the materiality of the speech act, in which the two should not become lopsided. Yet Césaire's conceptual narrative follows an Other-from-without going to Fort-de-France, capital of Martinique and so the symbolic heart of colonial discourse (and the antithesis that created him), and in that second moment of negation realizes the fallacy of Western logos and his own essence in the ventriloquism that encompasses the contradictions of his Creole subject status. Western discourse tries to name him an Other-from-without, but once he masters the speech of his estrangement, he becomes conscious of that discourse's monologic fallacy. Logically speaking, as an Other-from-without, he should not be able to ventriloquize the subject; because he can and *recognizes* that he can, the heart of his cowardice becomes the realization of his capacity, of being a totality rather than simply part of a cruel colonialist machine.

NEGOTIATING THE IDEAL AND THE MATERIAL

In comparing the use of masking, logos, and materialist versus idealist dialectics, one finds strong commonalities among the three works analyzed here. Du Bois, Senghor, and Césaire all use masking to signify the logical impossibilities of the binary of white subject/Black Other and to locate the moment of this paradox in the negation of the negation, which is also the moment where the Black subject achieves consciousness. All three men also conclude that, because the binary is false, the colonizer's claim to logos must also be false, and they deploy a material-ist critique of this idealist structure to emphasize this failing. There are differences, too, but it should be emphasized that these differences are not predetermined structures. In looking at the different types of Others that Du Bois, Senghor, and Césaire respond to, and taking their specific temporal and geographical moment into consideration, these discourses speak well to their circumstances. Yet the circumstances do not predeter-mine the discourses: one cannot conclude that counterdiscursive strat-egies are limited by how one is Othered, where one lives, and at what moment in time. The works of Du Bois, Senghor, and Césaire highlight the mass of contradictions in discourses that Other the Black, and thus the innumerable ways one can address and reformulate these paradoxes.

Du Bois's veil, while it marks the contradiction in Western discourse that Senghor and Césaire also locate, does not underscore, as theirs do, an ancestral link to Africa. Indeed, at the very beginning of *The Souls of Black Folk*, Du Bois reassures the reader that the Negro American's long-ing for synthesis is not based on the desire to "Africanize America." This does not mean that Du Bois is less interested in Africa, or that he has turned away from it: his reading is intent on responding to his status as an Other-from-within:

> actively we have woven ourselves with the very warp and woof of this nation—we fought their battles, shared their sorrow, mingled our blood with theirs, and generation after generation have pleaded with a headstrong, careless people to despite not justice, mercy, and truth, lest the nation be smitten with a curse.[61]

The veil emphasizes the contradiction specific to that status.

Senghor and Césaire both establish links to Africa within their coun-terdiscourses, although the former places more emphasis than the latter on this construction. Given Senghor's status as an African living in a colonized Africa, his strategy is to position European colonialism as an antithesis in a larger dialectic that begins with Africa. Here the masks transcend the colonial moment: they are not produced by the moment, and they speak directly to the failure of the European construction of logos as well as its deadly abilities. As an African still living in Africa, Senghor can easily establish the existence of the Black subject that pre-cedes colonialist discourse on the Other-from-without, as the latter can only operate on the assumption that the Black possessed no consciousness before encountering the European. While Du Bois's counterdiscourse focuses on demonstrating how the Black is part of the very "warp and woof" of America, Senghor draws a strict line between the African and the European. In responding to being categorized as an Other-from-without, Senghor would gain little by emphasizing the Black's role in Western civilization, as that line could be manipulated to underscore the need to validate the Black subject according to white guidelines. Instead, Senghor's masks emphasize the existence of a Black consciousness—inextricably bound up with African culture and history—that precedes the white and offers a wholly different yet equally viable epistemology and ontology of the Black subject.

Césaire, although also speaking to the position of being an Other-from-without, works somewhere in between these two other men, emphasizing both the Black's African ancestry and his place in the colonialist dialectic. Like Du Bois, Césaire must grapple with the contradiction of being Othered while being deeply implicated within an antagonistic and exploitative Western environment. If we read his counterdiscourse through the lens of his status as, like Senghor, a Martinican and an Other-from-without residing with a Black numerical majority, but also, like Du Bois, as one who occupies Western soil, his construction of the Black subject speaks well to both situations. Césaire uses ventriloquism to examine the status of the Other-from-without, and in deploying the Marxist reading of the negation of the negation, he is able to point to the failure of the idealist definition of the antithesis in that moment. The resulting subject is one who finds empowerment in his present moment and, through that, is able to establish links to both his future and his past. This is best embodied, I would argue, in the dance that concludes Césaire's text. The dance is the ultimate speech act, in that it merges communication and its manifestation, while also linking the Black to his African ancestry and the Creole culture that has sustained the past in the present.

Without the interventions of these three men, African diasporic counterdiscourses on the subject may have taken much longer to manifest themselves, especially within the theoretical negotiations that, above all else, signify the Black subject in the West. Although responding to different variations of being Othered, and operating on different interpretations of dialectical synthesis, Du Bois, Senghor, and Césaire did not reject the role of the Black in Western civilization. Indeed, as all of them make clear, the Black subject is not restricted to (and should not restrict himself) to Africa, because he is not only an intrinsic part of the West, but part of the world as a whole. Yet the nation and its misogynist discourse of collective identity formation remain. As the next two chapters show, especially with regard to the nation, gender, and sexuality, the tradition of African diasporic counterdiscourse on the subject was just beginning.

CHAPTER THREE

Some Women Disappear: Frantz
Fanon's Legacy in Black Nationalist Thought
and the Black (Male) Subject

For Du Bois, Césaire, and Senghor, the existence of the Black subject is demonstrated through the contradiction inherent within the idealist binary of the white subject and Black Other. Their use of a masking trope indicates the complicated relationship between idealist and materialist lines the Black subject must negotiate. All three also attend to the question of the Black and logos, but Senghor and Césaire respond more to the importance of a "Black" logos or speech act than Du Bois does. Before moving to a comparative analysis, I want to first analyze how, on the surface, Fanon provides a devastating reading of the effect of Western logos on the Black subject, but his deployment of a more materialist sensibility, one intimately tied to the Black and the speech act, forces us to reconsider his argument. Fanon is not so much maintaining the impossibility of the Black subject in the West as he is altogether rejecting the deployment of the idealist dialectic in the construction of counterdiscourse. This is first signaled by his adoption of *Aufhebung* to drive his dialectic rather than *Sehnsucht*.

Although Aimé Césaire and Frantz Fanon were born and raised in Martinique and thus were familiar with the colonialist discourse on the Other-from-without, their counterdiscourses on subjectivity are very different, reminding us that "Blackness" cannot be reduced to the sum total of either natural and/or nurturing forces. Whereas Césaire produces the Creole subject through an idealist dialectic whose synthesis is a merger between French and Martinican logos, Fanon does not believe that an idealist dialectic is capable of recognizing—much less producing—Black subjectivity. According to Fanon, a colonialist logos, even when merged, cannot help to produce a Black subject. Such a logos can only produce white subjectivity and, within the idealist dialectic that is the basis for that subjectivity, the colonized is always already Other. Fanon uses the metaphor of the mask to indicate as much, most memorably in his 1952 work *Peau noire, masques blancs* (Black Skin, White Masks).[1] In his introduction Fanon states that he wishes to examine the effects of colonialism on the Black man ("le Noir") through the idealist dialectic on which it relies to discursively locate the Black. The deployment of the Western logos, then, introduces the fundamental concerns of this work:

> We attach a fundamental importance to the phenomenon of language. That is why we consider this study necessary in that it can enlighten one aspect of comprehension in the dimension of alterity for the man of color. It is understood that talking is to exist wholly for the other.
>
> The Negro has two dimensions. One with his compatriot, the other with the white man. A Negro carries himself differently with a white man than with another Negro. That this disparity is the consequence of the colonialist venture, there can be no doubt. . . . That it nourishes the main artery at the heart of the different theories that wanted to accord to the Negro the retarded evolution of the simian, no one would dream of denying. These are objective items of evidence that make up the reality.[2]

By beginning with language (specifically French), Fanon is acknowledging the effects of the colonial experience, both in his production and in his statement. Ironically, it is Fanon's mastery of this language that allows him to perform its oppressive abilities, rendering through figurative speech the very dynamic that imprisons him. Besides its practical aspect with regard to publication and audience, by writing in French, Fanon is producing himself as a colonial subject now speaking from the metropolis. This is more intriguing if one analyzes his enunciating moment and the way that moment counters his reading of how the Black is supposedly rendered wholly abject by Western logos.[3] According to Fanon, Western logos positions him not as speaking subject but as spoken object. As the second line of the second paragraph indicates, both positions exist, indicated by and divided by language. When speaking with his "compatriot" he is an enunciating interlocutor ("un," or "one"), but he is quite literally "the other" when speaking with the White man ("la Blanc"). This is a linguistic system that finds its counterpart in the dialectic system of white subjectivity:[4] "the theoretical and practical affirmation of white supremacy is the thesis: the position of Negritude as an antithetical value is the moment of negativity."[5]

Fanon argues that the self/Other dynamic performs two tasks simultaneously. First, by positing the Black man as Other, the white man is himself able to come into subject status, bolstered by a language and system of thought supposedly based on abstract principles of truth, but in reality based on principles designed to justify and encourage the colonialist project. Second, this linguistic and philosophical dynamic teaches the colonized how to express himself within an immediately oppressive linguistic system and thus, even when speaking himself, he ultimately produces himself as the spoken. According to this system, "Blackness" is concurrent with being Other, and "whiteness" with subject status. In order to achieve some semblance of subject status, the Black man must put on a "white mask"—able to mimic, but never assume, the identity of that white subject. "Le Noir Antillais sera d'autant plus blanc, c'est-à-dire se rapprochera d'autant plus de véritable homme, qu'il aura fait sienne la langue française." (The black Antillean will be even more white—that is to say will be more approachable as a real man if he will make the French language his own.)[6] The relation between Black and white, Other and subject, is malevolently asymmetrical. As Fanon explains, although (white) subject status is contingent on the (Black) Other for its production, "Blackness," as object, remains as the shadow projected by that white subject to produce himself as subject.

In Fanon's view, the Black *is* in fact an Other, relegated there by whites and the Hegelian structure that asserts the Black as a mere moment in the white subject's dialectic of being. The Black puts on a mask in an attempt to be white and therefore be a subject. But it is only a mask. The Black, because he is Black in a white language, can only be Other. The mask the Black uses in his quest for whiteness (subject status) is language. Yet even as language allows him to mask himself as a subject, it simultaneously emphasizes his status as antithesis: "One understands that the Black's first action must be a reaction, and thus the Black is appreciated in reference to his degree of assimilation. One also understands that the recent arrival will only express himself in French. It is this that underscores the rupture that is nonetheless produced."[7] It is important to remember that the four counterdiscourses analyzed in these chapters begin with the subject either occupying a specific space or making a specific journey. Du Bois's Negro American is the first complete generation of freedmen and freedwomen now seeking recognition and legitimization of their sociopolitical presence. Senghor's masking poems begin and end with the Black subject in Africa now confronted with the European presence. Césaire's subject is returning from Paris, the center, to Martinique, the margins, according to colonialist discourse and praxis. Fanon's subject, however, is moving from Martinique to Paris, and therefore encountering a discourse he is familiar with, but he does not yet fully appreciate its many complexities and hypocrisies.

These differences are understandable when one moves outside the realm of abstractions. In Du Bois's formation, African slaves were brought to the space of the colonizer. Disallowed from freely participating in white society, slaves and freedmen alike created their own exclusive communities. These are the African American communities, or "spaces," that foreground Du Bois's theory of the African American subject and its relation to "masking." In Du Bois, the majority of African Americans who lived in these communities were employed by whites either as domestics or agricultural and industrial laborers. During the day, they occupied the colonizer's space, but at night returned to their own space. There they sustained and developed a culture that, although distinct from the culture of the colonizer, was not wholly separate with regard to language, gender roles, communal structures (nuclear and extended family formations), and the work ethic. Du Bois reads his formation as one within which two communities, and therefore two subjectivities, function side by side. Of course, the slaves in the Caribbean were also brought to a space where they developed their own communities. However, this "third" space was native neither to the colonizer nor to the colonized.[8] The society created by the colonizer is always already secondary to the society in the metropolis: it will always be a poor imitation of the latter. Unlike the situation in the United States, Caribbean Blacks outnumbered whites in such a proportion that, "because of their sheer numbers, Africans and their descendants converted many islands into little replicas of Africa." The colonized was considered more "natural" to the space than the colonizer.[9] As Other-from-without, the colonized was as exotic as the space to which s/he had been brought. Whereas the African American was deemed Other to the home space of the colonizer, the Black in the French or British Caribbean was deemed as Other (as) the space in which both colonized and colonizer existed. In addition, Fanon's use of masking foregrounds a history in which the colonizer brought slaves into a space from which the colonizer did not originate, directing the colonial project from the Western metropolis (Paris). For Fanon, this creates a dynamic in which the colonizer occupies two spaces: the invisible metropolis that nonetheless has a very visible, active influence with regard to language, government, and economics, and the colonial space that is shaped and formed by the former, becoming in many ways a projection of that metropolis, a colonial "Other" to the metropolitan "self."

Fanon begins with language in order to assert the French language as an ideological instrument that reinforces the notion of the metropolis as "self" and the colonies as "Other." In Fanon's reading, the establishment of the colonizer's language as the only legitimate means of communication (education, commerce, media, government) automatically erases all other languages, producing a colonized who can only express himself within terms that render him as an object. Because Fanon determines subjectivity through the French language, a language that determines the colonized as Other, there is no appreciable difference between himself and the collective. He uses a brief anecdote about a train trip to explicate this phenomenon of being indistinguishable from the collective. In the story, he goes to take a seat and is first put off by a young girl who screams that she is frightened by "le Nègre."[10] When he moves to sit down anyway, he finds that spaces have been cleared on either side of his seat:

> I existed in triplicate: I occupied the place. I went to the other, and the other evanesced, hostile but not opaque, transparent, absent, disappeared. I was suddenly responsible for my body, responsible for my race, for my ancestors. I placed myself under an objectifying lens and discovered my Blackness, my ethnic characters.[11]

As Fanon cleverly proves, his collective identity exists both in a spatial sense and in the more abstract realm of language. To the little girl, he is a

Black, and therefore possesses the stereotypes of the collective (whatever they may be in this case). The spaces that are vacated and thus meant to marginalize him ironically produce an opposite effect of multiplying his presence. Yet the effects are ambivalent: this lack of individuality, of being indistinguishable from the collective to the white subject, causes that subject to enunciate him as "Other."[12]

Fanon is not precluding the possibility of a Black subject, nor is he necessarily being contradictory about how masking and gender operate. This is not to say that Fanon's famous discussion on the role of the Algerian woman has been misread, nor that his deployment of the veil is not essentialist and sexist, only that there is less contradiction here than one might at first surmise. Fanon is rejecting the possibility of idealist dialectics, providing a space in which the Black subject can realize himself. Fanon's white mask was created by and for the colonizer and therefore possesses no aspect—no matter how alluring or promising circumstances might sometimes make it seem—through which a Black can achieve subjectivity on white terms. He can only possess the mirage of subject status, for within the idealist dialectic, the Black must always be Other. Many recent critiques of Fanon's pessimistic deployment of the veil conflate his "Algerian veil" with his "white mask." Without discounting the very useful critiques these analyses offer, I would nonetheless argue that Fanon's ultimately materialist orientation, producing analyses that are always scenario specific, only further underscores the necessity of keeping these two tropes separate. The Algerian veil, grounded in Algerian tradition that exists alongside but also precedes the colonizer (and so, Fanon, assumes, is wholly independent of the latter), *can* operate as a means toward liberation, the realization of subject status. While *Peau noire* spends much of its time "unveiling" the alluring deceit of the white mask, the end of the work largely dedicates itself to discussing how some Blacks have already achieved subject status, and how those still deprived can also move to realize themselves as subjects. To be brief, *Peau noire* is a work that begins with the idealist trap, where the Black can only speak by donning a white mask, but ends with materialist strategies to reclaim one's Black skin. In this light, using *Peau noire* as a call to revolution, we can understand why Fanon would prefer reading the drive behind the dialectic as upheaval—ultimately materialist in its sensibilities—rather than longing.

In this reading of counterdiscourses of the Black subject, Fanon's use of the mask stands out in relief because he describes the mask as *white* rather than a signifier of the Black subject produced out of a complex relationship between idealist and materialist dialectics. The mask in this text is not the same as the Algerian veil because the former is grounded in colonialist discourse whereas the latter is read by Fanon as produced from Algerian culture. At the end of the chapter I will discuss Fanon's reading of the Algerian woman, but it is important not to conflate the mask in *Peau noire* with that in his other two works, primarily because Fanon speaks quite specifically to the historical and economic position of the Antillean Black. This difference is key because Fanon locates the white mask as an idealist construct, whereas the veil, to his mind, is materialist. The white mask signals the debilitating effects of colonial discourse and praxis on the Black; the Algerian woman's veil is the embodiment of *action*—smuggling arms past French soldiers. If we remove this conflation from our reading of the colonial subject, *Black Skin, White Masks*, while difficult to interpret given the many contradictions within the text, nonetheless *does* provide us with a Black subject. Fanon is not rejecting the possibility of the Black subject, he is rejecting the possibility of achieving subject status by manipulating and countering the idealist dialectic of the white subject and Black Other.

Fanon begins by repudiating strategies that rely on locating the contradictory moment of the negation of the negation in the idealist dialectic: "l'homme n'est pas seulement possibilité de reprise, ou de négation" (man is not just the possibility of recuperation or of negation), moving on to argue that "l'homme est un OUI vibrant aux harmonies cosmiques" (man is the vibrant YES to cosmic harmonies).[13] In other words, subject status for the Black is not contingent on responding to being Othered because the Black subject already exists, brought into being by a higher, obscure power: "cosmic harmonies." A few pages later in the introduction, Fanon explains how idealist and materialist concerns play out for those with Black skin seeking what they think is subjectivity but is only white masks:

Before beginning this process, we must speak to certain things. The analysis that we are undertaking is psychological. In spite of this, it is immediately apparent to me that the true alienation of the Black man entails an abrupt recognition of social and economic realities. If there is an inferiority complex, it is the outcome of a double process:

—first of all economic

—subsequently, the internalization, or better put, the epidermalization of this inferiority.[14]

Quite clearly, material concerns speak first to the condition of the Black, not logos. There are systems that operate outside language that speak more effectively to the alienation of the Black—in this case, economics. Logos is secondary, and here Fanon inverts it, claiming that the sense of inferiority is not so much taken inward as splashed out onto the Black skin. Is this a difference without a distinction?

How we read Fanon's methodology plays very heavily into how we will understand *Peau noire, masques blancs*. Diana Fuss demonstrates how Fanon is using a materialist dialectic in his discussion of the Black in both this text and *Algeria Unveiled*, but she also reads him through the Lacanian principles that operate most directly on the Black subject and white Other.[15] In her recent reading of Fanon, T. Denean Sharpley-Whiting argues that Fanon is a psychologist not a psychoanalyst, and rejects poststructuralist readings of Fanon.[16] In this reading I want to argue that Fanon is not only doing a psychoanalysis of the impossibility of the Black subject but is also producing a Marxist critique of the idealist dialectic. After all, Fanon makes clear that the goal of this analysis is to *destroy* the "psychoexistential complex" that plagues the Black colonial. Even further, in the final paragraph of the introduction, Fanon insists that *Peau noire* be read only as it pertains to the Antillean Black, no one else, and not even himself necessarily. Earlier in the introduction, Fanon writes that many Blacks and many whites will not recognize themselves here, and that this analysis will not pertain to them. Despite the specificity on which Fanon insists, this is where his theory of the Black subject sharply delineates itself from his later works. While he too responds explicitly and implicitly to the colonialist discourse of the white subject and Black Other, his "white mask" operates only to reveal the awful paradoxes and oppressions of this binary—it cannot and will not signify the emergence of a Black subject in the midst of these paradoxes.

Further into the introduction of *Peau noire*, Fanon explains that in order to analyze not simply an individual but a group, he must combine "phylogenetic theory" with the "ontogenetic" perspective. In other words, in analyzing the situation of the Antillean arriving in Paris, his status as an Other to the (white) French subject must be placed alongside his economic and political disenfranchisement. Du Bois and the Negritudists use masking to combine the effects of the material and ideal on the Black subject. While Fanon also deploys both categories in his ensuing analysis, it is not in the same manner, and he makes clear that his interest in logos is far from amiable: "en analysant [le complexus psycho-existentiel], nous visons à sa destruction" (in analyzing [the psychoexistential complex] we look to destroy it, 9). This death by analysis makes up the bulk of *Peau noire*, but the final two chapters, Fanon explains, "sont consacré à une tentative d'explication psychopathologique et philosophique de l' *exister* du nègre" (are devoted to a tentative psychopathological and philosophical analysis of the Negro's state of *being*; Fanon's emphasis, 10). Briefly put, first we will destroy, and then we will build (a classic deployment of a Marxist *Aufhebung*), although both approaches come under the rubric of analysis. At first glance, it seems that Fanon's text is roughly imitating the very idealist dialectic he seeks to expose: he will begin with the Black Other, destroy that Other's antithesis, the white subject, and, in this negation of the negation, produce the Black subject.

Unlike the other counterdiscourses, Fanon begins with the Black Other ("the Black cannot be a man," he explains at the outset), an interesting inversion of Hegel's German subject in the *Philosophy of History* that suggests, given the conditions through which the Black Other was produced in order to realize the white subject, the Black subject must do unto the white subject as was done unto him. There is an important twist here in that Fanon begins with the *idealist* construction of the Black Other but wants to perform a negation of the negation that will bring about a *materialist* result: Black being. The antithesis here is the white mask and the synthesis will be the Black skin: how is this possible?

The bulk of *Peau noire, masques blancs* focuses on the pitfalls, traps, and humiliations that await the Black man or woman who attempts to become a subject as it is defined by colonialist discourse, and it is these earlier sections on which most scholars focus. In the concluding chapters "La Nègre et la reconnaissance" and "En signe de conclusion," however, the Black skin of Fanon's subject emerges from beneath the mask. In "La Nègre," Fanon deploys the master/slave dialectic from Hegel's *Phenomenology of the Spirit* by arguing that the Antillean Black was freed without the struggle for recognition Hegel posits as the prerequisite for the slave to gain consciousness: "historiquement, le nègre, plongé dans l'inessentialité de la servitude, a été liberé par le maître. Il n'a pas soutenu la lutte pour la liberté" (historically, the Black, plunged into the inessential nature of slavery, was liberated by the master. He did not battle for his freedom, 178). Fanon's brilliance will first provoke hilarity (in fact, it is hard not to believe many of his contradictory assertions are tongue in cheek): what are we to do when synthesis is achieved without its antithesis? We are then sobered by his conclusion: according to Fanon, the result, not exactly hilarious, is a Black who is always Other. Unlike in Du Bois and the Negritudists, the intersection of idealist and materialist dialectics does not signal potential, but foreclosure.

This reading does not apply to all Blacks, as Fanon makes clear at several points throughout the book. Unlike the "Noirs américains," he argues, who are currently engaged in the struggle for their freedom and consciousness ("they battle and are battled against"), Fanon is explicit in determining Antillean Blacks as Others-from-without and in fact uses some of the same devices deployed by Senghor in moving the Black from void to subject. Fanon, like Senghor, produces two different types of masks, and both writers posit one as white, or European, and lacking life, or as two-dimensional. Both argue that this mask is antithetical to the Black subject. They differ, however, in their use of the other mask: Senghor's mask is an originary synthesis of the speech act, an absolute within which the Black subject is established. Fanon's veil, in his writings on Algeria, *Algeria Unveiled*, although also of non-European origin, is action predicated on silence, not speech. Yet Fanon does not apply this veil to his Antillean Black, stuck as he is as an Other-from-without, an Other with a white mask. So how to escape this trap of logos?

Action. Whereas Du Bois, Senghor, and Césaire all tend to privilege the speech aspects of counterdiscourse, Fanon locates a greater and more powerful logos in the Marxist dialectic (in fact, he begins his conclusion with a quote on the history of social revolutions from *The Eighteenth Brumaire*). If the exploited Antillean Black will fight, he will be successful because "he will undertake it and lead it not according to a Marxist or an idealist analysis, but because, quite simply, he will be unable to conceive of his existence beyond the battle against exploitation, misery and hunger."[17] For Fanon, the weakness of the colonizer and the converse strength of the colonized are located in the present moment and what the colonized decides to do in that moment. The past and the future, Fanon argues, much like Marx, are determined by the present. On a certain level, all four theorists use the present moment of logos, or the speech act (the realization of their discourse in the act of reading), to point to a past that begins before the colonialist thesis of the white subject or self (in the idealist contradiction, the terms are often synonymous, anticipating the subject before its realization). Fanon is arguing that all of this is either unnecessary or doomed to failure, reading the manifestation of logos in a different order. In the three previous counterdiscourses, speech was the privileged component, used not only to reveal the inherent contradictions of colonialist discourse but also to counter the colonizing narrative of the Black with no past and no future, except as subordinate to the colonizer. In focusing on action as a counter to logos, Fanon is focusing on one of the common manifestations of logos in the present moment. Colonialist discourse must be endlessly repeated and reasserted, not only to continually disguise the past and manipulate the future but to misrepresent the present, to impute to the Black behavior and/or motives (aggression, degeneracy, criminality) regardless of what he is actually doing. For Fanon, the disruption from this dismal dialectic must begin with action, not words, because action disrupts the present moment, the act of repetition from which all other acts and narratives spring.

Diana Fuss's 1994 "Interior Colonies: Frantz Fanon and the Politics of Identification" argues that Fanon privileges speech in the construction of the subject, quoting from the chapter "The Negro and the Language" ("to speak is to exist absolutely for the other"). Yet in "La Nègre et la reconnaissance" (The Negro and Recognition), Fanon explains that the actual consciousness of the Antillean Black was not developed in the manner laid out in Hegel's *Phenomenology* because the Negro, in being handed freedom without a struggle, failed to achieve recognition from the white, and one needs both freedom and recognition to achieve consciousness ("To speak a language is to take on a world, a culture. The Antillean who wants to be white will be so as soon as he makes his own the cultural instrument that is language," 30).[18] Yet here that we can also understand Fanon as actually asserting that speech is always already colonialist in orientation and explaining that the Black desire to learn French is not for mimicry but for mastery. As both these quotations make clear, however, such mastery is heavily compromised. "*Assumer*," the French equivalent of to "take on," has two meanings. The first is the same as the English (take on a job, assume a position, etc.) but the second definition speaks specifically to a psychological state and means to consciously accept that state and its conditions—in other words, Fanon might not be saying that the Black comes to master the world or a culture but that in speaking the language he is accepting the conditions and limitation of that language, subsuming himself to it.

In emphasizing speech, Du Bois, Senghor, and Césaire see language as a force that operates outside Western logos and is therefore accessible to the Black to combat the system that Others him. For Fanon, the specific situation of the Antillean having been "handed" his freedom (a questionably cursory reading of the history of Caribbean Black, to say the least) by the colonizer means that he cannot help but inherit the same logos. The only way out is to move away from the counterdiscourse of speech and into the counterdiscourse of action. In Fanon's equation, we begin with the Black Other who moves from the margin to center, Martinique to Paris, to achieve the subjectivity on which whites seem to have some monopoly. In time, that Black will realize that he has not achieved subjectivity, only a white mask. At this point the Black must make a choice either to accept the terms and conditions of the mask and live forever as Other, or to discard the inauthentic promissory note he holds so dear and opt for action, namely, rebelling against all situations in which the Black must accept an inferior or exploited position. Fanon's remedy suggests he reads colonization as quite similar to Hegel's master/slave dialectic, proposing a materialist solution to an idealist dilemma: the Black must be recognized by the white in order to become a subject; however, he cannot attempt to achieve this recognition through language but through action. To make that choice is to *desire*, which Fanon predicates as the origin of action. Once the Black desires his freedom more than a white mask, according to Fanon, he becomes resistant to being Othered, and in that resistance and the formulation of that desire, he is now asking to be recognized. It's very simple, really: you have to act to get noticed.

The conclusion of *Peau noire* is structured like a series of mantras, in which the right of the Black to demand, desire, and act is continuously asserted, punctuated by denials that "whiteness" functions in any way as an Absolute. This is the moment of consciousness for the Black, a synthesis resulting from the "white-mask-wearing" Black encountering the limitations of logos and in that encounter developing the desire to be recognized—not according to white terms, which was the mask, but according to the terms of his action, on terms dictated by him. Action is the Black logos and the Black subject. One must first destroy the white logos by coming to recognize the trap one is in as Black Other and then rebuild based on that moment of desire. Fanon's emphasis on action spoke quite loudly to diasporic Blacks, whether revolutionaries, scholars, or most likely both, confirming that his work possesses a powerful theoretical component and that the speech act *is* key to the Black subject. The Antillean Black must destroy the speech in order to realize the act. While Du Bois's, Senghor's, and Césaire's discourses speak quite efficiently to respective categories of the Other as well as the specific temporal and locational nature of the Black subject, Fanon's discourse, also specific but with its emphasis on action, speaks broadly but effectively to African, African American, and Caribbean Blacks, Black Britons, and Black French, evidenced not only in the revolutions that the 1960s and 1970s witnessed across the diaspora but also in his resounding popularity in the discourses found within each community.

INCOMPARABLE MASKS

The trope of masking unites the counterdiscourses of Du Bois, Senghor, Césaire, and Fanon in that they use it to signify the plight of Blacks caught up in the position of the slave in Hegel's master/slave dialectic: the contradictory position of being named Other in an environment they have enriched and developed with their own hands. In their deployment of the mask, we can develop a sense of how each writer understood the structure of racist discourse. In *Souls*, it is a structural flaw, namely, the failure to honor synthesis-as-merger in the idealist dialectic. In Senghor's mask poems, it is the Eurocentric signifying chain that comprises the epistemology of the Western subject; in *Cahier*, it is the proscription of the empirical from the construction of the subject. In *Black Skin, White Masks*, it is the inherently racist nature of the idealist dialectic—on which the French language is based. Above all else, masking symbolizes the inability of the white to force the Black to succumb to logos, and the various opportunities available to the Black to counter this insidious discourse. While all four counterdiscourses can therefore be assembled together as a set of strategies that attend to much the same problem but in different circumstances, that does not mean that each counterdiscourse can *only* be applied to similar temporal and locational situations. Instead, it is important to underscore the brilliance with which all four authors use masking as a counterdiscursive strategy that reveals the critical fallacies in the Western discourse of white subject and Black Other. All four provide theories of the Black subject that white Western discourse would do well to recognize and incorporate into its discussions of the subject.

Deployed as a counterdiscourse to the colonialist binary, masking can work in a variety of ways to produce a Black subject without subsuming that production to its originary status as Other to the white. The mask produces a useful specificity for the Black subject to underscore the *historical* rather than *inherent* need to assert the Black as a subject and, in using that history as a frame, provides that Black with a cultural origin and intellectual substance that white logos is so desperate to deny. Masking not only reveals the contradictions in the discourse to which it is responding, it achieves a wonderful simultaneity through double significance. While pointing to the failure of Western logos, it also points to the triumphant existence of the Black over logos. By deploying the mask as a performance or process rather than a static term, a signifier for the *existence* of the Black subject rather than as a synecdoche for the Black himself, these counterdiscourses avoid positing the Black as eternally abject, created by racist discourse and praxis. Instead, the Black subject marks the failure of Western logos to categorize him as Other and the reasons behind the failure of that discourse in recognizing him as a subject. I am not suggesting, however, that this is the only way in which we can and should interpret the mask. Interpreting masking as possessing both a philosophical strategy and performance strategy provides us with an even greater understanding of the many ways in which Black writers in the West construct subject status.

DES FEMMES DISPARAISSENT

One final and equally essential aspect of masking as a counterdiscourse must also be kept in mind: some women disappear. Whereas white women feature prominently in these counterdiscourses, and white men are also prominently featured (or obviously implied), Black women, as agents, disappear altogether. At best, they are objects that are acted on; at worst, they simply do not exist. They thus become, as Michele Wallace has poignantly observed, the "Other of the Other."

Despite the central role Black women played across the Diaspora, sharing the work and often the same fate as the men for resisting and at times overthrowing the yoke of slavery and the colonial culture, all the texts discussed here depict them only as abject (Du Bois's Josie and Fanon's reading of Mayotte Capécia) or malevolent, as in Senghor's and Césaire's reading of women as liars and deceivers—who at times use the mask, like the European, against the Black man. In Fanon's body of writing, the only exception is the Algerian woman, who is praised for remaining silent in the service of her man. Just as the racist discourse on the Black ignored the evidence of Black "self-consciousness," the four theorists ignored the vital presence and contributions of Black women in their discussions of race, citizenship, and nationality. Although all four thinkers emphasize the materialist negation of the negation and how thesis and antithesis must both be present in the resulting synthesis, their discourses retrieve the very idealist negation they are decrying when we consider their reading of gender. In all of the counterdiscourses outlined above, whether it is assumed or posited, men beget men: white men beget their Black antithesis, and Black men beget other Black men.

It is important to make a distinction here: that the absence of the Black female subject in the theories of any of the preceding figures is not selfsame with ignoring women as a whole. Du Bois, for example, supported women's suffrage throughout his entire career, and in his discussion of the Black oppression he rarely failed to omit women from his discourse. Frantz Fanon also incorporated issues of gender into his theories of the white subject and Black Other, most unforgettably in his indictment of Black women who become involved with white men (he determined them to be self-hating) and his reading of Algerian women as strangely invulnerable to the destructive effects of masking with regard to subject status.

Yet theorizing the Black subject, neither Du Bois nor any of the Negritudists discussed here allows a space for the possibility of the Black female subject. The failure to consider gender, like those theories of subjectivity that ignore race, is not simply an error of omission, an appendage that must now be fitted on to make their theories "complete." The failure is far more critical than that: gender is an integral dynamic in the production of identity in the era of colonization, as demonstrated by

Ann Laura Stoler's analysis of the role of women within and without colonial discourse in the Dutch West Indies (*Race and the Identification of Desire*) and Jennifer Devere Brody's recent discussion of the discourse on Black women in Victorian culture (*Impossible Purities*). If gender is excluded, the critical results can only yield at best a partial, at worst a wildly erroneous, series of pronouncements on the formation of the subject in the African diaspora. As the preceding chapters argue, race and identity are only two parts of the necessary triumvirate for any analysis of race and the modern subject. The construction of the nation is the necessary third component, and gender figures heavily into this construction. By returning to the moment of consciousness from each of the counterdiscourses analyzed above, I want to show how an *idealist* construction of the nation operates in each of the moments, quite contrary to the more materialist sensibilities that enable such strikingly useful constructions of the Black subject. By ignoring the very same paradox in *nationalist* discourse that they locate and deconstruct in the colonialist discourse of subjectivity, these four theorists produce Black subjects that can only be male and, therefore, heavily compromise their constructions in terms of applicability.

Looking at Du Bois's anecdote in *The Souls of Black Folk* in which a young white girl refuses his calling card and thus brings home the ugly reality of racial discrimination, Claudia Tate's *Psychoanalysis and Black Novels* asks why all the literary critics who have analyzed this famous passage have failed to remark on perhaps its most crucial element, namely, the gender play. In recounting what is most likely (according to David Levering-Lewis) an apocryphal anecdote, Du Bois deploys the figure of a young white girl to symbolize the rejection of the Negro American (who, in this case, is quite tellingly male) by his nation. Gendered discourses on nationhood and nationality are, of course, as old as the concept of a sovereign body. In *Imperial Leather* Anne McClintock points to the very poignant ramifications of this gendering in the age of Western colonization. McClintock argues that, since the eighteenth century, Western nations have relied on the image of the white female to justify, construct, and deploy the devastating campaigns of enslavement, colonization, exploitation, murder, and disenfranchisement against peoples of African descent. *Imperial Leather* argues that the gendering of the encounter between white and Black over the past 275 years served perversely to reverse the roles of oppressor and oppressed, so that Western crimes against other peoples could be translated into benevolent acts of civilization or, when naked violence was to be used, the scene could be understood as a defensive measure against murderous savages.[19]

The suppression and oppression of the Black becomes necessary in order to deny him sexual access to white women and prevent him from forcing himself on her to propagate a bastard species that could contaminate the racially pure citizenry. To look at this from another angle, the Western obsession with miscegenation was not scenario-specific but linked to larger fears concerning the meaning and definition of the Western nation. It therefore makes sense that, in their readings of white women and Black men, Du Bois, Senghor, Césaire, and Fanon are expressing more than sexual desire: they are focusing on that relationship as emblematic of the Black man's position in the West. Consider, for example, that famous anecdote from Du Bois's *Souls*:

> I remember well when the shadow first swept across me. I was a little thing, away up in the hills of New England, where the dark Housatonic winds between Hoosac and Taghkanic to the sea. In a wee wooden schoolhouse, something put into the boys' and girls' heads to buy gorgeous visiting-cards—ten cents a package—and exchange. The exchange was merry, till one girl, a tall newcomer, refused my card,—refused it peremptorily, with a glance. Then it dawned on me with a certain suddenness that I was different from the others; or like, mayhap, in heart and life and longing, but shut out from their world by a vast veil.[20]

If we are to understand this moment as an allegory of the nation, what we see is clear: on reaching the age of sexual maturity (when boys and girls stop truly despising one another and only pretend to do so) and thus potential citizenship, Du Bois discovers that the nation rejects him alone out of all his classmates. The Black male is not wanted as a citizen of his nation even though the only difference between himself and his classmates is color. Du Bois's anecdote is, like most of his writing, impressively strategic. He sets it in New England, his actual birthplace, of course, but also a region embedded within the American imagination as a state relatively free of that "peculiar institution" of the South, and supposedly synonymous with all that is best about America's democratic tradition. Any man can become a citizen, so long as he shows he is fit for society and willing to work. The anecdote leaves no doubt as to Du Bois's meeting these qualifications, as he is in a schoolhouse, educating his mind and interacting quite merrily with his fellow future citizens. His rejection is abrupt and meaningless—unless the reader acknowledges the often unspoken but loudly crude manner of Northern American racism.

Fanon situates his anecdote on coming to Black consciousness not in a schoolroom but in the Freudian setting of the phallic train, where a little white French girl and her mother pass by:

> "Mommy! Look at the nigger, I'm scared!" Scared! Scared! So that is how one begins to fear me. I had wanted to laugh to the point of suffocation, but that had become impossible. I couldn't any longer because I already knew the legends, tales, history, and above all *historicity*, which Jaspers had taught me. Thus the corporeal scheme, attacked at many points, collapsing, ceding its place to the racial epidermal. In the train, it wasn't about an awareness of my body in third person, but in tripled person. In the train, instead of one, I had been left two, three places. I hadn't discovered feverish coordinates in the world. I existed in triplicate: I occupied the place. I went to the other, and the other evanesced, hostile but not opaque, transparent, absent, disappeared.[21]

Like Du Bois, Fanon shapes his story as almost incidental but clearly belying an ugly and determined history of white racism, also rendering its effect as bizarre—in this case, multiplying himself. Here, again, white women are deployed to symbolize the rejection of the Black male as a citizen/subject by the white nation. Just as Du Bois gestures toward America's democratic tradition through his New England schoolhouse setting, Fanon invokes both imperial and modern France, an old woman and a young one, who in turn manipulate him into a grossly overreaching specter of the Black race and a host of African ancestors—savages to these two females, who clearly read him as the living embodiment of these frightening hordes. Situated in the telling trope of Western civilization, modernization, and expansion, the train, these women shrink from the Black that they are metonymically expanding to such magnificently frightening proportions. They have returned to the land of the savage and invoked the primitive, the powers of these imperial subjects such that they can (re)create this modern Black man and reduce him to nothing more than the fear that has been passed from generation to generation, from the antiquated racist discourse of the old empire to the equally anachronistic but nonetheless modern fear and hatred of the Black embedded within this twentieth-century Western republic.

In *Cahier d'un retour au pays natale*, Aimé Césaire also places his scene on public transport, in this case a streetcar in the capital of Martinique.[22] Because Césaire's Creole subject is the culmination of white oppression and Black abjection, his scene differs from Du Bois's and Fanon's by having a proactive narrator. Nonetheless, he too uses the figure of white womanhood to symbolize the denigration of the Black male from subject to object in the gaze of the Western nation. As noted earlier, the object of the narrator's derision is clearly a landscape, falling into Hegel's conflation of Africa and Africans: they are all natural landscape rather than nations with subjects. While Césaire's narrator is openly conscious of the practice of racism, its effects on him are no less striking, and his moment of consciousness arrives when he finds himself speaking for those who despise him. Through his narrator, Césaire shows how racism pushes ugly oppressive thoughts and ugly words through the heads and eyes of its victims.

In *Imperial Leather*, Anne McClintock provides a feminist critique of the gendered discourse that could also apply to the anecdotes above, limiting white women to the role not of actively electing but being delegated by the male electorate: "women are figured as property belonging to men and hence as lying, by definition, outside male contests over land, money and political power."[23] Yet there is a crucial distinction between white women and Black women to which McClintock does not attend. All three of the above anecdotes hit their target in communicating to the reader, in a direct and unforgettable way, the bizarre and complex ramifications of racism and how it rejects its Black male citizenry. Yet, in drawing on the gender discourse of the white woman as nation, the white male as her citizen, and the Black male as the interloper, these anecdotes effectively bar Black women from the discourse. While the Black woman might be allocated a role as Africa, the mother country, in the two anecdotes where Africa is evoked (Fanon's and Césaire's), it is the Black male who signifies Africa, again returning to

Hegel's conflation. In short, whereas white women *always* figure into this racist and misogynist discourse, Black women are prone to remaining barred altogether. As we have seen, being determined Other still leaves room to respond and create a counterdiscourse as subject-misrecognized-as-Other, but how does one respond when one is not even part of the original narrative?

This patriarchal construction of the Black nation finds echoes in the era of the Black Arts movement, the subject of the next chapter. Without overlapping too much in terms of content, we can briefly remark the same construction operating in what is likely the most famous and influential play to emerge from that era by the movement's most influential artist, Amiri Baraka. In line with Césaire's and Fanon's anecdotes on coming to consciousness, we see Baraka's *Dutchman* echoing and complicating Césaire's trap of mimicry and Fanon's surreal pessimism as the Black male protagonist encounters and alternately ignores, flirts with, woos, and is betrayed by a cleverly cruel white woman who stands not so much for womanhood as the schizophrenic racist nation the hero must claim as his own. In this unforgettable play, Baraka brilliantly renders the relationship of the Black male to the American nation: sought out by her, alternately attracted and repelled by her strangeness and promise, trapped and forced to interact and, of course, in the end murdered, with no protest from the onlookers.

However, Baraka also reinforces the gendered discourse of the Western nation, in which the Black woman does not matter and the white woman is evil incarnate. Yet if *Dutchman* infuses Lula with a supernatural talent for cruelty, his protagonist—aptly named Clay—is also selected for critique. Clay is a malleable fellow, well-educated and too eager to please. Within the first few pages of the play, Lula has accurately pegged Clay:

> *Lula*: You look like you been trying to grow a beard. That's exactly what you look like. You look like you live in New Jersey with your parents and are trying to grow a beard. That's what. You look like you've been reading Chinese poetry and drinking lukewarm sugarless tea. [*Laughs, uncrossing and recrossing her legs*] You look like death eating a soda cracker.

And, a moment later, when an astonished Clay assumes that Lula, knowing him so intimately, must have been talking to his friend Warren Enright:

Lula: Is Warren Enright a tall skinny black boy with a phony English accent?

Clay: I figured you knew him.

Lula: But I don't. I just figured you would know somebody like that. [*Laughs*][24]

Combining Clay's pathetic attempts to grow into manhood by growing a beard, Lula's devastatingly accurate observation that "you tried to make it with your sister when you were ten," and his friendship with the pretentious Warren (in a world that may be Black but replicates American ignorance and insularity, the only Black who speaks with a British accent must be a pompous Black American), we are given a Black man who is not quite a man and not quite Black. As the play ensues, Clay's attempts to impress Lula, to play the supermasculine Black male she knows he is not but perhaps wants him to be (specifically with regard to sexual prowess), lead him further into her trap and, in the end, add him to her list of Black male "kills." Although the two causes can be conflated, we are made to understand that it is not just Lula's wiles but Clay's inauthentic Blackness that have led to this tragic end.

By framing their moments of consciousness within the construction of a patriarchal nation, these five theorists (including Baraka) effectively ignore and erase the ways in which Black women, over the past three hundred years, played a leading role in the formation of Black communities in the West. The central and vital role Black women played in the history of the African diaspora is suddenly rendered moot. Frantz Fanon, the central influence and inspiration of the Black Arts movement, offers no more than a compliant, silent, and veiled woman as a model for female activism. Less important but not forgotten, Du Bois's, Senghor's, and Césaire's theories offer only women with agency, or, like the Other-from-within, an agency that is wholly malevolent. The challenge that the Black Arts women faced would be to both recuperate the erased sociopolitical legacy of their mothers and to make themselves visible again in this new discourse of the Black nation in the West. As the "Other of the Other," they were deprived of the strategies used by Du Bois, Fanon, and the Negritudists. *Getting ovah*, it is clear, demanded a whole new set of theoretical tools if the Black female subject were to come into being.[25]

In *Too Heavy a Load* and *Black Women Novelists and the Nationalist Aesthetic*, Deborah Gray-White and Madhu Dubey, respectively, argue that the 1965 Moynihan Report found a perverse resonance among Black male activists such as Eldridge Cleaver and Amiri Baraka in their construction of the Black woman.[26] Gray-White writes that, while more explicit than previously, the misogyny in the Black nationalist circles and white national discourse was far from new and, in fact, had been in the making, "at least since Frazer's critique of black middle class women and Moynihan's matriarchy thesis. African-American men, from Black Panther Eldridge Cleaver and sociologist Calvin Hernton, to psychiatrists William Grier and Price Cobbs, to ideologue Frantz Fanon, accused black women of harming and holding back the race."[27] Madhu Dubey concurs, underscoring the depressing similarities between Moynihan and Black nationalist leaders by noting that "Black nationalist leaders not only echoed this masculine emphasis, but identified the black woman as an active agent of the black man's economic and social emasculation. This move was sanctioned by the Moynihan Report, which represented black women, statistically the most economically powerless group in the country, as a dominant force that indeed hindered the economic progress of black men."[28]

Earlier in this chapter I argued that masking operated as that "single complex unit" from the 1900s to the 1950s as a way to both respond to and reject the Western categorization of the Black as Other and to explore the basis for Black (male) subjectivity in the West. Even though Du Bois's, Césaire's, Senghor's, and, most influentially (with regard to the 1960s and 1970s), Fanon's counterdiscourses provided useful models for resistance and response, their (re)construction of a gendered agency in nationalist discourse disabled the possibility of a Black female subject at the same time that it enabled the Black male subject who, like his white male counterpart, comes into being through the denial of another's subjectivity—in this case, Black women. Hegel's, Gobineau's, and Jefferson's concepts of the white nation and white subject operate in an elision of the material and the ideal so that the Black could be figured as the idealist Other to the white subject. Whether unwittingly or not, Du Bois,

Césaire, and Fanon also allow the ideal to elide the material presence of active Black women in the nation, effectively negating *their* status as Other, but not negating that status for "other Others"—in this case of African diasporic counterdiscourse, the Black woman.

DOES THE BLACK SUBJECT BELONG TO
THE NATION OR THE DIASPORA?

Here we return to the same observation that greeted us in the first chapter: the ugly exclusion on which nationalist discourse—Black or white—must necessarily rely. With the resurgence of academic interest in the concept of an African diaspora, theorists of the Black subject have an alternative to the nation as the signifier for the collective subject. This does not mean that the term "diaspora" inherently signifies a different type of subject. Indeed, many contemporary works on belonging and identity vis-à-vis Africans and peoples of African descent either implicitly or explicitly use the term "diaspora" as synonymous with nation. Using these terms synonymously does us little good, especially when one considers how nationalism necessarily relies on a mythic concept of homogeneity, of Others, and of women as passive helpmates to the male subject. As a multivalent, international, intranational, multilinguistic, and multicultural space, diaspora suggests a movement away from homogeneity and exclusion toward diversity and inclusion.

Although the term "diaspora" literally means a "scattering of people," I want to qualify it further, arguing that it can offer a preferable construction of community as opposed to the exclusivity that is the mainstay for Black nationalist thought. The first two chapters of this book demonstrate how the (white) Western concept of the nation is inextricably intertwined with the concepts of the subject in that both are constructed through the dialectic of self/Other. Difference becomes the means by which a dominant group can assert its identity by exterminating, oppressing, marginalizing, or simply ignoring those it wishes to exclude. Nationalist unity always demands an enforced homogeneity and an intolerance of difference. By contrast, the concept of diasporic unity, as it has been advocated by such figures as Audre Lorde and Paul Gilroy, bases itself on a dialogic model, in which difference is recognized as a necessary reality for putting unity into praxis and as a source of strength, and where homogeneity is revealed as an oppressive and disabling myth. While I disagree with Jean-Paul Sartre's patronizing statement in *Orphée Noir* that the fallacy of a homogeneous Black identity stems from our internal racism, as chapter 2 has shown, I am inclined to believe that the assumption of homogeneity can operate as a useful strategy in limited contexts. I also believe, however, that positing a binary of Blackness most often returns us to the oppressive stereotypes in dominant Western discourse.[29] In Gilroy's and Lorde's (to name only two) constructions of diaspora, the bases for coalition are established on the grounds of diversity through unity. As Maryse Condé writes, "If we are not allowed to be diverse and different, we cannot be united."[30]

In the introduction to the English edition of *Farbe bekennen: Afro-deutsche Frauen auf den Spuren ihrer Geschichte* (Showing Our Colors: Afro-German Women Speak Out), Audre Lorde underscores how the differences between Black communities in Germany and in the United States are not only integral to our understanding of one another, and to a constructive future, but are also to coming to understand the many and equally valid meanings of both Black and feminist identities: "In the face of new international alignments, vital connections and differences exist that need to be examined between African-European, African-Asian, African-American women, as well as between us and our African sisters. The first steps in examining these connections are to identify ourselves, to recognize each other, and to listen carefully to each other's stories."[31] In *The Black Atlantic*, Paul Gilroy asserts a similar opinion concerning theoretical explorations of the Black diaspora, or "Black Atlantic": "In opposition to both of these nationalist or ethnically absolute approaches, I want to develop the suggestion that cultural historians could take the Atlantic as one single, complex unit of analysis in their discussions of the modern world and use it to produce an explicitly transnational and intercultural perspective."[32]

There are many ways, of course, to construct the "single, complex unit" that forms the basis for diasporic explorations of Black consciousness in the West, and many scholars, such as Simon Gikandi and Natasha Barnes, have taken exception to Gilroy's defining that unity exclusively through the slave experience.[33] The following chapter, by focusing on some of the work by Lorde and Rodgers written during the Black nationalist era, pursues the continual transformation of the "complex unit" established in the first two chapters, namely, the ways in which the Black diasporic tradition has responded to and moved beyond Euro-American discourses of Othering and the denial of subject status through intellectual conversation and the deployment of tropes that deftly move in and out of both idealist and materialist, essentialist and antiessentialist definitions of "Blackness" and subjectivity.

CHAPTER FOUR

How I Got Ovah: Masking to Motherhood
and the Diasporic Black Female Subject

FROM OTHER TO MOTHERS,

DIALECTICS TO DIALOGICS

The erasure of Black women from African American discourses on the subject and the nation has been a central topic of debate since the 1960s, and Michele Wallace is one of the most influential theorists in this arena. In "Variations on Negation and the Heresy of Black Feminist Creativity," Wallace responds to the critics of her book *Black Macho and the Myth of the Superwoman.* While Wallace agrees that her assertion that Black women have been complicit with Black men in their own denigration is too broad to be wholly accurate, she nonetheless insists that the heart of her argument remains true: "black feminist creativity is routinely gagged and 'disappeared'."[1] Wallace argues that Black women are the "Other of the Other," "dangerously unspeakable," and "resistant to theoretical articulation—hence the black feminist fear of theory, the invisibility of Black feminist interpretation in the realm of dominant discourse, and the way Black feminist literature prioritizes variations on negation."[2] While Wallace's claim that Black feminists are afraid of theory would surprise Hortense Spillers, Barbara Johnson, Claudia Tate, Hazel Carby, and Angela Davis among others, the "variations on negation" are the focus of this chapter as we move from dialectic to dialogic structures of Black subjectivity.

In dialectical discourse, Wallace's "Other of the Other" is a devastating reading of the limits of the dialectical subject because it offers little to no hope for alternative (read Black female) subjectivity. However, Du

Bois's, Césaire's, Senghor's, and Fanon's counterdiscourses perform an elision between the idealist and materialist dialectics in their deployment of the nation as the collective identity for the subject, Black or white. The inability of the dialectic to accommodate an "Other of the Other" stems from a logical fallacy in its construction of the subject and the nation. The dialectic of the subject—and those counterdiscourses analyzed in the previous chapters—deploys a version of chronology in what Mikhail Bakhtin identifies as the simplest chronotope, or "adventure time"—in other words, a narrative that has the *appearance* of sequence but in fact is independent events externally ordered in a way that belies their "random contingency," as Bakhtin puts it. In "Forms of Time and Chronotope in the Novel," Bakhtin looks at the "simplest" chronotope as it operates in the Greek epic and its hero, noting that "all the events and adventures that fill it, constitute time-sequences that are neither historical, quotidian, biographical, *nor even biological and maturational.*"[3] Bakhtin's critique of this particular ordering of time and space is similar to Friedrich Engels's critique of Hegel's idealist dialectic. Engels observes that Hegel's synthesis is often suspiciously similar to his original thesis, suggesting that his antithesis is little more than ephemeral, theoretically moot by the time synthesis is reached. In his discussion of the chronotope, Bakhtin points out that this ordering of the temporal and locational allows, for example, the heroes of the Greek epics to operate outside of the "normal" passage of time and the limitations of space.

The manipulation of time and space to legitimate philosophies of the subject is central to the structural origins of the Black Other and the Black subject. Hegel, Gobineau, and Jefferson all rely on the same fantastical chronotope to realize the white subject within a progressive narrative and dislocate the Black as Other and therefore outside this narrative. Hegel is more specific in his explanation from the *Philosophy of History*, arguing that there are two types of chronotopic history, or the ordering of spaces according to time: Western Europe possesses an analytical history, meaning that the passage of time is explicitly marked in the ordering of space—the modern state being the most recent ordering. By contrast, Africa exists in prehistoric mist, where time passes without any effect on space, and where progress and development have not occurred. This is why Europeans and Americans have the right to enslave Blacks: they are simply helping them progress. The counterdiscourses constructed by Du Bois, the Negritudists, and Fanon take issue with this reading, either arguing that Blacks have always existed within chronotope of progress (Senghor) or that Blacks in the West *had* progressed despite racist denials or (as Fanon argues) that some Blacks have progressed and others would do so as well, once they reject the Western chronotope that forever positions them as primitive and act in their own self-interest.

These debates on the relationship of the subject and Other to various chronotopes all exclude women from anything but the most superficial consideration. Posited as a passive landscape, an ally to white men, or ignored altogether, both Black and white women remained relegated to variations of Hegel's "African time," but with an important difference, for Hegel holds that Europeans must at least try to help the Black to progress. In *Notes*, Jefferson argues that nature has marked the Black as one whose biology would remain unchanged from its primitive nature. In *Algeria Unveiled*, Fanon posits that women could gain freedom for their Black men by remaining in what he determined to be their "traditional" role: veiled, silent, and subservient. In the Black nationalist discourse of the 1960s and 1970s, a similar philosophy also dominated: Black men must fight for their rights and Black women should be satisfied with their subordinate roles as assistants, lovers, and mothers.

How does this relate to Bakhtin's "adventure time" chronotope? In both (white) Western discourses on the nation and the subject and Black counterdiscourses, men are the only active agents; women are either passive or invisible. In narrative form, then, the story of the nation is always and only the story of men, rendering the nation's birth, its origins, its present, and its future wholly in the hands of men. Women are only the mothers and mates needed to create male heirs. Indeed, we can see this movement away from the material and wholly into the ideal—whenever women are discussed—in looking at the counterdiscourses of Du Bois, Fanon, Césaire, and Senghor. As a result, this wholly masculine lineage is not smooth and unbroken; rather, as Holquist puts it, it is a series of "separate adventures," where the father, in the absence of a woman, seems to spontaneously (re)generate a son. As Bakhtin explains it, "time is organized from without," that is, according to a masculinist timeline. In deploying the masculinist "adventure time" chronotope, Du Bois, Senghor, Césaire, and Fanon begin their narratives with men, men who miraculously spring from nowhere as there are no Black mothers in their narratives, only ineffectual or victimized sisters, or desirable, deceitful sex objects, Black or white. Dialectically speaking, in erasing the female from discussion, they perform the same idealist "negation of the negation" for which they took Hegel to task. The famous opening pages of Du Bois's *The Souls of Black Folk* reflect this masculinist sensibility when the narrator assures the reader that the Black *man* would not "Africanize America." While this is clearly a reference to white fears of Black men marrying white women, the fact that it is women who would produce these fearful children, not men, is quietly elided.

This passage is a conversation between men, one that assumes women will do as they are told and not operate on their agency. Even for Césaire's Creole subject, mixture becomes the result of the encounter between two men, colonizer and the colonized. The agency of women as mothers, as the *only* "material" conduit for the progression of a lineage (childbirth), is carelessly ignored, for these narratives explicitly depend on women without agency. Frantz Fanon's discussion of interracial encounters (despite its deliberately inflammatory descriptions of Black hands squeezing white breasts) nervously elides the potential result from that encounter: the white woman giving birth to a child of mixed-race ancestry. As Bakhtin notes, biological exigencies become impossible in the "adventure time" chronotope; men "beget" other men instead of women birthing children of both sexes and almost any racial heritage.

The leaders of the Black Arts movement would continue this idealist "negation of the negation" in their dialectic of the Black subject and Black nation. In his famous essay "The Black Arts Movement," Larry Neal explains that a complete and total break with (white) America and its culture is essential to this new Black movement:

> The Black Arts movement proposes a radical reordering of the western cultural aesthetic. It proposes a separate symbolism, mythology, critique and iconology. The Black Arts and the Black Power concept both relate broadly to the Afro-American's desire for self-determination and nationhood. Both concepts are nationalistic. One is concerned with the relationship between art and politics; the other with the art of politics.

Like other forms of Western nationalism, this one also insists on a clean break with the past that enables a discourse of "new" beginnings. Neal then moves to explain that this rift is hardly a loss because "the Western

aesthetic has run its course: it is impossible to construct anything meaningful within its decaying structure. We advocate a cultural revolution in
art and ideas."[4] However, it is not simply the white American past with
which Neal is eager to cut ties. In the following pages, he moves on to
echo the sentiments expressed two years earlier in Amiri Baraka's essay
"The Myth of a 'Negro Literature' " by arguing that previous generations
of Black intellectuals must also be estranged:

> The new aesthetic is mostly predicated on an Ethics which asks the
> question: whose vision of the world is finally more meaningful, ours
> or the white oppressors? What is truth? Or more precisely, whose
> truth shall we express, that of the oppressed or the oppressors? These
> are basic questions. Black intellectuals of the previous decades failed
> to ask them . . . much of the oppression confronting Third World and
> Black America is directly traceable to the Euro-American cultural
> sensibility. This sensibility, anti-human in nature, has, until recently,
> dominated the psyches of most Black artists and intellectuals; it must
> be destroyed before Black creative artists can have a meaningful role
> in the transformation of society.[5]

Fanon's masculinist and nationalist sentiments are invoked implicitly
and explicitly throughout the essay. With the exceptions of Aisha
Hughes and Carol Freeman (who are only mentioned in passing), Neal
concentrates his discussion on Black male artists and, in one case, praises
a text in which Black women are crudely portrayed as white female
wannabes. His concept of the nation is also masculinist in that it underscores the necessity of eliminating the past in order to begin anew. The
myths of clean and clear beginnings and of being able to break irrevoca-
bly with the past are central assertions used in the trope of the (founding) father. Finally, Neal's invocation of "Blackness" throughout the
essay reveals an implicit belief that there is only one correct Black identity, and that this identity links all Black peoples across the world. Although Neal is addressing the peoples of the Black diaspora, this is
nonetheless a nationalist sensibility, where unity is forged through an
enforced homogeneity, and difference is established through dichotomies ("Black" versus "Western" cultural sensibilities).[6]

By ignoring the agency women possess as the only group that can give
birth, and ignoring how biracial children are often the common result of
races encountering one another, Black nationalist leaders were able to

perpetuate two myths: that masculine power is absolute, and that a nation's history can be (and in some cases has been) racially homogeneous. Nationalist discourse, whether white or Black, relies on certain strategic exclusions. By excluding the role of the mother, nationalist discourse can grant its male citizens fantastic powers, albeit ones wholly located within the ideal, or discursive, realm rather than the material, or realm of praxis. By erasing the mother as an agent, masculinist discourse can grant men the power to determine the race of their offspring and the ability to establish finite origins and ends to the national narrative. While tropes of founding fathers rely on linear constructions of time, the trope of the mother speaks to circularity, connecting peoples not only to future generations but to previous ones. In a striking imitation of the American myth of the founding fathers (which constructs the nation as wholly and originally white and simultaneously denies past and previous intermixtures), American Black nationalism constructs a history in which those whose lives and contributions fail to correspond to its conservative gender and racial dichotomies (masculine versus feminine, Black versus white) are condemned and/or ignored altogether. By erasing mothers, both nationalist narratives, whether Black or white, perpetuate the myth that men hold absolute power over their origins and therefore are the natural leaders over the present and future of a supposedly "pure" race. Of course, no one can create his or her own material lineage, and no one possesses that vaunted power of logos, in which the speech is simultaneous with the act. The agency of the mother, so studiously avoided in narratives of the nation and the subject, so potentially disruptive and destructive, nonetheless always haunts Black and white nationalist discourses.[7]

Theoretical explorations of female agency through Bakhtinian dialogics is increasingly becoming an established tradition in Black feminist thought. In her famous essay "Speaking in Tongues: Dialogics, Dialectics, and the Black Woman Writer's Literary Tradition," Mae Gwendolyn Henderson formulates a Black female subject through Bakhtin's dialogic principles that intersect with Hans-Georg Gadamer's dialectic of the "Thou." Henderson's model is especially useful in its articulation of diversity as a means of unity—that is, it is Black women's heterogeneity, rather than homogeneity, that enables an "omnivocal" subjectivity. Instead of logos, which enables the subject to delineate and reject others, "omnivocality" possesses the far greater power of being able to connect with others and *recognize* their subjectivity. Here we can see an important step beyond Hegel, whose own exploration of recognition was hindered by the idealist master-slave dialectic in which recognition can only be enabled and thus ultimately defined by the master, leaving the slave with a secondary subject status on achieving consciousness.[8] In their counterdiscourses, Du Bois, Senghor, Césaire, and Fanon all played with the negative aspect of recognition, which, in their narratives of the subject, defines the moment when the Black becomes aware that he is *Other*. In her heterogeneous model, Henderson provides a new type of recognition, wherein difference becomes the means by which one can speak with, recognize, and thus be recognized by a variety of subjects. Because dialogue cannot be created without two speaking subjects (whether inner or outer voices), recognition becomes the means by which a unity based on diversity can be achieved. Moving away from a logos-based subject also means a move away from the binary of the nation, in which the line between subject and Others is quite clear. Instead, what Henderson provides here is the framework—through Black female subjectivity—for a *diasporic* subject, one who deploys dialogue instead of logos.

Anticipating Henderson's dialogic model for the Black female, two celebrated poets and essayists, Carolyn Rodgers and Audre Lorde, deployed the trope of the Black mother as a variation of Bakhtin's dialogic discourse to enable and explore Black female subjectivity. This trope, now nearly thirty years old but long overlooked, challenges, to put it in Madhu Dubey's terms, the "black folk culture" that "was assigned a certain ideological value to make it amenable to nationalist intentions."[9] Identifying that "ideological value" as the construction of the Black subject and the Black nation outlined above, Rodgers and Lorde challenge Black nationalist constructions of the subject, providing an alternative discourse that enables a Black feminist subject within a more inclusive understanding of a politicized Black collective. In other words, Rodgers and Lorde reject dialectic constructions of the subject in favor of a dialogic structure, which, as a "variation on negation," goes beyond the bounds of nationalist discourse to situate Black subjectivity within a heterogeneous model of the Black collective. By rejecting a system in which Black subjects can only be produced against Black Others and embracing the concept of diverse Black subjects, Rodgers gestures toward, and Lorde fully deploys, diaspora as the new collective model for Black subjectivity.

Rodgers's and Lorde's trope of the Black mother enables Henderson's model of the diasporic subject and also implements Dubey's reading of subtextual (counter)discourse. Henderson's "simultaneity of discourse" is achieved through the mother's conflated position as speaking for both herself and her children—as well as *through* her children. Bakhtin's theory of internal dialogue is explored through the mother as a subject who literally produces other subjects—and Gadamer's dialectic model of conversation of mutuality and reciprocity takes shape here through the mother as one who offers recognition through unconditional love but *not* unconditional agreement. Difference can be explored between the mother and her interlocutor without imposing delineations in the resulting dialogue. Using the mother as a trope in Black Arts poetry implicitly challenges the nationalist discourse's myths about origins and absolute power.

This trope of the mother, while hardly new or uncommon to any literary era, achieves a special significance in the poetry of Carolyn Rodgers and Audre Lorde because it enables a dialogic shorthand, providing an alternative to the lengthy novelistic narrative so that the Black Arts poem can also provide the multiplicity of voices and chronotopes necessary for the dialogic subject. Unlike the novel, Black Arts poetry can exploit the immediacy of performance, the power of the present that is almost wholly controlled (barring interruption from the audience) by the performer. While, on one hand, the novelist has the freedom to choose multiple narrators *and* simultaneously slip into the background, the poet cannot so easily disguise his or her racial and gender category. At the same time, that poet's speaking presence is more difficult to obscure or deny, as the performance is nothing less than the deployment of his or her agency—even if some of the audience would like to deny that agency. Control over audience reception also changes: while a reader can put down the novel and control the pace of reading, the audience at a poetry reading (and, to some degree, the reader of a poem) must accept the pace, volume, and literal parameters of the poem determined by its author. Because the immediate is impossible to categorize (it becomes the past if reflected on, the future if anticipated), the poet possesses the power to determine not only the chronotope of his or her work but also the time and space of the audience, relegating them to past, present, or future. Unlike the novel, time is performed, not constructed, and the traditional linearity imposed by Black nationalism can be upended quite quickly—if only for the moment—by the speaking poet (and the written poet, to a large degree, as breaking off reading midpoem most often runs the risk of complete disorientation. If they are not in epic or narrative form, poems rarely have the equivalent of chapter breaks, scheduled rest times).

"FOR MUH' DEAR": INTERSUBJECTIVITY THROUGH
MOTHERS AND DAUGHTERS

Although no longer as famous as her contemporaries Nikki Giovanni, Sonia Sanchez, and, of course, Audre Lorde, Carolyn Rodgers did garner critical praise in the 1960s and 1970s, perhaps most famously with *How I Got Ovah*, a collection of poetry written between 1968 and 1972 that finally brought her to national attention with its publication in 1975. It was also her first collection written after her break with Chicago's Organization of Black American Culture (OBAC), which, like most Black Arts organizations, was largely controlled by Black men. These poems challenge the masculinism of Black nationalist discourse that operated in both OBAC and other Black Arts organizations. Nonetheless, as the literary critiques written at that time reveal, Rodgers's collection was interpreted as performing dialectically, despite the obvious dialogic model that *How I Got Ovah* follows. Angeline Jamison's "Imagery in the Women Poems: The Art of Carolyn Rodgers" and Betty J. Parker-Smith's "Running Wild in Her Soul: The Poetry of Carolyn Rodgers," from Mari Evans's critical collection *Black Women Writers* (*1950–1980*), read *Ovah* as the narrative of a rebellious daughter's ultimately successful search for meaning and identity in her reencounter with her mother's church.[10] While both these readings offer rare close analyses of specific poems ("For muh' dear," "The Revolution Is Resting," "Jesus Was Crucified or It Must Be Deep," "IT IS DEEP," "U Name This One," "Poem for Some Black Women," "Masquerade," "FOR WOMEN," and "how i got ovah II/It Is Deep II"), they presume a dialectical structure to this collection in which the relationship between the mother and daughter is oppositional, thesis and antithesis, and the conclusion provides synthesis or reconciliation between revolution and religion in the Black community.[11]

A dialogic reading of *How I Got Ovah* provides a very different assessment of Rodgers's exploration of Black female consciousness in an era of "masculinist ethics."[12] Rodgers positions her mother and daughter in dialogic rather than oppositional relation to create an intersubjectivity that reclaims and recuperates the history and contributions of Black women past and present. This in turn exposes the multiple meanings of Blackness. Much in line with Bakhtin's dialogic, *How I Got Ovah* does not offer a "moral center," an omniscient or divinely wise narrator to offer the "correct" message from the series of dialogues between mother and daughter. The mother, like the daughter, is a central but ambivalent figure, as is her sometime signifier, the church.

The collection opens with "for muh' dear," a poem that immediately establishes the contextual nature of "Blackness": "today Blackness/lay backin/& rootin," suggesting that on other days Blackness performs differently, is perhaps not so relaxed ("lay backin") or so grounded and/or supportive (rootin). In this particular chronotope, time and space intersect to create Blackness as a chorus of supporters—or, at least, that is how the narrator chooses to see it. As the poem progresses, we learn that "today," as an unstable moment, also reflects the instability of the meaning of Blackness, for the narrator and her mother are in disagreement as to exactly what Blackness *is* doing, as well as what it *should* do. The narrator's assertions of Black pride and the performance of identity are met with a mother's pessimistic wisdom in the stanza following a pregnant pause of space on the page:

told my sweet mama
to leave me alone
about my wild free knotty and nappy
hair
cause I was gon lay back
and let it grow so high
it could reroute its roots
and highjack the sky!

she sd. why don't you let it grow
right on down to the ground, honey chile,
grow yo' self a coat of hair fuh winter
matter fact you so BLACK now, huh!
why don't you jest throw
a fit
of BLACK lay backin & rootin.[13]

The narrator is signifying—literally and figuratively—on Blackness as a dynamic spirit that evinces itself in her "free knotty and nappy hair." The mother plays this image to an extreme of grotesque hilarity, sarcastically yet lovingly addressing her daughter as "honey chile," ending with the complex observation that her daughter might as well retire to her equally grotesque egotistical creation of a "BLACK lay backin & rootin." The final stanza is a contemplative synthesis: "my mama gives some boss advice. . ./i think we all ought to do that." This is the entrance to the rest of the collection, a musing smile framed by a consciousness of self and the collective, indicating the impractical exuberance of the narrator without rescinding its terms. The ambiguity of these final lines—should the readers *follow* her mother's boss advice or *give* boss advice?—is the basis for a dialogic analysis in which Black women's voices are enjoined to speak together and to one another, even if they are in disagreement. In direct contradiction to the assertions made by Larry Neal and Amiri Baraka in their essays on Black art, Rodgers's poem suggests that "Blackness" is not a monolithic entity and that, even further, revolutionary consciousness, as exemplified by the daughter, does not need to be wholly in opposition to older Black generations.

Whereas Du Bois, Fanon, and to a degree Césaire carefully outlined racist discourse either rhetorically or structurally, "for muh' dear" is far more ambiguous and ambivalent. The title itself points to a comfortable and loving familiarity. The phrase suggests a mother's words to her child, but the narrator is quite clearly the daughter, allowing for both possibilities. The ambiguity of the speaker also allows for a doubled reading: the mother, not the narrator, frames the terms of an exchange where the mother ventriloquizes the daughter. Because the collection of the poems establishes the narrator as the daughter, we must necessarily understand the doubled reading as the daughter *ventriloquizing the mother ventriloquizing the daughter*. Of course, one can only ventriloquize so much before distinguishing voices from one another becomes an impossibility. Because the reader/audience can no longer determine exactly who is framing whom, they must accept the overlap between mother and daughter, their inherent intersubjectivity that, at the same time, is not based on shared political sentiments. Henderson's "simultaneity of discourse" begins to emerge in this poem as the "simultaneous ventriloquism" that enables a nonlinear reciprocity, or dialogism, in the mother's and daughter's subject positions.

Rodgers is not only arguing that our diverse political beliefs, our differing interpretations of "Blackness" do not need to divide us, she is further suggesting that our intersubjectivity is not necessarily based on shared ideology. For audiences of Rodgers's time and today, the sarcastic, witty, and multivalent commentary of the other is immediately familiar ("matter of fact, you so BLACK now . . . "), and while perhaps exasperating, it is hardly threatening and perhaps even a little heartwarming. The complexity of mother-child relationships is truly the focus of this poem, and it is a complexity that many members of the audience, Black or white, can immediately comprehend as one that cannot be reduced to a binary of, as Amiri Baraka famously put it, "Negroes and blacks." Biologically speaking, the daughter cannot sever ties with her mother, because her mother is part of who she is. The bond that the mother and daughter share in this poem encompasses their different politics—a concept to which Rodgers gives more than a little push by beginning the poem with "*today* Blackness" (my emphasis).

The material and somatic metaphors Blackness evokes are also considered here. The trope of the woman as landscape produces itself in the cognitive divide between the narrator and her mother. The narrator pictures herself literally transcending landscape with a literal extension of her "Blackness": her hair. Her mother counters this ideation by reducing hair to a primitive extreme. Blackness is turned in on itself, growing out of the Black body as hair that then covers that same body. At the same time, the mother suggests that her daughter simply manifest this Blackness, "throw a fit" of it, which simultaneously points to an expression of anger and an expression of madness. This is reminiscent of one of the nineteenth-century racist discourses in which Blackness is a psychosomatic quality that is irrational, savage, and therefore dangerous to the tempered European. Thomas Jefferson's worried excursion into the hatred that Black slaves must necessarily bear their masters, and Hegel's and Gobineau's later depiction of the crazed Negro find reflection in the revolutionary era in which *How I Got Ovah* was written. Yet this disagreement does not provide a delineation between the two voices here. The dialogic structure of "for muh' dear" reshapes the Black subject. While the masking counterdiscourses use dialogue and ventriloquism to assert the Black subject through his possession of logos, here dialogue signals the establishing of a Bakhtinian "intersubjective" subject. There is no delineation of discourse and counterdiscourse, nor is the exchange in this poem simply limited, like much Black Arts poetry, to the terms dictated by Black nationalist thought. Instead, by producing a poem in which mother and daughter discuss hair, the impact of the past (not just the mother's generation) and the way it informs their discussion is also brought into play—contravening the belief expressed by Neal in "The Black Arts Movement" that revolutionary consciousness operates independently from its antecedents. Hair, Blackness, and the manifestations of both in this poem are informed by debates and discussions that long preceded the 1970s' romance with the Afro, or "natural."

"Blackness" introduces itself as an independent dynamic that modifies the external dynamic of the narrator's ambitions. Describing it as "lay backin & rootin" suggests that it is "laid back," but because "backin" is written in a vernacular gerund, this Blackness could simultaneously be supporting ("backing") something or someone—possibly the narrator and her individual and collective identities. "Rootin" has a clear double meaning, pointing to the roots of the narrator's hair and heritage, combined to indicate a seriocomic will reminiscent of Hegel's German subject and Gobineau's Aryan. Just as Hegel's German and Gobineau's Aryan are credited with manifesting the racially inspired power to transform thought into being, Rodgers's narrator manifests the power of her Blackness through the simple act of allowing her hair to grow and "highjack the sky!" The mother, on the other hand, counters this dizzying declaration of Black will with the sarcastic suggestion that this hair may best be made into a coat to both protect and accommodate such powerful desires and demands.

Hair also works as an overdetermined trope within the sociopolitical discourse of African Americans in the 1960s and 1970s (as it had earlier and would continue to do). Resisting the integrationist images of Black women with straightened hair or a short and therefore manageable natural, the Black media, in line with African American sociopolitical trends, encouraged women to explore less traditional hairstyles. Like Black men, many African American women adopted the large Afro in all its diversity, often using decorative accoutrements and/or braiding. Using West African or specifically African American techniques also became more popular and visible across urban landscapes. The phrase "Black Is Beautiful," used by both Black and white media, attached itself to this new Black woman, who ostensibly had done away with the previous oppressive dictates of hairstyle. Obviously, this had an ambivalent effect on Black women: on one hand, beauty standards were no longer so strictly tied to illusory white models; on the other, it returned them to the category of the beautiful, consumable object. For the narrator of "for muh' dear," her "wild free knotty and nappy/hair" is the literal and figurative embodiment of her Black pride, defying any and all popular beauty standards by transcending them. For her mother, this wild hair is Rabelaisian in its immense size and uncombed condition; rather than to defy and transcend, the mother can only read her daughter's hair as a dangerous throwback to racist understandings that still operate today. In other words, there are necessarily a variety of counterdiscourses that, while responding to the same racist discourse, are sensitive to different aspects of it, and even possibly at odds with one another in their responses.

For reasons too long and twisted to explore thoroughly here, white American society has issued strict dictates on Black women's hair. Ranging from the ubiquitous and telling image of the mammy in a handkerchief, hair invisible, to the approved, staid image of the Black woman with straightened hair, to the demonic stereotypes of the angry Black women with her hair in its "wild" (read natural) state, African American women's hair has always been read as a dangerous excess that must either be hidden or else made to imitate true ("white") femininity.[14] Unlike Black men, therefore, Black women were encouraged and coerced, by white and sometimes Black communities, either to straighten their hair or to hide it. By focusing on hair as a trope for Blackness, Rodgers is able to indicate a history of repression and critique specific to Black women in which they played the role of both oppressor and oppressed. While the problems and complexities wrought by this stigma are now the problems that Black women must address, some Black women participated and still participate (as this poem shows) in attempting to regulate "acceptable" hairstyles.

The narrator's final lines in "for muh' dear" ("my mom gives some boss advice/i think we all ought to do that") makes clear that she is not offended by her mother's words but takes them to heart. This strong and complex bond between mother and daughter is all these lines convey clearly. The most distinct difference between Rodgers and the counterdiscourses analyzed in the previous chapters is the establishing of a Black female context in which the daughter looks both to herself and to her mother in her exploration of the nature and power of the Black identity. Within this female tableau, another question is allowed to emerge, namely, that of individual versus collective identity for the Black subject. "For muh' dear" engages with this question by inserting a series of qualities into Blackness that allow it to operate within the individual, gesture at the collective, and maintain a subtle sense of independent force. Blackness is also framed as the product of discourses that seek to posit the Black as the radical Other—and/or as a benevolent, redemptive force. Quite simply, Blackness is an ongoing dialogue possessing an ambivalent past, a complex and energetic (if uncertain) present, and a boundless future. "For muh' dear" clearly functions as the introduction to Rodgers's collection of poems, but it also stands alone as a thoughtful and engaging brief treatise on Blackness constructed between generations and history, and as an irresistible entranceway into further exploration of these themes.

The title of this collection, *How I Got Ovah*, asserts an obstacle (or a series of obstacles) overcome; on that level, it suggests poems will be in some wise explanatory, possibly an instructive narrative for those also seeking to "get ovah."[15] Gender and subjectivity must grapple with a history of presence and invisibility, a revolutionary era that complicates the minority's relationship to an oppressive and antagonistic federal authority, and the relationship between Black men and women, as well as Black women among themselves. "For muh' dear" begins with a unique premise: the narrator asserts an energetic and unproblematic agenda for her "Blackness" that is critiqued by her mother, who ushers in the sobering history of its construction, suggesting it is not so easy to overcome racist discourse when its counterdiscourse overlaps with it. Du Bois, Senghor, Césaire, Fanon, and Baraka create counterdiscourses that look at both the ideal and material aspects of Black identity. Rodgers continues this approach (as does Lorde, as I will later demonstrate), but with a key difference: the ideal and material are not assumed to be in a dialectical relationship but rather in one that is dialogic—that is, both conflated and simultaneous.[16] A discourse and counterdiscourse are introduced within the context of a dialogue between women of different generations, and the final line, "i think we should all do that," encourages a collective identification with this exchange. As we move forward to establish a Black identity in the face of antagonistic and countering forces, we must turn to the previous generation (still very much alive and active, as this poem attests) still dispensing "boss advice."

Gadamer's dialectic finds resonance in an exploration of the complex terrain of the Black female who shares aspects of the Black male's oppression but also has been subjected to her own unique Othering and erasure. The challenges and dangers all African Americans face must be established and linked to those sets of oppressions specific to the Black female at the same time that the Black female subject is brought to the fore in her own right. Rodgers structures youthful exuberance and sobering history as thesis and antithesis, but not in an oppositional relationship to one another. That is to say, one does not cancel out the other but combines with it even as both sentiments retain their individuality as they dialogue with one another. The final lines assert the legitimacy of the mother's warning, but obviously through standards that are self-generated, although the "self" must always already be understood (to some degree) as an extension of the mother. This "biological" (overlapping) framework of generations subverts the more linear understanding of Hegel and his respondents who fail to examine the theoretical dilemma of a thesis as an Absolute starting point. Because Rodgers destabilizes any claim on the part of the thesis, or an Absolute origin, what follows is equally ambiguous. After all, what is the meaning of the final two lines of "for muh' dear"? Does the narrator intend to begin her investigations with her mother's complex warning, wrapped in a coat, or is her eye still on highjacking the sky? We must look to the succeeding poems for clarification.

Several poems that follow continue to explore the archetypal relationship between the narrator and her mother, who together (re)produce the "Greenwich Mean Chronotope" of this collection. The daughter is the revolutionary who questions the limitations and silences of the past by focusing her intelligence on the present and its future ramifications.[17] The mother, on the other hand, is *also* focused on the present but frames it within past experiences and the wisdom of previous generations to question her daughter's reading of the present. In "JESUS WAS CRUCIFIED, or/It Must Be Deep/(an epic pome)," the narrator, ill, is telephoned by her mother, who urges her to pray for herself and all the hate that lies within. Here, the difference between generations is expanded: the daughter acknowledges that she is in fact quite angry, an emotion the mother rejects:

and she sd if she had evah known educashun
woulda mad me crazi, she woulda neva sent me to
school (college that is).[18]

The mother then begins a clichéd and simultaneously powerful litany of
her struggles, from working in the "white mans factori," to her daughter's uncouth behavior and questionable company ("THEY COMMUNIST
GIRL!!! DON'T YUH KNOW THAT???"), to her observation that not all
whites are bad and not all "negroes" are good. In a painful and funny
passage, the mother argues her point by describing a Black grocery clerk
who failed to pack a "colored lady's" ice cream in the proper protective
bag, contrasting him against a white bank clerk who deposits the mother's hard-earned money "fast and nice."[19]

    This poem, as read by Jamison and Parker-Smith in conjunction with
"IT IS DEEP," exemplifies the cognitive rift that Black nationalism asserted between the supposedly humiliating acquiescence of the older
generation and the "real" Black revolutionaries who will achieve what
their parents and ancestors had dared not seek. Yet "JESUS WAS CRU-
CIFIED" refuses to propose a simple dichotomy between a self-hating
older generation and their righteous and revolutionary offspring, whom
they castigate in misguided anger and fear. After urging her daughter to
read the Bible, bidding her goodbye, and hoping that "we don't have to
straighten out the truth no mo," the mother drops a telling anecdote:

> she sd, I got tuh go so I can git up early
> tomorrow
> and go tuh the social security board to clarify my
>   record cause I need my money.
>   work hard for 30 yr.s and they don't want
>   tuh give me
> $28.00 once every two weeks.
>   I sd yeah . . .
> don't let em nail u wid no technicalities
>   git yo checks . . . (then I sd)
>
>   catch yuh later on jesus, I mean motha!
>
>   it must be deeeeep . . .[20]

The mother's determination to receive her social security check from—who else but—The Man, and her daughter's playful slip "catch yuh later on jesus," force one to question exactly who is crucifying whom. More importantly, Rodgers argues that economics and everyday experience necessarily create different ideas and expressions concerning the state of the race. The narrator is college-educated because her mother scrimped and saved her wages from working in the "white mans factori" (a fact that is underscored in the poem "Portrait"), forcing the reader to remember and/or consider that revolutionaries are rarely self-made, let alone self-funded. This is a dialogue between generations about *change*, through which we are reminded that revolution and repression are related, and the subject status of both mother and daughter rely on an unpleasant and confusing history. Spiritual strength and the role of the Black church also play a key role in this dialogue. Christian doctrine strengthens and sustains the mother while the daughter dismisses such teachings with a playful yet patronizing sarcasm. All the same, it would be difficult to read the teasing verbal slip at the end of the poem as laughing dismissal, because the narrator is also recognizing her mother's struggle and sacrifice, even in the face of their own ideological struggle. This is a final, dizzying play of intersubjectivity, for we see how a mother's support and a college education necessarily lead to a serious cognitive rift between mother and daughter, as the latter moves to question the beliefs and actions of the former. Rodgers uses education to explain how the daughter, even while disagreeing with her mother, is nonetheless a product of her mother's achievement: providing her children with the education she was denied.

The poem that follows, "IT IS DEEP (don't never forget the bridge /that you crossed over on)," continues this theme, only this time in a language integrating Black vernacular with that infamous poetic styling of the college undergraduate, where simplicity and immediacy are waylaid by painfully rigid phrasings and an enchantment with "new" archaic words ("My mother, religiously girdled in/her god"). The contrast is deliberate, for Rodgers moves from the final musing and playful enunciation of "JESUS WAS CRUCIFIED" ("it must be/deeeeep . . .") to a formal structure introducing itself with painful delicacy and traditional grammar. This move encourages us to understand the many layers that comprise this dialogic voice. Although "IT IS DEEP" sustains the theme of a caring mother critical of her daughter's political stance, the narrator's analysis of her mother is both more focused on the mother's painful past ("I heard the tears when/they told her a high school diploma was not enough") and more prone to simplistic analysis and thus dismissal ("[she was] not able to understand, what she had/been forced to deny"). Education, as we see, combined with the gap in years, can cause one generation to misread and misunderstand the other, even as education constructs the words in which the previous generation's struggle is movingly portrayed.

"For muh' dear" introduces the conflation of generations, and "JESUS WAS CRUCIFIED" and "IT IS DEEP" reveal that generations are not a progressive linear order. These poems are ultimately grounded in a dialogic sensibility where variances in speech point to the variations in subject positions one can occupy. The narrator of the first poem is far more flexible and subtle, less inclined to Other the mother as an atavistic throwback to an intolerable time. The repeated phrase "it must be deep" (with a growing number of e's) in "JESUS WAS CRUCIFIED" contrasts against the assertive theme of its successor, "IT IS DEEP." The first phrase asserts uncertainty in the face of certainty, whether "it" signifies the divide between herself and her mother, or the history that has produced such a complex mother. Here the narrator gives larger voice to her mother, allowing for the full paradox and complexity of the mother's subject position as spoken (supposedly) from her own lips. The second poem asserts only the divide between mother and daughter, not the complexity of the mother, despite the paean in the final stanza:

My mother, religious-negro, proud of
having waded through a storm, is very obviously,
a sturdy Black bridge that I
crossed over on.

Unlike its antecedents, this poem contains only the narrator's viewpoint, a master discourse that will determine the meaning and role of all it chooses to observe and analyze. Consequently, the mother is produced as a strong but deluded individual whom the narrator believes to have surpassed. In the face of the narrator's college-age claim to omniscience, the final lines are clearly compromised: the narrator asserts her highly questionable right to walk over her mother, trampling her underfoot in order to move beyond her.

Yet move beyond to what? In a departure from "for muh' dear" and "JESUS WAS CRUCIFIED," the narrator of "IT IS DEEP" proposes a move forward very much along Hegelian lines in which the thesis overcomes the antithesis and congratulates itself for (supposedly) having achieved synthesis. Unsurprisingly, we find that the antithesis is never allowed to express itself, thus permitting an easy and trouble-free move through a dialectic—which, as Rodgers shows, simply returns us to the thesis, not beyond. By contrast, "for muh' dear" and "JESUS WAS CRUCIFIED" are dialogic, expressing themselves through internal dialogue; even if the narrator is doing no more than ventriloquizing her mother, she is incorporating a discourse that defies her own. The voices match one another in their wit and complexity, battling over ideology and blending in reaffirmed family ties, and, as the final lines reveal, neither voice can have the last word. This dialogic ending does not so much refuse as find itself confounded by a long and confused history incapable of a simple solution.

This circular mother-daughter chronotope, framed through a Bakhtinian internal dialogue, also defines the very heart of Rodgers's Black female subject. "The Children of Their Sin (an exorcise)" is the point at which *How I Got Ovah* most closely parallels the anecdotes related by Du Bois, Césaire, and Fanon that trace their moments of consciousness and establish their dialectics of Black subjectivity. The poem opens with a long quote from Ezekiel Mphahlele's *Death, Somewhere, and Homeward Bound* in which predictions of ghettoization and slow extermination of Blacks by whites are followed by questions of vengeance. The narrator then enters, implicitly suggesting that racial lines are not so easily delineated, relating how

> I moved and went
> and sat next to
> a white man
> because
> the brother who
> sat down beside me looked
> mean and hungry.[21]

This brief anecdote becomes the repetitive refrain and backdrop to four sections that narrate a childhood recollection of her mother's purse being stolen and the devastating financial effect. The narrator of "The Children of Their Sin" seems unable to reconcile her present act of racial "betrayal" with that distinct memory. As the anecdote repeats itself and the memory gains clarity, both become more vivid, painful, and therefore irreconcilable. It finishes in a rage and anguish of conflicting emotions:

> I moved and sat next to this
> white man today
> > away from that MEAN NIGGER
>
> WHO STOLE
>
> > MAMAS MONEY
>
> I moved to sit next to this white man
> the white man
> WHO MADE THAT AFRICAN NIGGER BROTHER/jump
> > that fence and git gone
> and the rage and burning shame of conflict
> set my teeth on ice
> and strove to liquefy the
> marrow in my bones.[22]

There is no resolution here, even when provided with a counterdiscursive structure that directly ties Black crime to white oppression. This knowledge does not reconcile the painful paradox of automatically and insipidly reading Black suffering as a potential well of violence—an equation made famous by Thomas Jefferson—and recalling the long-lasting effects of Black on Black violence. Through internal dialogue we are shown the painful aspect of the mother-daughter chronotope where the absence of clear delineations between time and space burdens the narrator with the tortures of the past and the ambivalence of present affinities and alliances. The narrator is tormented by the "shuffling shadows" in her soul,

> a coliseum of women
> screamingMERCY
> in tongues, from the whips

and the panoply of subject positions that cry out. The child shouts accusations at the "MEAN NIGGER WHO STOLE/MAMAS MONEY," the socially conscious and personally involved revolutionary denounces "the white man/WHO MADE THAT AFRICAN NIGGER BROTHER" flee with the purse, his back turned to her mother's pleas, and the college-educated poet describes, as with gritted teeth, "the rage and burning shame of my conflict" that "strove to liquefy the/marrow in my bones." The intersubjective contains a broad swath of subject positions, and no one realization can achieve supremacy here—there are too many others, too many selves speaking both internal (within the Black individual) and/or external (within the Black community) ambivalence.

Like Aimé Césaire, Rodgers selects a moment of betrayal to amplify her coming to consciousness, although unlike Césaire's narrator, her narrator was not previously beset by shame and self-loathing for homeland and history. Contrary to the ideology of "betrayal" in Black nationalism, we see it is not a woman but a man who acts "against" his race. Even further, Rodgers reverses the terms: it is the Black *mother* that is betrayed by the Black man. However, this is not a simple inversion. The betrayal portrayed here is not malevolent, and not the result of an alliance with white men: it is the result of a poverty of circumstances. Unlike Du Bois and the Negritudists, Rodgers does not use this moment to signify an important change in the narrative structure of her collection: the poems that precede this one range from "for muh' dear" to darker musings on Black pride and white oppression. After all, Rodgers does not pitch white against Black in this piece but splits open two sides of her own consciousness to reveal a central contradiction produced by Black on Black violence derived from the long experience of African Americans. Césaire also blurs the line between Black and white by ventriloquizing the two white female passengers; Rodgers speaks only through Black voices to produce the immediacy of this paradox in the Black subject.

In the manner of Du Bois, Césaire, and Fanon, Rodgers also constructs her moment of consciousness through a conflict between a man and a woman. However, there are two telling differences: first, the conflict is not interracial but between two African Americans, indicating that the Black subject can and will encounter conflict and the moment of consciousness within his or her own racial identity. Second, the conflict does not have sexual overtones but instead situates itself within socioeconomic strife. Rodgers's dialogic moment of consciousness, unlike those of Du Bois, Césaire, and Fanon, does not rely on a binary in which the Black, as thesis, encounters the antithetical white in order to achieve a synthesis. "The Children of Their Sin" asserts that the conflict that engenders consciousness is not so easily resolved as a war between races because it cannot be so easily externalized. Although the poverty of African Americans is the obvious result of centuries of white oppression and exploitation, Rodgers does not use this reading to explore the means by which the Black subject creates itself. Instead, she locates this moment as one that signifies the complexity and the contradictions of history and economics, and the resulting wide range of voices that construct a dialogue of Blackness. Du Bois and the Negritudists (as well as many other intellectuals of the previous generation) have already established and brought into public consciousness the wide-ranging effects of white colonization on the peoples of the African diaspora. Rodgers has shifted the focus, moving beyond the trope of the gendered nation and into the complex dialogic of the Black subject within the Black *community*.

"U Name This One" (which follows "The Children of Their Sin") provides a brief and disturbing narrative of Black failure enmeshed in the culture of the blues, as the title relinquishes the author's right to frame the discourse, suggesting that the audience must make its own frame. It ends with a short, exhausted stanza that could best sum up the Greenwich Mean chronotope for this collection:

> let uh revolution come.
> couldn't be no action like what
> I dun already seen.

Subjectivity is both always already present and constantly coming in to being, derailed and reasserted by the paradox of the Black experience.

This concept of a mutually informing "intersubject" becomes more apparent in *How I Got Ovah*'s combination sequel (perhaps the first of its kind): "how i got ovah II/It Is Deep II" is the final sequence between the narrator and her mother—much to the chagrin of the latter. The poem begins:

> just when i thought i had gotten away
> my mother
> called me on the phone
> and did not ask,
> but commanded me
> to come to church with her.

The narrator then confesses:

and because i knew so much
and had 'escaped'
i thought it a harmless enough act.

Yet she finds herself unable, or "not prepared," to witness baptism and communion, "and so I went back another day/trying to understand the mysteries." Upon return, the narrator is "touched" just when the choir sings "oh oh oh oh somebody touched me":

and when I turned around to
see what it was whoever touched me wanted
my mother leaned over and whispered in my ear
    "musta been the hand of the Lord"

At first glance, it seems as if serious questions have been foreclosed by humor—the narrator's soul-searching and consternation reduced to a mother's sleight of hand. Instead, as Lisa Gasbarrone has noted in her article comparing the subversive uses of laughter in Bakhtin and Hélène Cixous, "'The Locus for the Other'," we see laughter upending the dialectical imperative that a clear, decisive, *individual* consciousness must be achieved. Instead, what this poem provides is an intersubjective moment of recognition and understanding. The narrator returns to church clearly jittery and is reassured by an obvious maternal sleight of hand. Because the poem ends on this moment, we can assume that the narrator also finds the gesture reassuring albeit comic. Yet what is the resolution for a poem burdened with such an ambitious title—or, rather, two ambitious titles? "How i got ovah II/It Is Deep II" is only the second to last poem: like its predecessors, it does not constitute a border of this collection but plays a vital part from within. The narrator and her mother are not an aggregate of insidious oppressions but complex "intersubjects" informed by and informing each other through a host of assertions and contradictory meanings.

Rodgers's intersubject also breaks from the tradition of using masking to signify the metaphorical line between Blacks and whites. Instead, Rodgers argues that an attempt on the part of the intersubject to deceive will necessarily result in self-deception; such is the nature (if a little bit preachy) of subjects who are not and cannot be wholly individual in their consciousness. In "Masquerade," the mask is the device Black men and women use by mutual agreement to deceive one another and thus deceive themselves, a poignant example of how the intersubject, in acting against others or Others, necessarily acts against him or herself. As in Fanon, masking is self-deception, but its origin is obscured and not directly traced back to a colonizing impetus. It is a shield—as the tradition has understood it—but it must be dropped now because

> it is not enough for me.
> it is not enough for you.
> together we must plunge
> deeper into our pain for more—
> for the more pain we attempt to escape
> the more joy we automatically negate.[23]

Exploration and understanding are produced here as useless unless they are mutually informing. Yet mutuality should not be understood as a coalition, either in defense or offense. As the last lines make clear, to act in concert as if one (rather than as two in constant dialogue, constant negotiation) can only lead to an unhappy result. By attempting to escape pain intersubjects do not reach joy; instead, they are reduced to its negation, that is, pain. Escape, then, is not an action that moves intersubjects forward but keeps them immobile. Rodgers conflates escape and individualism here, and thus immobility and individualism. In the search for meaning, the individual must understand him or herself as a composite, as she writes in "Living Water":

> there is no way to find your selves, except this
> accept this
> plunge in life and deep at that
> and then swim until you reach some
> momentary imaginary shore.[24]

As in "Masquerade," confrontation and intersubjectivity are also conflated, suggesting that attempts at homogeneity—whether that means ignoring pain to focus on joy, or attempting to ignore mutuality to focus on the individual—lead one nowhere. As opposed to the idealist dialectic subject being spurred by either longing or the desire to overcome, which often results in a homogeneous synthesis-as-thesis, the dialogic intersubject is spurred by the desire to confront, engage in contrasts; in short, to be in dialogue, not monologue. In the last line of "Living Water," the emphasis on the momentary points to the relatively static state of synthesis in a dialectic structure. "Getting ovah," this collection argues, is not a static synthesis but an unending process of change and renegotiation. For the intersubject, epiphanies are fleeting.

SPACES BEYOND NATIONS: AUDRE LORDE AND THE VISION OF DIASPORA

During her all too brief lifetime, Audre Lorde—poet, activist, essayist, and scholar—inspired millions with both her words and deeds. Barbara Christian and Mae Henderson point out how Lorde used her many identities—working class, Caribbean, African American, lesbian, mother—to produce an activist politics that speaks to a wide array of women across the African diaspora. Lorde refused to understand her differences as separate or that which marginalized her from the center or "norm"; for her, diversity opened up possibilities for alliances and unity rather than foreclosing them. In spite of this, Lorde is most often located in white feminist scholarship as the token Black lesbian on the reading list, and even in African American and Caribbean studies she is rarely considered outside discussions of queer theory. In the wake of a resurgent interest in diasporic thought and subjectivity, Christian's and Henderson's call to reach all women across racial, ethnic, sexual, national, and class lines becomes ever more important.

Here I will be looking at Lorde's early work as a poet during the Black Arts era to examine her contributions as a diasporic intellectual who also attended to the question of Black subjectivity, and Black female subjectivity in particular. Although both Rodgers and Lorde use the trope of the mother to explore this subject status, the differences in their approaches suggest the degrees to which sexuality and circumstance can impact constructions of Black female subjectivity. In *How I Got Ovah*, Rodgers, focusing on Black communities, uses the mother as the dialogic counterpart to the protagonist, her daughter, in order to retrieve and recuperate both Black female subjectivity and the generations that precede her revolutionary peers. By contrast, the poems collected in Lorde's *Coal* (which includes poetry from her first volumes, *The First Cities* and *Cables to Rage*) and *The Black Unicorn* speak to the larger construct of the American nation and the African diaspora, most often to posit the protagonist as a mother, using that position to unify Blacks across the communities and national borders, underscoring their links to Africa, one another, and to Black men (who often appear as sons).

Neither *Coal* nor *The Black Unicorn* is wholly focused on constructing the Black female subject. Lorde is also working on giving voice to the Black lesbian (who is easily the Other of Michele Wallace's Other of the Other) and exploring human desire in the conflated boundaries between heterosexual and homosexual desire, between romantic love and platonic love. In *Coal* these desires collide with the hostile American milieu where being Black, female, and gay make her a triple target, and Lorde often links this exclusion and exploitation to the patriarchal construct of the white nation. In *The Black Unicorn* these explorations are also tied to her diasporic construct, rendering lesbian desire in America visible through the West African cultures where Western taboos on homoerotic interaction find little resonance. While Lorde, like Rodgers, explores these themes through a semiautobiographical context (they both use the first person most often and draw parallels between their personal lives and those of their protagonists), *Coal* is more explicit in its analysis of the Black female subject in the white nation, and *The Black Unicorn* underscores the Black female subject's diasporic nature, linking Black women across time and continents. Unlike Rodgers, Lorde does not use an African American vernacular, rather standard English grammar and terminology, nor do these poems conform to the "slam" style that a majority of Black Arts poets, both male and female, used. Although most of the poems from *Coal* analyzed here (*The Black Unicorn* was first published in 1978) were written contemporaneously with *How I Got Ovah* and explore similar themes, Lorde was not, strictly speaking, a Black Arts poet and is clearly addressing audiences across class, community, and color lines. Finally, unlike *How I Got Ovah*, the majority of these poems were not written in the same time period and linked to explore a common theme. There are many themes and addresses in these two collections; I focus on those poems that address the themes outlined by Madhu Dubey (the relationship between the individual and the collective; the oppressive past and revolutionary future; and absence and presence in subjectivity) and the trope of the mother vis-à-vis the Black female subject.

Lorde, like Rodgers, assumes a dialogic relationship between the ideal and material aspects of Black identity. In the title poem from *Coal*, she implicitly takes the derogatory phrase "black as coal" to compose an introductory statement on the relationship between her individual Black identity and its relationship to the Black and white collective. Coal is contextualized as the originary state of a diamond, hence possessing both rare and great value and a multifaceted aspect. She muses,

> There are many kinds of open
> how a diamond comes into a knot of flame
> how sound comes into a word, coloured
> by who pays what for speaking.[25]

Lorde expertly maneuvers between the dangerous divide of the essential and the construct, making clear that her words are "coloured," or Black, but this is not a biological difference, rather an experiential one, depending on what one risks or "pays" for certain enunciations. Diamonds, after all, are produced only after experiencing extraordinary heat and pressure. The image of a diamond in the light also reflects a positive rendering of the diversity of Black discourse. Because Lorde does not draw on a Black vernacular, these poems immediately signal an important difference between her and the Black Arts poets. Here, she quietly argues that her words are another type of Blackness, but she links them to all Black people and links her specific life experience to the experiences of those who look like her, ending with the lines, "I am Black because I come from the earth's inside/now take my word for jewel in the open light." This statement of unity deliberately capitalizes the "b" in Black, implicitly making common cause with the Black Power movement and the philosophy of Black pride. The "command" in the final line is evidently addressed to both Black and white audiences. As Phil Harper argues in *Are We Not Men?*, many Black Arts poets, such as Larry Neal and Amiri Baraka, attempted to split Blacks into two groups, the "authentic" and the "inauthentic," defining these categories in terms of who subscribed to their platform and who rejected it. By refusing to disguise her status as a lesbian and feminist in her poetry, Lorde is clearly not with the program. Any exclusion, as this poem makes clear, is not of her own making: she identifies with all of her Black brothers and sisters.

The Black Unicorn also begins with its title poem, but the solid, logical signifying chain enabled by the natural (that is, having to do with nature) metaphor of coal is traded in for a mythological beast that operates as a more explicit entry into the dialogue on race. Besides being fictional, unicorns are always white, suggesting that the fiction of race is directly tied to white constructs rather than biology. Yet, as essentialists often fail to understand, a fiction is just as powerful as any reality when you can compel enough people to believe in it and act on it. The power of the fiction, as Lorde suggests through the image of this animal, stems from its misleading visual similarity to perceived realities. A unicorn (whose name is wholly based on its difference) almost seems real because it looks so much like a horse. Racial difference can be ballooned into all sorts of outrageous beliefs because one can often *see* color difference and therefore assume its difference must possess some sort of meaning. Lorde overturns another assumption with her "Black" unicorn: rather than assign it ideal traits or the purity of the martyr, she asserts that the black unicorn is "greedy," "impatient," and "mistaken/for a shadow/or symbol," suggesting that idealist constructions of race are always inadequate.[26] The horn of the unicorn, the poem suggests, should not be mistaken for a phallus but a double signifier for race *and* gender, implying that these differences occupy overlapping categories and so the same signifier. It is also possible that the horn signifies sexual difference as well, given its sexualized context (and playing on the stereotype of the lesbian as masculine woman possessing a fictional phallus). The final stanza of the poem hints that the Black women portrayed in the following poems will not satisfy any expectations of femininity:

The black unicorn is restless
the black unicorn is unrelenting
the black unicorn is not
free.

This final stanza—especially the final two lines—provides the dynamic for the rest of the collection, in which Black women and lesbians are moving against their oppression.

Both "Coal" and "The Black Unicorn" address a Black and white audience, and this blurring of racial lines continues in "The Woman Thing" and "Oaxaca"; but this is not the only conflation. Although separate poems, these two works share a common theme and a distinctive style of an allegory narrated in the third person. Both suggest more than they explicitly state, ambiguously describing a preindustrial culture where male hunters make "fresh tracks for their children's hunger," leave "bloody footprints," are "snow-maddened, sustained by their rages," and "in the night after food they may seek/young girls for their amusement" ("The Woman Thing"). In "Oaxaca" the men are farmers, but in both poems they fail at their attempt to provide. In "The Woman Thing" their frustrations target prepubescent ("unbaked") girls, who flee from them in terror, but the poem ends with the narrator claiming that

> the woman thing my mother taught me
> bakes off its covering of snow
> like a rising blackening sun,[27]

suggesting that a Black matriarchal resistance is manifesting itself. Linking the male hunters with coldness and snow, and the girls and women with an approaching heat, this poem's symbolism conflates with "Oaxaca" (which directly follows it), where women are recalled in the act of sowing:

> Growing their secret in brown earth
> spread like a woman
> daring
> is weary work for still-eyed men
> who break the earth
> nursing their seed.

The male planters, on the other hand, struggle against the effects of heat ("a dry season"). The act of planting suggests the sexual violation of women and possibly the usurping of a woman's prerogative to nurse and give birth. Put together, these two poems construct a narrative in which an early patriarchal culture that moved from hunting to planting violated and denigrated its women but, drawing on themselves as a source of heat and power ("Oaxaca" twice warns that "lightning comes" and also speaks of a known storm and "brewing thunder"), these women have yet to be fully conquered.[28]

This narrative recalls the suspiciously simplistic narratives many professionally trained and amateur scientists have proposed (on the basis of what they admit to be incomplete evidence) to justify the suppression and oppression of women in Western cultures recorded in our earliest written histories. The majority of the stories begin with a hunter /gatherer culture in which the superior strength of men (it is assumed) automatically accorded them the position of providers for the tribe through hunting. As the fable goes, a particularly long absence from their women caused the men to realize that women do not give birth spontaneously but needed men to "fertilize" them. This (as well as other subsidiary external factors, such as environment) led to the creation of primarily agrarian societies, where men became planters so as to ensure the continuation of offspring; thus, the natural evolution of patriarchal culture. By contrast, Lorde's counternarrative suggests that it was the failure of hunting that led men to violate women when they pleased ("injustices drip from their mouths") and led women to become gatherers ("the woman thing my mother taught me") and possibly planters, which, in "Oaxaca," the men attempt to usurp but also seem to fail to do so. In Lorde's fables, the violence of patriarchal culture is highlighted, reading its domineering practices not through the pseudo-Darwinian lens used by dominant discourse but through the cruelty of those practices and their negative outcomes (failure of hunting societies, the violation of human beings—specifically young children—and the consequent rupture of community through the use of terror as a means of control). Lorde reconfigures the trope of women as "gatherers" and passive landscape much the same way she reconfigures coal, pursuing the natural metaphor through to its logical and positive manifestations. In a logical series of signifiers reminiscent of Senghor's mask poems, Lorde makes the following argument: if women are earth, then it follows that they are enriching, active, and of course warm, a source of heat. As a source of heat, they are also a source of light, and as a source of light, they are lightning, active, powerful elements that transcend the earth and able to challenge their oppressors. The most explicit manifestation of this power is in sound, described as the "brewing thunder" and threatened in the "thunder's eve." Whereas "Coal" located the narrator's logos in words, like diamonds, they were also described as "sound," suggesting that women, at least, possessed logos long before written and spoken language. Thunder is created, of course, in the encounter between hot and cold air, pointing to an interpretation of the origin of this women's power stemming directly from their forced confrontation with domineering men. While Rodgers's use of the vernacular in *How I Got Ovah* operates as a logos bounded by and manifested in specific time and place (and so at least in passive agreement with Neal's assertion in "Black Arts" that the true Black revolutionary's consciousness must manifest itself in the present, not the past), Lorde eschews this idea in favor of a transcendental logos where it is the power and force of sound, not words themselves, that matters. Put together, both interpretations agree with Bakhtin's reading of dialogue as something that is both scenario specific *and* transcendental.

"Oaxaca" refers to a city in Mexico famous for both its precolonial and postcolonial history, culture, and architecture; in invoking it, Lorde is suggesting that oppressive pasts are not wholly defined by race, and that men, whether colonized or colonizer, are often indistinct in the eyes of women when they attempt to invoke masculine privilege. But these poems are not passive protests: they warn of a retaliatory female strength that lies in the very place where men have located feminine weakness, namely, in nature. Patriarchy, Lorde argues, is not natural: its violence is not a biological imperative but the result of failure and frustration. In like kind, its gains are at best temporary: the men in the poems, although they dominate their women, are not thriving, and although they can terrorize women, they cannot wholly control them. Lorde seems to suggest that if any sociopolitical movement, Black or white, models itself on a patriarchal model (and at times Neal and Baraka, among others, tried to justify misogynist praxis with a strategic reading of West African culture just as Lorde counters this with her own exclusionary readings) it cannot and should not count on women as its passive allies.

The poems in the first section of *The Black Unicorn*, "From The House of Yemanja," "Coniagui Women," "Dahomey," and "125th Street and Abomey" offer another response. The glossary provided at the back of the collection reveals that these names, unlike the black unicorn, are neither mythical nor invented but instead refer to past and existent African nations that were not patriarchal in their structure, contrary to the assumptions of Neal, Baraka, Addison Gayle, and others. On an immediate level, these poems overturn Western myths. "Coniagui Women" (as well as the self-explanatory "The Women of Dan Dance with Swords in Their Hands to Mark the Time When They Were Warriors") shows how African women occupied roles such as warrior and hunter, which are traditionally understood in the West as inherently and exclusively male, while "Dahomey" (and the glossary explanation) conveys that the Amazons were not in fact a myth but actual women feared in battle and respected throughout West Africa. Lorde's image of the black unicorn achieves a deeper meaning here, becoming the symbol of a counterdiscourse to Western myth, the white unicorn. The black unicorn is here to provide factual data and recuperate histories from which all Americans have been severed. Operating as a specifically Black female (and possibly lesbian) icon, the black unicorn is also in dialogue with the myths of Black nationalism, quietly demonstrating how a supposedly independent, nonwhite ideology is at least partially grounded in white fictions, that is, patriarchal structures as both originary and normative.

"To a Girl Who Knew Which Side Her Bread Is Buttered On," the final poem in *Coal*, uses humor explicitly to upend masculine domination (again bringing to mind Lisa Gasbarrone's reading of Bakhtinian laughter). Recalling both the slightly atavistic tone and agrarian setting of "The Woman Thing" and "Oaxaca," this highly condensed poem narrates an archetypal male antagonist ("He, through the eyes of the first marauder") who spots a young girl and immediately moves to assume ownership ("his catch of bright thunder").[29] Lorde juxtaposes lightness and weight here, the Mother Goose–like rhyme and invocations of scones, tea, and bread with an explicit mistrust of masculine desire, reading it as synonymous with the Black nationalist assertion that the past should be left behind. This desire to begin anew is translated as a blatant dismissal of the importance of ancestry and coupled with the Black nationalism's argument that a woman should be defined only in relationship to the man who is her mate. It is this linear thinking, this specifically masculinist hubris, that leads to his downfall. Assuming that the "bones" are asleep (and failing to read them beyond their negative connotations as irrelevant and mere artifact), he ends up "trampled into the earth" by them while the girl "with a smile of pity and stealth/ . . . buttered fresh scones for her guardian bones." As in "The Woman Thing" and "Oaxaca," the defeat or destruction of the male is initiated by his own aggressive behavior, a not so subtle allegory for the more masculinist precepts in Black nationalism. At the same time, Lorde posits this aggression as unnatural, unjustified, and, as underscored in *The Black Unicorn*, not so much ancestral or African as Western. Of course, her choice of referents here is strategic, as she avoids those West African cultures that were and remain patriarchal.[30] She interrogates the more complex history of our slave and colonial past by depicting the young girl preparing very English scones and tea, unaware of or deliberately ignoring the nationalist and economic histories that inform this repast.

The oppositional relationship between men and women that "The Woman Thing," "Oaxaca," and "To a Girl" posit is only one of several relationships between men and women, old and young. Like *How I Got Ovah*, the majority of the poems in *Coal* move from more external observations to become increasingly prone to self-examination and critique as well as more inclusive. In "Generations" Lorde again speaks from a feminist perspective but, in deeming these women symbolic mothers, addresses this new generation in a gender-neutral tone that enables an exploration of social connections across gender lines. The title points toward mutually informing definitions, the continuous act of rebirth and a group of people defined by the era in which they were born and came of age. The poem's message, pessimistic in its outlook, does not address this new Black Power generation (it is even suggested that they would not listen in any case) but addresses its peers: those women who came of age in the 1950s to wage war on a virulently racist, misogynist, and homophobic society. In the meaning that is created between the two definitions inherent in the title, Lorde suggests that the differences between generations are minimal in importance ("How the young attempt and are broken/differs from age to age") compared to the painful similarities:

How the young are tempted and betrayed
into slaughter or conformity
is a turn of the mirror
time's questions only.[31]

Like the two poems that precede it, "Generations" focuses on the relationship of the past and the present, directly countering two of the most famous aspects of Black ideology that flourished from the 1940s into the 1970s and have never completely disappeared: that in order to build a strong and united Black community Blacks must return to the patriarchal "norms" of our African ancestors; and that this generation has little to learn from its supposedly abject history of enslavement and Jim Crow.

However, Lorde does not argue that the successes of her generation are the lesson; instead, it is the generation of failure and the overwhelming power of oppressive forces that they must heed. They must (very much in line with Carolyn Rodgers's presentation of generations) recognize that they are not unique in their desires or aspirations and that others have passed before them and others have failed. Contrary to expectation and ignorant assumptions, it is the generation of young

Black women who do not symbolize a slave past ("We were brown free girls") and who were also lesbian ("and the wind has made us golden /made us gay," although this is only slyly hinted at in a double entendre) that most closely resembles these new warriors. Yet "Generations" is not simply a critique of this new generation—the focus is actually on Lorde and her peers for their almost dismissive attitude toward those who are now following in their bloody and scarred footsteps and their complicity in enabling their own invisibility, their erasure from contemporary history. Lorde asks:

But who comes back from our latched cities of falsehood
to warn them that the road to nowhere
is slippery with our blood
to warn them
they need not drink the river to get home
since we have purchased bridges
with our mothers' bloody gold;—
for now we are more than kin
who come to share
not only blood
but the bloodiness of our failures.

Here Lorde underscores the inherent intersubjectivity of generations and the responsibility that parents (at least in the metaphorical if not strictly biological sense) bear toward their children (a term she uses in the poem). If history repeats itself, Lorde says, and failures are repeated, the blame does not solely lie with those only looking forward; it lies also with those who can only look back. Knowledge must be shared, of both successes *and* failures. A third definition of the title suggests itself at the end of this poem: because so much is shared between these two groups, ultimately they are not separate from one another but simply one single "generation." This poem, striking in its honesty, begins to modify the more defiant and aggressive stance of Black feminist power. We move from this power as a veiled threat to one that has the agency to effect change. The invocation of the mother in "Generations" achieves greater repetition and expansion of meaning in "Now That I Am Forever with Child" and "Story Books on a Kitchen Table." The potential to teach these "children" the hard lessons that the parents have learned becomes the positive manifestation of the rage brought about by masculine violence and men's attempts to erase female consciousness, and thus female subjectivity. The focus has also narrowed, moving from the larger, deliberately ambiguous allegorical cultures of "The Woman Thing" and "Oaxaca" in the Black community and the era of Black power. At the same time, Lorde begins to focus on the specific qualities of a woman's power in the form of the mother.

In "Now That I Am Forever with Child," the intersubjective (and timeless, as the title indicates) nature of motherhood is explored as the narrator recollects her pregnancy and

> the swelling changed planes of my body
> and how you first fluttered, then jumped
> and I thought it was my heart.[32]

The development of the fetus is paralleled with the development of the narrator's increasing awareness of her maternal identity. The chronotope of intersubjectivity is asserted in the final stanza, where a specifically maternal consciousness arranges the time and space of intersubjectivity:

> Since then
> I can only distinguish
> one thread within running hours
> You, flowing through selves
> toward You.

Time and space are circular in this maternal consciousness—the "You" flows into the "You," with the mother and the endless conflation of selves mediating. The running hours are compressed into a single thread (perhaps the umbilical cord?) so that intersubjectivity and the consciousness of motherhood become synonymous. Like the relationship Rodgers proposes between her mother and daughter in How I Got Ovah, intersubjectivity is not a simple merging of two into one (the synthesis in an ideal dialectic) but the conflated coexistence of two subjects, defined by, through, and against one another.

Contrary to the comforting image suggested in its title, "Story Books on a Kitchen Table" provides another and very different reading of the mother and child relationship, suggesting, like "Generations," that biology is not the deciding factor in the identity of motherhood. Lorde's turbulent and strained relationship with her own mother, as documented in her "biomythography" *Zami: Towards A New Spelling of My Name*, seems to be the inspiration for this poem, in which she relates a daughter's pain and terror at being left alone by her mother. The reasons for her mother's neglect are not specified, but the beginning lines of the poem suggest that, whatever the external reasons might be (a job, family duties), the narrator believes that the primary impetus is a mother who resents the duties of her position:

> Out of her womb of pain my mother spat me
> into her ill-fitting harness of despair
> into her deceits
> where her anger re-conceived me
> piercing my eyes like arrows
> pointed by her nightmare
> of who I was not/becoming.[33]

While the relationship between mother and daughter in *How I Got Ovah* is not always harmonious, Rodgers's depiction of an always loving and supportive mother casts an idealistic light on an alliance that relies on the Western discourse that deliberately conflates biological imperative with the socially constructed imperative that mothers must be guided by a deep and abiding love for their natural offspring. Although the obvious semiautobiographical style of the collection suggests that Rodgers is being more descriptive than prescriptive, she does not address this conflation and the many examples of women and girls who, for whatever reason or circumstance, are far from embracing their status as mothers and/or do not possess that sacrificial and often self-negating love.[34] From the beginning of "The Woman Thing," Lorde has already hinted at the cruel and painful ways in which one can become a mother (for example, being raped as a child) and now explores how different mother-daughter relationships also affect the chronotope of intersubjectivity. As the first stanza of "Story Books" indicates, the narrator's mother gives birth in two stages. First, the daughter is "spat" out and then *re-conceived*, a striking description that contradicts the passive figuration of the mother in social (and an atavistic biological) discourse (where the passive egg is fertilized by hyperactive sperm, waits nine months, goes into labor, and has the baby removed by a doctor).[35] Instead, the mother in this poem can actively manipulate the development of the fetus, delay and/or divert its conception—and violate it with an anger that is as palpable and powerful as any weaponry.

Second, while the mother can control the circumstances within the womb (and without, as the poem suggests that this re-conceiving may also take place during childhood), she cannot alter the destiny of her child, no matter how much it frightens or angers her. One can retroactively provide one interpretation of this anger as her mother's rejection of Lorde's dark skin, features that did not fit the definition of traditional beauty (as Lorde's sister did), and even, perhaps, her burgeoning homosexuality. From this perspective, the spitting out of her daughter can also be Lorde's banishment from her own home when still a young adult. While time and space are still circular, the manifestation of the mother's anger and her concomitant refusal to recognize, unlike the mother of the previous poem (most likely Lorde), signal that her daughter, though part of her, is also distinct from her.

The "selves" invoked in the final stanza of "Now That I Am Forever with Child" become the "iron maidens" that protect Lorde in her mother's absence, but this protection is ambivalent: an iron maiden is a medieval instrument of torture in which the unfortunate prisoner is locked in a steel cage of humanoid form. The collective spirit between women assumed in the earlier poems is now broken in a scenario where it is not just a woman but a mother who is the oppressor. Informed by this chilling tale, the Blackness so positively interpreted in "Coal" becomes negative in the final line, where the lack of compassion and love, as well as a "vanished mother," make the reader feel sorrow and pity for this "Black girl," rather than awe and respect. This sense of loss, stemming from a deliberate withholding, is also part of The Black Unicorn, most memorably in "From the House of Yemanja," where the narrator cries

Mother I need
Mother I need
mother I need your blackness now.[36]

The Black Unicorn also provides one of the most striking statements on dissociation and a sense of estrangement not only from one's mother but the Black community. Located toward the end of the collection, it retroactively redefines the most romantic descriptions of West African culture in the earlier poems and, in turn, can be interpellated by those poems, encouraging the reader to develop a complex understanding of the African legacy. "Between Ourselves" begins with the narrator's painful description of "walking into a room," a common allegory used in discussions of an individual's various social allegiances ("if you walked into a room where there were three groups of people . . . which group would you go to first?"). The first stanza argues that nowadays there is no group for her:

> where shall my eyes look?
> Once it was easy to know
> who were my people.

Lorde then thinks this moment with the era of the African slave trade and, like Rodgers, locates the betrayal in the actions of a Black man against a Black woman:

> Under the sun on the shores of Elmina
> a black man sold the woman who carried
> my grandmother in her belly.

Like Rodgers, Lorde examines how her anger encourages her to Other her brother, deny him his humanity:

> When I see that brother behind my eyes
> his irises are bloodless and without color
> his tongue clicks like yellow coins
> tossed up on this shore
> where we share the same corner
> of an alien and corrupted heaven
> and whenever I try to eat
> the words
> of easy blackness as salvation
> I taste the color
> of my grandmother's first betrayal.[37]

Again like Rodgers, she traces the motivation of that betrayal in money and implicitly suggests that racial capitalism is at its root, but Rodgers's "brother" is portrayed in a far more sympathetic light, as he is less likely in search of financial profit and most likely simply seeking funds to feed and shelter himself. At the same time, How I Got Ovah constructs a strategic delineation from certain conflations of the subject. While Rodgers's "Poem for Brother/for the Nation" suggests that the loss of a good Black man is a shared one, the narrator is indicted only for failing to prevent this downfall. She distinguishes between passive complicity and the more active engagement in committing the crime, prevented from doing so by her intersubjective status. Lorde's "Between Ourselves," however, does not allow itself this delineation. The greed and the corruption of the slave trader, while not a trait she honors, is nonetheless part of her:

> I have forgiven myself
> for him
> for the white meat
> we all consumed in secret
> before we were born.

Rodgers's narrator cannot forgive herself, but the "crime" is easier to bear (of a passive, almost unconscious complicity), to say the least. Lorde depicts the origin of this betrayal in a far more chilling way, namely, cannibalism for the sake of personal gain, and, in order to retrieve herself, must forgive both the slave trader and herself, for he is also part of her, his betrayal the flesh of her flesh.

Both *Coal* and *The Black Unicorn* endlessly renegotiate ideal and material mothers, synecdotal for the ideal and material relationships both women share with one another and their communities. By "material" I mean the everyday reality of economic and political strife that human bodies must negotiate. In Lorde's poems the celebration of African matrilineal and/or sexually equitable cultures with inspirational mother figures and maternal aspects is deliberately juxtaposed against recollections of her own mother, who was far from ideal. *Coal* ends on a more definitive but far less balanced note, suggesting that Black women, like the protagonist of "To a Girl," is safest with her ancestors, even as this brief poem leaves us with the unsettling feeling that these ancestors are also demanding and restrictive, from a past that is less than liberatory, and that the girl tends to them perhaps less out of spontaneous love than duty. The most definitive statement in *The Black Unicorn* is in the final stanza of "Between Ourselves," where Lorde writes

> if we do not stop killing
> the other

in ourselves
the self that we hate
in others
soon we shall all lie
in the same direction.

The final lines evoke both a restrictive uniformity and the grisly image of mass graves. Yet this is not the poem Lorde chooses to end her collection, and the three poems that follow, "Future Promise," "The Trollop Maiden," and "Solstice," focus on the necessity of constant change, confronting loss and hardship and, most importantly, incorporating it. As the final stanza of the last poem intones,

May I never remember the reasons
for my spirit's safety
may I never forget
the warning of my woman's flesh
weeping at the new moon
may I never lose
that terror
that keeps me brave
May I owe nothing
that I cannot repay.[38]

The only two words that Lorde allows to be capitalized here are "May" and "I," emphasizing both the strength of the subject and its contingency on those external forces that are nonetheless conflated with it. Renewal, loss, and regeneration become the mantra for the Black female subject, and the strongest riposte to Black nationalist theories of the Black subject: the past is always with us, negotiating with the present and future. Its terrors bring us courage, and while the present allows us to "never remember," we must simultaneously never forget, for it is within this circularity that our future lies. In *Black Women Novelists*, Madhu Dubey locates much of the ambivalence surrounding the mother in the novel's mirroring of the way in which the mother functions as a symbol of lack. Rodgers and Lorde offer a different reading by transforming lack into loss, which in turn spurs a circular process of retrieval. As such, the mother achieves a different significance with these two poets: it is not dominant ideology but her own humanity that defines her.

While Carolyn Rodgers and Audre Lorde offer tropes of motherhood that are far less ambiguous and ambivalent than those found in the novels of their time, they are not superficially idealistic either. *Coal* argues that women are agents who share common cause in a sexist nation, but it also underscores how some women can and will use this agency to hurt and harm not only one another but their offspring. *How I Got Ovah* explores the ideological (in this case, synonymous with generational) rifts between a mother and daughter, using the abiding love of a mother and child as the basis for their dialogues. In *Coal* the rift is emotional and, in an almost perfect inversion of Rodgers, quietly suggests that the abuse between women is caused by their failure to understand the common origin of their oppression. That is, that they *should* share a common antisexist ideology.

Not unlike the Harlem Renaissance, which drew on a distinct African ancestry and some of the cultural differences between Black and white Americans, many leading Black Arts writers and Black nationalists constructed themselves in relation to dominant racist ideology as Others-from-without the American nation. Figures such as Larry Neal, Addison Gayle, Hoyt W. Fuller, and Amiri Baraka pointed to their political and social disenfranchisement and the very different circumstances under which most of them arrived in America. They also underscored their political, social, and ancestral commonalties with Blacks outside the United States (as opposed to their white countrymen). While they did not deny their American heritage and did not explicitly call for a separate nation within a nation for perpetuity, Black Power movements and their artistic wings nonetheless found it strategically useful to emphasize the need for Black communities to look to themselves for empowerment and sustenance, not a white government and citizenry who, through both legal and illegal measures, revealed their desire to keep the Black population abject and marginalized. As in the work of Du Bois, Fanon, Césaire, and Senghor, this Black Other was most often assumed to be male, while the Black female operated as the "Other of the Other." In the discourse that manifests itself in the Moynihan Report and in the more explicitly misogynistic aspects of Black nationalist ideology, the Black female became the Other-from-within. Whether the ally of the white male or the emasculating Black mother, the Black female was nonetheless constructed in racist and misogynist discourse as a malevolent agent located *within* the American nation regardless of that nation's construction as either white or Black. Carolyn Rodgers, a Black Arts poet, and Audre Lorde, a Black poet who explicitly shared common cause with some Black Power ideologies and practices, do not counter this trope with a wholly opposing construct but instead explore the stereotype. Both Rodgers and Lorde locate the Black mother as within the nation, but both also underscore the historical lineage located outside the United States. Rodgers's invocation is admittedly vague, yet present, gesturing toward the Middle Passage and slave women in "how i got ovah II/It Is Deep II" and "Living Water," while Lorde's *The Black Unicorn* explicitly describes historic and contemporary African cultures that lost populations to the Atlantic slave trade.

The Black mother, as seen in Rodgers's and Lorde's poetry, projects a very different set of values for the Black subject. Neither Rodgers nor Lorde ever position her as an absolute origin—rather, she is the point of orientation for all Black subjects, the medium through which, willingly or not, they negotiate their intersubjectivity. As a result, space becomes a series of conflations rather than strictly defined borders between subjects, races, and nations. Both *How I Got Ovah* and *The Black Unicorn* construct the moment of consciousness as twofold: as in the theories examined in the last two chapters, they first confront their "Other"—in this case, the Black male—but they do not achieve consciousness until they recognize that this Other cannot be delineated from them. In short, the Other is also a subject who overlaps with their own subjectivity. Recognition, as first defined by Hegel, achieves an even more complex meaning here: whereas Hegel and Fichte both explored the realization of the subject as contingent on recognition from the Other, the trope of the mother locates this Other as *within* the subject rather than external to him or her, and in recognizing this conflation comes to realize that Other's independent subject status. In other words, one achieves subject status first by encountering the Other and realizing that, because they overlap with one another, they are intersubjective.

This construction anticipates one of the most famous mothers in American fiction: Toni Morrison's Sethe in *Beloved*. In her essay "Redeeming History," Helene Moglen analyzes the way in which the mother, as a central figure in Western literature and its exploration of subjectivity, has until recently been deployed in wholly negative terms: "In the fundamentally misogynistic mode of the fantastic, that moment has been ambivalently identified with the primal mother: the origin of all difference and the site of ultimate loss, so powerful that her presence can never be directly known but only mediated through the fears and longings of her sons and daughters."[39] Agreeing with this, Margaret Homans argues that *Beloved* is part of the "fantastic fiction" that proceeded realist fiction and moved beyond the binary of self and Other to "[dissolve] the distinction between self and other by revealing how the Other serves as an instrument in the construction of the self."[40] Like Rodgers and Lorde a decade earlier, Morrison "lifts the primal mother out of that prelinguistic space and returns her to history."[41] Here the mother functions in the subject's moment of consciousness in the same way Rodgers and Lorde construct her and in the way Bakhtin imagines consciousness:

> In dialogism, the very capacity to have consciousness is based on *otherness*. This otherness is not merely a dialectical alternation on its way to a sublation that will endow it with a unifying identity in higher consciousness. On the contrary: in dialogism, consciousness *is* otherness. More accurately, it is the differential relation between a center and all that is not that center.[42]

What this statement also implies, of course, is that consciousness is not linear, not a singular and defining moment but a continuing process of encountering others and realizing one's (inter)subjectivity. In Lorde and Rodgers, this process begins with the mother, recognizing her as both Other and conflated with oneself. This is reminiscent of the Lacanian mirror stage and the moment when the child realizes s/he is not one with the mother. However, where Lacan then engages a dialectic series of ramifications (the most famous being the phallus and the law of the father), Rodgers and Lorde engage dialogic structures. In all three collections of poetry discussed here, the mother is a recurring trope, a recurring process of consciousness even as that subject encounters "other others" (in all three collections, usually lovers, but Lorde also incorporates men with whom she has had both romantic and platonic relationships). The trope of the mother enables a more complex realization of circular time, belying the myth of origins as clearly delineated and controlled by founding fathers. The trope of the mother both recuperates the history of female achievement erased by Black nationalist ideology and favors a dialogic structure for subjectivity, which in turn enables a truly diasporic structure to produce Black subjects united across national boundaries and united through diversity rather than homogeneity. Unlike the trope of the founding father, mothers point to the endless line of ancestry that precedes and overlaps with each subject: all human beings emerge from the mother, are conflated with and distinct from her—and are therefore an undeniable product of the past, shaped by it without being wholly controlled.

Although their approaches differ significantly in various respects, both Rodgers, in her award-winning collection *How I Got Ovah*, and Lorde, in her early collections *Coal* and *The Black Unicorn*, use the trope of the mother to upend nationalist discourse, enable the Black female subject, and provide what Michael Holquist has referred to as a "Greenwich Mean Chronotope," the definitive intersection for time and space against which oppositional chronotopes are both acknowledged and critiqued. The mother, as signifier for the past, present, and *future* generations becomes the standard for time and—as one who gives birth and thus also signifies the space through which subjects overlap—the standard for space. Anticipating Lorde's later work on diasporic unity through diversity, as well as Gilroy's prescription in *The Black Atlantic*, Lorde and Rodgers create specific readings of the mother to serve as the cornerstone for their alternative visions of individual and collective Black subjectivity.

As Margaret Homans has noted, the lack of total reconciliation is the necessary outcome of rejecting binaries and the illusion of homogeneity. Whereas Du Bois, Césaire, and Fanon provide a moment of consciousness that reveals the racially determined nature of the subject, both Lorde and Rodgers deploy the intersubjective nature of the mother to underscore the differences *within* Blackness, its complex and often contradictory nature (and, specifically in the case of Lorde, the mother of biracial children), the inherent fiction of clearly delineated racial categories. After all, not only can Black women give birth to biracial babies, so can white women—a striking fact difficult to incorporate into any ideology that argues for homogeneous racial identity. There remains, however, a severely flawed aspect to Lorde's and Rodgers's dialogic theory of Black female subjectivity. The men in *How I Got Ovah*, *Coal*, and *The Black Unicorn* are often demonized. At best, they are held at arm's length and studied; at worst, they are portrayed as irretrievably malevolent, angry in the face of failure, and in search of a convenient target. Although both Lorde and Rodgers "convert" that Black male Other into a subject in the second step of "coming to consciousness," the biological ramifications of the mother as the determining trope of subject status automatically position the Black male—who cannot be a biological mother—as subsidiary, a tool through whom the black female can come into being.[43] In *How I Got Ovah* the narrator's voice changes dramatically when addressing male lovers; "Breakthrough" and "Masquerade" both underscore the deep distrust that exists between the sexes. Rodgers locates the masking performance between the sexes rather than between the races. She writes:

> you want to wrap your self
> up in me/i in you and we
> we will hide behind each other
> and that will be the only
> truth between us.
> we, us, ducking and hiding and
> running and blinding ourselves.[44]

Here we see a negative intersubjectivity, impelled not by recognition but the need to hide and/or disguise oneself. We must pause at the fact that this negative example is between an adult man and woman (as opposed to, say, a mother and son). It is important, of course, to note that this inability to fully incorporate the Black male is a reaction, rather than an action—because subjectivity is constructed through dialogue, Black nationalist discourse and its difficulty in recognizing the Black woman as a subject become part of Black female subjectivity. Both Lorde and Rodgers address individual men in their poems to underscore the respect, love, and care these men have inspired in them, but, as a collective, Black masculinity is described as having very few saving graces. Part of this is deliberate: Rodgers and especially Lorde are at pains to show the degree to which this supposedly "Black" masculinist stance is barely distinctive from the way in which dominant (white male) discourse constructs males and females, and, subsequently, the fiction of a "pure" and homogeneous Black identity.

Despite the sexist underpinnings of Black nationalism, both Lorde and Rodgers would have been very different poets—if artists at all—had it not been for the gains and sacrifices of Black Power movements, the Black Arts movement, and even Black nationalism. Although flawed in some ways, the success of these sociopolitical movements and their revolutionary discourses is quite evident today, both in the United States and across the African diaspora. The political rights we have gained, the increasing social freedoms and dizzying triumphs in African American literature, music, performing arts, and sports can all trace the majority of their impetus from the Black men and women who stood and spoke so boldly in the face of violence, imprisonment, and death. Black Power, in turn, owes much to the sacrifices, actions, and ideologies of Du Bois, the Negritude movement, and Frantz Fanon (among others).

The ideological rifts within the Black community that both Rodgers and Lorde underscore, in addition to the critique of the gendered discourse of national belonging they implicitly provide, calls into question what *does* make a subject "Black" if not politics or a specific way of un/belonging in the West? By substituting the Black mother for the mask as the Black subject's trope, Lorde and Rodgers are arguing that it is our West African ancestry, rather than our tortured relationship to the Western nation, that links us. Much in line with Fanon, these two women argue that it is recognition, rather than disguise, that accords subjectivity to the Black. While this helps erase the lurking ramifications of Black subjectivity discussed in the previous chapters (namely, that it is white racism, and our location as Other, that unites us), the invocation of West African ancestry rests on uneasy ground because it must remain vague and, to a certain degree, rely on Western categorizations.[45]

In the final chapter I examine discourses that address the problem of competing and/or unequal epistemologies with regard to the ontology of the Black subject. In other words, how does one construct an African diasporic subject within a West that in many ways is still firmly attached to the myth of the nation as a homogeneous activity located in a progressive linear history?

CHAPTER FIVE

The Urban Diaspora: Black Subjectivities

in Berlin, London, and Paris

STRANGER IN THE VILLAGE: NATIONAL MYTHS
AND DIASPORIC REALITIES

The scope of this chapter is admittedly ambitious, even though I do not
pretend to offer an exhaustive account of these three Black communities
but rather a restricted look at how Black novelists, poets, and essayists of
the 1980s and 1990s in Germany, Britain, and France have addressed the
question of subject status. The goal of this relatively brief comparative
analysis is to explore the common themes, tropes, and strategies in all
three literatures and to highlight the differences specific to each community and its history.

Although they possess different histories, the Black writers in Germany, England, and France featured in this chapter all critique the nation as an atavistic—and even mythological—construct that implicitly, if
not explicitly, (mis)reads borders as racially defined. Whereas Black theorists such as Du Bois and Fanon locate the nation as central to the
formation of Black Others and subjects, the writers in this chapter understand the Black subject as first and foremost part of the African
diaspora. Their productions of that subject update the famous observation made by James Baldwin in "Stranger in the Village," that those rural
Europeans for whom the Black is still a novelty represent the bygone
days of provincial isolation. "This world," Baldwin writes, "is white no
longer and will never be white again."[1] Like Baldwin, these authors agree
that the Black is no longer *a* stranger in the village but, as the title of his
essay argues, it is the village that has become "stranger," rooted in colo-

nialist myths that locate the Western Black in the "African jungle" rather than at the center of the urban diaspora where most now reside.[2]

THE IMPOSSIBLE MINORITY: AFRO-GERMANS

The German racial imagination is both similar to and different from that of its (white) Western counterparts. Given its immigrant roots—coupled with a doctrine of Black inferiority—the United States misunderstands race as a dichotomy between Black and white, with whiteness as a blanket term to cover any and all non-Blacks, non-Asians, and non-Latino/as. French discourse, as we will see later in this chapter, moves to exclude certain "newly arrived" Mediterraneans and Eastern Europeans, but its reading of whiteness shares much of the same definition of those who are "not Black."[3] Britain, too, has some of its own quirks about which non-Blacks and non-Asians qualify as white in addition to its deployment of who is English (white) and who is British (white and nonwhite colonials), but in relation to Germany, British racial discourse is closer to the same vague, general ideas about white identity one can find in France and the United States.[4] By contrast, Germany is not so vague, and in recalling Gobineau's dizzyingly complex hierarchy of categories of whiteness (beginning with different types of Aryans and moving down in purity and superiority), as well as Hegel's location of Germany as the most superior of all Western nations, we can understand how white Germans do not read themselves as racially selfsame with other white Western Europeans but rather as a distinct *Volk* with a specific cultural and *racial* heritage. In determining who does and who does not belong to the nation, Germans do not focus only on physical signs of "whiteness" (skin color, hair texture, or facial features) but also on racial/cultural (with the cultural speaking more to the myth of racial memory than specific practices) heritage. Indeed, the guidelines for German citizenship routinely exclude both whites and nonwhites born and raised in Germany, perhaps even after several generations, but welcome people of "German ancestry" who have never lived in Germany and do not speak German. The Americans, French, and British, to one degree or another, most often pretend to (and to some degree do) overlook race in determining national belonging, instead bringing in a different set of signifiers such as political beliefs, cultural mores, and economic status (all of which are read as indicators of the willingness to assimilate). Germany, on the other hand, while not prohibiting all non-Germans from becoming citizens, nonetheless has trouble viewing those who do not share a specific racial heritage as "true" Germans. As a result of this narrow and fixed idea of "Germanness," Black Germans, despite having been born and raised in Germany and belonging to no other culture or nation, are often read not as German but rather as "African" (as if a continent of 750 million people and 1,000 languages is a homogeneous community).

Nor is this practice of exclusion strictly a phenomenon of the twentieth century. Germans of African descent are not exactly a new addition to the German landscape: as the foundational anthology *Farbe bekennen: Afro-deutsche Frauen auf den Spuren ihrer Geschichte* (Showing Our Colors: Afro-German Women Speak Out) notes, "unsere Geschichte nicht erst nach 1945 begann. Vor unseren Augen stand unsere Vergangenheit, die eng verknüpft ist mit der kolonialien und nationalsozialistischen deutschen Geschichte" (our history did not begin after 1945. Before our eyes stands our past, closely bound with colonial and national socialist German history).[5] *Farbe bekennen* and other later works have pointed out that some Afro-Germans can trace their roots back to the nineteenth century, if not before.[6] At the same time, many of those who identify as Afro-Germans are the product of an interracial liaison occurring in one of three major moments of German history: the Allied occupation of the Rhineland after World War I, the Allied occupation of Germany after World War II, or the postwar years (1950s to present). As Carol Aisha Blackshire-Belay writes, "to speak of the African-German community may be a misnomer. Although there are 300,000 African Germans, there is no community of African Germans equivalent to the African-American communities of North Philadelphia, Detroit, or Harlem. However, there is, in a sense, a community of culture, or a psychological attachment to community, based on a similarity of experiences."[7]

For almost a century, the German nation has consistently rejected Black Germans as anything other than foreign or, more specifically, "African." Indeed, when one looks at the history of these three generations of Afro-Germans, we can see exactly how anti-Black discourse renders the history of these native-born Blacks as foreign. In "Blacks in Germany and German Blacks," Rosemarie Lester focuses on the reception of the *Rheinland Bastarden*, or "Rhineland Bastards," the first "generation" of Afro-Germans born to white German women and the Black soldiers who made up part of French occupying forces. As Lester writes, basing much of her argument on the research of historian Reiner Pommerin, French use of Black troops "so incensed racial feelings of Europeans as well as white Americans that it soon ballooned into an international scandal under the catchword *Die Schwarze Schmach* ('The Black Disgrace')."[8] Unsurprisingly, rumors soon abounded about the savagery of these Black soldiers (later disproved by a formal inquiry by the American commissioner in Berlin and the American commander in Coblenz, as Lester informs us), not the least of which were claims of wanton rapes committed by a disproportionate number of Black soldiers on helpless (white) German women. As Lester and others have reported, Black soldiers were, in fact, less inclined to rape than their white counterparts, indicating that the outcry over these crimes was fueled less by a concern for German women and more by racism. While the children of these interracial encounters number somewhere between 375 and 500, May Ayim reports that only one German woman reported rape as the cause of her pregnancy.[9] It is important to clarify that, while rape can never be justified and the color of the rapist has little or no bearing on the crime, the discourse surrounding the Rhineland Occupation makes clear that the rape of white women by white men is not a crime but any coupling between a white woman and a Black man could only be rape.

Unlike the white German children fathered by the Allied occupation forces, the "Rhineland Bastards," as they soon came to be called, were seen to be as foreign as their fathers. As Monroe H. Little Jr. reports in "The Black Military Experience in Germany," despite their mothers' German citizenship, the children were treated as outsiders by the German citizenry and government alike: "as the birth of these children attracted increasing attention, ostracism and attacks on them and their mothers also grew in number."[10] The fates of these children varied, although the majority were forcibly sterilized according to the dictates set down by the Nazi regime. Robert W. Kesting refers to the "missing 'Rhineland mulattos'" in his discussion of Black soldiers and citizenry who were murdered by German and Hungarian troops.[11] Other accounts point to death camps, while still others, such as *Farbe bekennen*'s interview with Doris Reiprich and Erika Ngambi Ul Kuo, or Hans J. Massaquoi's recent autobiography *Destined to Witness*, indicate that some Black Germans remained as part of the German wartime population, albeit most often denied jobs, ration cards, or any other means of subsistence.

The *Besatzungskinder* or "Occupation Babies" of the Second World War fared little better in the decades that followed the defeat of the Nazi regime. As in the previous generation of Afro-German children, efforts were made to have them adopted by Black families overseas, as their skin color was viewed as incompatible with German identity. In her memoir *Daheim unterwegs: Ein deutsches Leben* (On the Way Home: A German Life), Ika Hügel-Marshall, the daughter of a white German woman and an African American soldier, writes that her mother sent her away to a Catholic home for children, most likely because of the racial intolerance of the community, not to mention the likely pressure from her new husband, a former officer in Hitler's SA (Sturm Abteilung, literally "storm section," Hitler's private army).[12] Hügel-Marshall recounts how, throughout childhood and adolescence, her skin color caused her fellow Germans to understand her as an outsider, an exotic object, but never simply a German. In the personal narratives by Afro-Germans in *Farbe bekennen*, their status as outsiders despite their German background is a common theme.

We can see a striking contrast between Germany and the United States, Britain, and France in the genealogy of the Black presence. Whereas other Western nations trace their Black presence back to moments of colonial glory that, while morally compromised, nonetheless recall the nation at a moment of political and economic strength, the entrance of the Afro-German occurs in moments of Germany's resounding defeats. In addition, the fathers of these Black Germans were members of "enemy" troops and therefore are easily translatable into the nationalist allegory of the (Black male) invaders who held the German nation (white and female) under siege. The result of the encounters between Black American and West African soldiers and female civilians easily lend themselves to nationalist discourse where Germany's humiliating defeat becomes synonymous with the entrance of the black rapist onto German soil.

The constructions of Black Others and white subjects in national discourse discussed thus far rely on the convenient erasure of history (for example, most African Americans could point to an American pedigree that far outdistances that of most white Americans). As all the Afro-German autobiographies published to date reveal, the stubborn and often violent public and informal rejection these Black Germans encounter tallies all too well with the way in which nationalist discourse constructs subjects and Others. Locating their origins at a point in time in which the German nation was under siege by non-German occupants, the autobiographies of Black Germans such as May Ayim, Helga Emde, Astrid Berger, Miriam Goldschmidt, Laura Baum, Corinna N., Ellen Wiedenroth, Raya Lubineztski (all published in *Farbe bekennen*), Ika Hügel-Marshall's *Daheim unterwegs* and, at times, Hans-Jürgen Massaquoi's *Destined to Witness* broadly or even specifically locate the obstacles that stand in the way of recognition and subject status within the bizarre and forbidding logic of nationalist discourse.[13] More specifically, these writers all share a common narrative of confronting the ways in which both familial and social discourse locates them as Other. The majority of these women recollect the very ambivalent regard with which they were held by their white German mothers. Despite their complete self-identification as German, even to the degree that some admittedly feared or reviled any and all peoples of African descent, many, such as Hügel-Marshall and *Farbe bekennen*'s Wiedenroth, Corinna N., Ayim, and Raya Lubineztski, recount how they were sent away to orphanages. Whether they were sent away or remained at home, all these authors describe the troubled relationships they shared with their white German families.[14] Regardless of their shared biology, culture, and language, their location as "outsiders" to the nation erased or at least complicated those other considerations that so clearly indicated their belonging.[15] In her collection of essays *Grenzenlos und unverschämt* (Borderless and Brazen), May Ayim provides a striking example of the degree to which the Afro-German is rendered Other through German nationalist discourse. "Das Jahr 1990: Heimat und Einheit aus afro-deutscher Perspektive" (1990: Home and Unity from an Afro-German Perspective) opens with the author living in Berlin right after the collapse of the Berlin Wall, witnessing the euphoric mood attending German reunification. Juxtaposed against the elation, the general atmosphere of joy and goodwill, is a rising tide of anti-Black violence and the increased scarcity of anything other than white faces in the normally racially diverse streets of the capital:

> In the first days after November 9th 1989, I noticed that hardly any immigrant women or Black Germans could be seen in the city, especially those with dark skin. I asked myself, how many Jewish women were (not) on the street. I ran into a couple of Afro-Germans whom I

had met in East Berlin the previous year, and we were delighted at this opportunity to meet again. I was the only one on the way to somewhere, wanting to breathe in a little of the excitement, absorb the historical moment, and share my reserved joy. Reserved, that is, because the forthcoming aggressive actions from the Legislature against immigrant women and refugees were also directed at me. I knew, just like other Black Germans and immigrant women, that a German passport alone did not represent an invitation to the East-West celebrations. We felt that with the forthcoming internal German unification, an increasing demarcation would push us outside—an outside that would enclose us. Our participation at the party was not questioned.

The new "we" in—as Chancellor Kohl loved to put it—"this country of ours" hadn't had and still had no place for everyone.

"Get out of here, nigger, don't you have a home?"

For the first time since living in Berlin I was forced, on almost a daily basis, to resist blunt offenses against me, hostile stares and/or openly racist defamatory remarks.[16]

This sense of being relegated to a space "outside" the nation is a leitmotif to the majority of Afro-German autobiographical texts. As the authors detail their move into adulthood, their stories often intersect at those key moments in which German racist discourse reminds them that their "Blackness" overrides any and all other commonalities. The concept of "Blackness" as an artificial and therefore unnatural coloring on the skin (rather than a natural shade) is quite common in Germany. Corinna N. writes that schoolchildren would comment " 'You must have fallen in some cocoa'; or 'Can I touch you? Can I see if your color rubs off?'," while Ellen Wiedenroth explains "for brown skin, the German language only has terms borrowed from eating and drinking, like 'chocolate brown' or 'coffee brown'."[17] This in turn tallies with German children's stories in which children misbehave by getting dirty, find the dirt will not come off, and so "become Black," which is viewed as punishment for their bad behavior.[18]

The linking of darker skin to colonial commodities (coffee, chocolate) and degraded objects (dirt) is hardly unique to Germany, but racist discourse in France, Britain, and the United States is more likely to look at Blackness in terms of behavior and ability, for example, poor communication skills, low intellect, lack of strong social and familial ties, violence, and an overactive libido. While these stereotypes are far from unknown in Germany, I would suggest that the differences between Germany and the other three countries is in large part linked to their respective histories of minority presence. As slave historians have noted, a Western discourse justifying the enslavement of Blacks did not fully develop until the late eighteenth and early nineteenth centuries. Prior to that time, many slave owners admitted that there was no moral defense for the practice, only an overriding economic need. From the 1830s onward, however, the rise in the slave trade and colonial holdings starkly contrasted with the democratic fervor and widespread belief in human suffrage that French, American, and English philosophers, artists, and even politicians supposedly held dear. Although no direct tie could ever be proven beyond a reasonable doubt, I nonetheless maintain that it is more than coincidental that the rise in anti-Black discourse paralleled the West's move toward supposedly democratic governments that nonetheless derived great wealth from their slave and colonial holdings. In other words, the French, British, and American anti-Black discourses reflect an awareness of the Black presence within their respective "empires" and the need to reconcile their egalitarian political philosophies with their oppressive and racist practices.

Others-from-Within from Without: The Challenge of a Counterdiscourse. The German presence in Africa was relatively brief and less widespread than its French and English counterparts, and the origins of the Afro-German population are not concentrated in this colonialist moment. The German discourse of linking Blackness to valuable colonial commodities and defining it as an external, abnormal physical state (Blackness as the result of drinking too much cocoa, becoming dirty, etc.) reflects a history that reveals that, unlike the Black in Britain, France, and the United States, the "German Black" is not read as an Other-from-within, but an Other-from-*without*.[19] An experience that recurs throughout almost every personal narrative found in *Farbe bekennen*, as well as Hügel-Marshall's and Massaquoi's autobiographies, best epitomizes this. In "Three Afro-German Women in Conversation with Dagmar Schultz: The First Exchange for This Book," from *Showing Our Colors*, the English translation of *Farbe bekennen*, Laura Baum and May Ayim, despite their widely varied backgrounds, bond over a common experience:

May: It often happens with me that people have their own expectations and ignore what I say. When I tell them that I grew up here and have spent my entire life here, the question might still come afterward; "Yes, and when are you going back?"
Laura: People think I'm a foreigner. If I speak flawless German, I get this "admiration."[20]

Encountering this inability on the part of white Germans to understand so simple a concept as one being both Black *and* German is most likely unique to the Afro-German experience and presents a complicated challenge to a counterdiscourse.[21] The refusal to understand Afro-Germans as German, much less as equals, is the cornerstone of the German discourse on the white German subject and the African Other. The African American has been and still is considered an American problem; the Afro-German barely exists in the German imagination.[22] As many of the authors in *Farbe bekennen* complain, many white Germans, especially those from rural areas, seem psychologically incapable of conceiving of someone who is both Black and German. White Germans, even after a detailed explanation from their nonwhite interlocutor, still attempt to determine what African country the subject comes from. In short, the Afro-German identity is not the *antithesis* in the dialectic of (white) German subjectivity: *it is simply nonexistent*. Whereas African Americans function in white American racist discourse as the Other-from-within (they are recognized as having been born and raised in the United States, even if racists believe they do not belong there), a significant number of white Germans insistently and consistently misrecognize Afro-Germans as Africans, or Others-from-without, even though they obviously share the same language and culture. In other words, unlike African Americans, Afro-Germans must confront a racist discourse directed at Africans rather than Afro-Germans. There is not, technically speaking, such a thing as an anti–Afro-German discourse, only an anti-African discourse, raising the question of how one, as an Other-from-within, should respond to a discourse that posits one as an Other-from-without.

To date, there are only a few Afro-German counterdiscourses that elaborate an identity beyond the most efficacious method of response, namely, with a narrative of one's life that challenges and confounds German assumptions. As Blacks born and raised in Germany, with all its attendant uniqueness, Afro-Germans face a different type of Othering; being misread as African Others-from-without means they cannot deploy the same strategies we have seen deployed by Du Bois, Fanon, the Negritudists, American Black nationalists, Carolyn Rodgers, and Audre Lorde. Their most common strategy has been autobiography, and the literal writing of oneself into the nation. Carolyn Hodges argues that the strategy of autobiography as used by these Afro-German women speaks directly to the concept of *métissage*, or "unified plurality," as developed by Françoise Lionnet.[23] This "unified plurality," I would argue, can be more specifically rendered as diasporic identity. In the rest of this section I will show how both anti-Black German discourse is best countered through a diasporic model of counterdiscourse and how Afro-Germans enable this model in both their literature and their sociopolitical activities.

Beyond autobiography, Afro-Germans have had recourse to other genres, for example, the compilation of narrative histories, though not in great proliferation.[24] *Farbe bekennen* and Katharine Oguntoye's 1997 *Eine afro-deutsche Geschichte* (An Afro-German History) provide detailed histories of Blacks in Germany, but the only Afro-German to approach this question through literature rather than nonfiction has been May Ayim. May Ayim's poems "Afro-Deutsch I" and "Afro-Deutsch II" are structured as transcripts from a conversation between a white German and an Afro-German, although this "transcript" only gives us the statements and responses, underscoring the metaphorical erasure of self, or material existence, the Afro-German undergoes in German racist discourse. This dialogue-as-monologue Ayim constructs highlights the insistent misreading and redefinition that operates in the German imagination: the Afro-German is consistently and stubbornly recast as an African. In the first lines of "Afro-Deutsch I," the white German, using the polite "you," comments:

Sie sind afro-deutsch?
. . . ah, ich verstehe: afrikanisch und deutsch.
Ist ja 'ne interessante Mischung!

(You're Afro-German?
. . . ah, I understand: African and German.
There's an interesting mix!)

The German moves from astonishment and incomprehension toward a formula he can understand by (re)producing the identity as a binary: "African and German."[25] In the following stanzas, we see the Afro-German's identity, as it is understood by the white interlocutor, forcibly simplified and reduced to an "African" identity. The white German first translates the Afro-German identity into a derogatory category with roots in nineteenth-century race science, simultaneously performing and disclaiming the starkly racist overtones—and still using the polite form of "you":

Wissen Sie, manche, die denken ja immer noch,
die Mulatten, die würden's nicht
so weit bringen
wie die Weißen

(You know, some [people], they still think,
Mulattos, aren't
so far along
as Whites).[26]

This hypocritical disclaimer (identifiable to most African Americans by the preface "I'm not racist, but . . . ") is yet another way in which the minority interlocutor is silenced. If confronted with his racist assumptions, the white German can simply respond that *he* doesn't personally believe that sentiment, he is simply pointing out how *other* people feel— thus skirting the real issue at hand, that if those views are not one's own, why would one feel compelled to air them, speaking for those with whom one supposedly disagrees?

From the schizophrenic deployment of insults disguised as reports from a third party who is not present, the white speaker moves to redefining the Afro-German as African, and as one who does not belong on German soil:

Wenn Se fleißig sind mit studieren,
können Se ja Ihren Leuten
in Afrika helfen: Dafür
sind Sie doch prädestiniert

(If you work hard at your studies
you could really help your people in Africa
you were just predestined for it!)[27]

The geographical disconnect of (re)locating the Afro-German subject to Africa from Germany is accompanied by a temporal disconnect, as the white German urges, almost commands the interlocutor to devote his or her life to a career as a goodwill worker in Africa, carrying on the colonizing mission to civilize the savages. In a subtle move, the formal German "you" (*Sie*), becomes lazily obscured as *Se*, suggesting that the speaker is slowly but steadily invoking a racialized hierarchy in which he, as white and "really" German, takes up the "white man's burden," only this time instead of going himself, he charges the half-breed to educate him or herself and then spread that civilizing influence.[28] In arguing that the Afro-German is predestined for this type of mission, the speaker's understanding of racial difference as biological and hierarchical is fully revealed.

There is a space between the last two stanzas, and the final one begins with ellipses and a question, "Wie meinen Sie das?" (How do you mean that?), suggesting the Afro-German has responded to this Carl Peters– like address.[29] The speaker's response is angry, rejecting the (implied) accusation of racism to argue that the Afro-German does not have the right to cast the first stone, as it were, and therefore should remain silent altogether. As "Afro-Deutsch I" 's "conversation" quietly reveals, the Afro-German has never really been allowed to speak in the first place. Yet by placing the focus on the white German's discourse, Ayim highlights how that discourse elides an obvious reality (the Afro-German), so that it may retreat into a fantasy of colonialist binaries where all the Germans are white, and all the Blacks are African primitives.

Diasporic Strategies. There is another, equally important challenge Afro-Germans must grapple with: not only the white German perception of Blacks and Blackness but Afro-German history as well gives the Afro-German subject certain unique aspects, aspects that should play heavily into any comparison we make between Afro-Germans and other Black subjects in the United States, France, and England. Relative to the shared slave and/or colonial histories that produced African American, Black British, and French African communities in the West, Afro-Germans are a diverse group. They were born and raised apart from one another and, although they share knowledge of German racism and ignorance most whites and non-Afro-Germans cannot fully know, they all come from a wide range of class, ethnic, geographical, and even historical backgrounds. Some Afro-Germans have Afro-German parents, some have adoptive parents who are all white; some, although born in Germany, grew up all over Europe, the United States, and/or East or West Africa. Some come from upper-class backgrounds, others grew up fully destitute; some were raised as West Germans, others born and raised in the former Eastern bloc.

While this large number of differentials may strike some as yet one more obstacle to securing an identity or subject status, the Afro-German response to the diversity seems to have moved them beyond the more nationalist and restrictive understanding of "Blackness" that operates in many Black communities outside Germany and further toward what Paul Gilroy and Audre Lorde have identified as a "diasporic" understanding of the Black subject. Although the term "Afro-German" is commonly used to denote someone of both African and German ancestry, there is a wide variety of terms by which Black Germans define themselves, include others, and explicitly identify with other groups of people both within and without Germany. "Black German," a term coming into greater currency, speaks to all Germans who identify as racial minorities, most often including peoples of Turkish and South Asian descent. The term "Afro-European" is also becoming more prevalent, deployed specifically to make common cause with peoples of African descent all over Europe, as well as those (such as Katharine Oguntoye) who have lived in other European countries as well as Germany. One also finds Germans of African descent identifying as "African" and German (some are nation-specific, indicating the specific country of origin of their family, such as Ghana or Cameroon), or simply as "African," or simply as "German." Still others identify as African American, pointing to their fathers' citizenship.[30] Most often, Afro-Germans identify themselves differently depending on the context or group, understanding themselves as connected to a rather rich array of nations, ethnicities, and communities.

This process of identification is far from passive in its construction: there are a number of Afro-German and Black German sociopolitical movements and groups that reach out to Black, gay, and women's communities across the world. At the moment, the two largest groups are ADEFRA (Afro-Deutsche FRAuen, or Afro-German Women), with its focus on the intersection between antiracism and feminism, and the ISD (Initiativer Schwarze Deutsche und Schwarze in Deutschland, or Black German and Blacks in Germany Initiative), which is open to both men and women.[31] The strategy of elective affinities is explicitly stated in each, as, for example, on the first page of ADEFRA's Web site:

> ADEFRA is a forum in which we, as Black women, can develop our strengths and unfold our identities together. Therefore, our necessary strong points are mutual exchanges of histor(y)/(ies), culture(s) with everyday Black women (in West Germany and worldwide) through our similarities and differences (age, socialization, origin, lifestyle, etc). It is also important for us to make public the perspectives of Black women in politics and history.[32]

Given this explicit construction of their group as diasporic rather than national, it is not surprising to find that Afro-German activists most often point to Audre Lorde, after May Ayim, as one of their most inspiring leaders and organizers, from the time she arrived in Berlin to teach two seminars in minority women's literature at the Frei University in 1985 until her death in 1993.[33]

This diasporic orientation can also be found in Afro-German autobiographies and histories. The majority of Afro-German writing traces the subject as s/he narrates the diasporic past and future, locating the national origins of parents and grandparents, and then retracing those steps as s/he visits both nuclear and extended family in the United States, Ghana, Cameroon, Togo, Italy, England, and elsewhere. As I noted earlier, on a smaller scale these texts narrate the Afro-German in search of a subject status in conflict with German nationalist discourse. On a much wider scale, these personal narratives "perform" the diaspora by giving us a dialogic narrative of identity, beginning with its entirely nationalistic origins with Germans, Cameroonians, Ghanaians, etc., then moving to compound national identities (most often in the arrival of French African troops and African American soldiers during World War I and World War II respectively), and finishing with the "mature" identity wholly diasporic in its nature, most often evinced through the Afro-German, who is a product of intersecting national and ethnic identities (for example, an Afro-German mother and African American father) that also importantly intersect with gender and sexual categories.[34] More than seeking inclusion and protesting exclusion, these texts, in "performing" the Diaspora, reveal to us the increasing uselessness of restrictive definitions that confine themselves to the heteropatriarchal mythologies of race and nation.

Although her poetry addresses a range of issues, Ayim also makes a point of providing an effective counterdiscourse for the Afro-German subject. In "Afro-Deutsch I" and "Afro-Deutsch II," Ayim uses a strategy also located in Du Bois and Aimé Césaire: ventriloquism. Yet she uses it to different ends, to reveal the illogical spatial and temporal assumptions that emerge from those subjects who are unable to comprehend, much less speak, the material, performed truth of diasporic identities that do not so easily align with monologic definitions of race and nation. In their use of ventriloquism, both Du Bois and Césaire adhered to concepts of race and nation that, while not as monologic as its white Western model, nonetheless read the Black subject in the West as a synthesis of these two concepts. As a member of a generation that has benefited from the struggles and victories of previous generations of Blacks in the West, Ayim can now go further by mocking the white speaking subject as the one who is sadly misguided by outdated and outmoded concepts based on a binary, nationalist understanding of the subject and Other. She demonstrates her fluency with this German discourse not only by writing in her native language (a "strategy" that we must admit to be largely intuitive rather than carefully planned) but by writing a *spoken* German with its contractions and colloquialisms. Like Rodgers and Lorde, Ayim also accesses other historical eras, but in this case only to locate the white German as a retrograde reactionary whose language and thought locates him squarely outside the contemporary discourse. In Ayim's counterdiscourse, the ideal is marked not only by its reliance on racial and national myths but by its retrograde constructions. Whereas Senghor, Césaire, and Lorde use the West African past to help constitute the Black subject, Ayim's African diasporic ties are present and alive in her, and it is the white German (nation) that lives in the past.

INVERTED EMPIRE:
BLACK BRITONS AND "REVERSE COLONIZATION"

The "*Windrush* narrative" is the story of what critics and scholars alike have identified as the first generation of Black British writers. The "*Windrush* generation" was named after a recently retired warship used to transport just over a hundred Black West Indians to England in 1948, the first of many ships to do so.[35] The Caribbean modernists George Lamming and Samuel Selvon are the most famous writers of this generation; their texts set the tone for succeeding Anglophone writers by offering a multivalent view of immigration that subverts the notion of racial, gender, national, and sexual binaries. But while we may see the publication of Selvon's and Lamming's novels as foundational, the immigration experiences they narrate were not the first, because the arrival of the *Windrush* does not mark the first immigration of West Indians to England.

Yet, as Barnor Hesse argues in "Diasporicity: Black Britain's Post-Colonial Formation," "in this narrative, whether via the celebrations of the *Windrush* or its condemnation, the proximate, contextual idea of pre-existing, settled, regionalized Black communities simply vanishes."[36] More specifically, the "*Windrush* narrative" effectively erases not only the Blacks who served Julius Caesar in Britain but those who served under British forces during the American Revolutionary War and then accompanied the returning troops to Britain as per the British government's promise (thus escaping death or enslavement from the freedom fighting Americans).[37] Those purchased in English slave ports such as Liverpool and Preston eventually became domestic servants in local white households (although many Black Britons, slave or free, found themselves captured and sold to the Caribbean plantations), and still others came, through various means, to settle in England during the sixteenth, seventeenth, and eighteenth centuries.

At the same time, there is not a "correct" discourse. After all, as the presence of African American expatriates, Yoruba, Ifi, Indians, Pakistanis, Bangladeshis, Ceylonese, Jamaicans, Trinidadians, and others from the Anglophone Caribbean (who are also excluded, Hesse notes, by the "*Windrush* narrative") reveal, there is more than one way to be both Black and British. All the same, the use of the term "Black" to denote those of South Asian ancestry is decreasing, and while authors such as Buchi Emecheta and Ben Okri will write about the experience of being Black in Britain, they also understand themselves as Yoruba and Ibo respectively. Further, although all the authors and all the groups mentioned above do in some way investigate their role as Other in the British mind-set, the majority of the literature that focuses on the dichotomy of the white self and Black Other created by dominant British discourse is written by poets and novelists whose parents come or they themselves hail from the Anglophone Caribbean. While Selvon's and Lamming's texts interrogate the conditions for a Black and British subject, their focus on Black men meant that Black women's voices had yet to find substantial representation.[38] While Grace Nichols, Louise Bennett, and other Black women from this era recuperated these lost voices, it is in Joan Riley's *The Unbelonging* (1985) that we find the first extensive and most influential analysis of how gender produces different Black British subjectivities. Riley's novel reflects Michele Wallace's formulation of the Black woman as the Other of the Other, especially as she, like Wallace, looks at how nationalist discourse can at times bar the Black female, but not the Black male, from subject status.

Riley's deft weaving of race and gender issues in her analysis of Black British subjectivity produces a novel that is a bildungsroman of the Black female body being interpellated through a variety of white British, Black British, and Pan-Africanist nationalist discourses. As such, *The Unbelonging* is a progenitor to those novels that would follow a decade later to both build on and reconfigure the production of the Black British subject in England and the diaspora at large. Riley's protagonist, Hyacinth, moves through a series of dominant discourses—produced in the doctor's office, grade school, the orphanage, and university—that reveal to her that she is not only Other but the Other of the Other.[39] Yet while Audre Lorde and Carolyn Rodgers, Riley's contemporaries across the Atlantic, addressed these same issues through engaging and wholly likable narrative voices, Hyacinth is not so easily embraced. As she becomes gradually and more painfully aware of her status as Other, Hyacinth does not reject the discourse that posits her so but rather seeks to locate herself in it. While Riley's unhappy ending is ambiguous in its moral message— does Hyacinth remain Other because she has failed to reject the dominant discourse or because there is no way she can become a subject—*The Unbelonging* reveals how both dominant and counterdiscourses are guilty of naming the Black as Other in order to achieve subject status.

The Black female protagonists in later novels—Maxine ("Max") in Naomi King's *O.P.P.*, Jacqueline ("Jack") in Jo Hodges's *The Girl with Brains in Her Feet*, and Faith in Andrea Levy's *Fruit of the Lemon*— encounter the same combination of race and gender bias that besets Hyacinth, but they reject the notion that the Black female belongs nowhere. Riley's text argues that both British nationalist discourse and Pan-Africanist discourse produce subjects through Others and, as Other of the Other, Hyacinth can never achieve subject status. Ultimately, the largest difference between Riley's novel and those immediately following is in their interpretation of Black collective identity. Responding directly to both white and Black nationalist rhetoric, *The Unbelonging* argues that Black men can find spaces of their own (albeit compromised ones), but Black women lack any such space. Riley first broaches this topic in her portrayal of Colin Matthews, a favored alumnus of her halfway house-cum-orphanage who, Hyacinth is surprised to discover, is also Black. Hyacinth's confusion comes from her own treatment at the orphanage, where her Blackness is constantly referenced in negative and forbidding terms. In an encounter between Colin and Hyacinth, Colin makes a point of explaining his dislike of Black women and preference for all things white, and then nonetheless attempts to bed Hyacinth. Through Colin, Riley argues that Black men can at times achieve a compromised subject status by speaking the Black woman as Other. She also suggests that Blackness can in fact be gendered, as evidenced by Colin's superior status in the eyes of Auntie Susan, the orphanage administrator, who reserves her racist epithets for Hyacinth alone (Colin and Hyacinth are the only two Black adolescents at the orphanage). Yet in demonizing both Colin and, earlier in the novel, Hyacinth's physically and sexually abusive father, Riley also points to the particular ways in which Black men are emasculated in dominant discourse and so seek to reclaim masculinity by claiming power over Black women's bodies. As *The Unbelonging* makes abundantly clear, Hyacinth is not a victim because she refuses to act as these men have done but because she is unable, as "the Other of the Other," to claim mastery over any body, including her own.

Following her eviction from the orphanage, Hyacinth claims her birthplace of Jamaica with even greater ferocity and, tellingly, simultaneously claims the friendship of a young Jamaican woman named Perlene. Questions of space focus themselves into questions of sovereignty as Hyacinth, now a university student, at first cultivates and then rejects her South Asian university clique and begins to socialize with Black students and date Black men, all of whom define themselves through Pan-Africanist politics. In the company of Zimbabweans, Kenyans, and fellow Jamaicans, Hyacinth has several exchanges, especially with Perlene, on this new discourse. With regard to gender, little has changed: Black women are treated as helpmates, not equals, by their Pan-Africanist brothers. Perlene explains to her incredulous friend that all Black people are Africans, homogeneous and inextricably linked, no matter how disparate their geographical origins, and therefore must cohere to the sociopolitical guidelines of the Pan-Africanist discourse (which are insufferably heteropatriarchal and provincial). At the same time, not all people whom Hyacinth used to consider Black are equally so: as she learns from Perlene, her beau Charles and Dr. Walter Rodney, light-skinned Blacks, especially those who can "pass for" white, must be understood as traitors to the Pan-Africanist cause and therefore to all Black people. While willing to accept this stance from the rest of the African world, Hyacinth rejects any such criticism of Jamaica, insisting it is a Black utopia where skin tone bias, poverty, corruption—in fact, any sort of ugliness—does not exist. She is then alternately confronted and then patronized by her friends as someone who, though born in Jamaica, has been tainted by her years in England. Devastated by this pronouncement and by a sexual encounter with Charles that she cannot separate from her memories of childhood rape, Hyacinth resolves to return to Jamaica.

As one who was transplanted from Jamaica to an entirely hostile country where she is scripted as Other by whites, South Asians, and Blacks, Hyacinth does not, of course, find in Jamaica her long-awaited refuge. She is bewildered by the accents, the energy, repulsed by the poverty and crime, devastated and repelled to discover her beloved Auntie Joyce and Florence grimy and starving, her childhood friend Cynthia long since dead. These Blacks, whom she imagined as both possessing subject status and able to grant it to her, are now, under her English gaze, Other. The novel concludes with Hyacinth running to the cave she used to dream about, this time alone, haunted by the voices of her friends: "She could hear the weak sick voice calling out to her, pleading for help, bitter anger and hostility in the other one. . . . So she sat there, full of guilt and horror, not knowing what to do."[40] *The Unbelonging* is devastating because it argues that there is no space, no refuge, no counter-discourse for those Black women who are excluded from a nation's social majority. The white male is produced as selfsame with dominant discourse, most memorably in the doctor who diagnoses Hyacinth's bed-wetting and in Peter, the social worker. Both men, under the guise of helping Hyacinth, are merely there to confirm what they already know: she is abject, an outsider with no chance of changing her status. Their only desire, it seems, is to hear her speak this status. The white female characters are more present and more human than their white male counterparts, but their role is not terribly different: vis-à-vis the Black *woman*, Riley argues, white British women do not offer a different discourse.

Riley's critique of the white nation differs in an interesting way from the ideas discussed in the two previous chapters. Du Bois, Fanon, and Césaire produce Otherness in terms of being rejected by the white female, but in Colin Mathews, Riley opines that Black men will not always be rejected by white women so long as those men uphold (rather than work to undermine) the racist and sexist status quo—an inversion of the Moynihan Report and its unwitting Black nationalist allies. Carolyn Rodgers and Audre Lorde argue that nationalism, no matter what form it takes, necessarily constructs antagonistic differences and that a diasporic outlook, dialogic in design, is the only means by which Black women can hope to have their subjectivity acknowledged alongside Black men. While the absence of a Black mother and the abuse of a Black father in *The Unbelonging* would seem to corroborate this sentiment (without a mother Hyacinth is completely vulnerable to the dialectics of patriarchy), Hyacinth does not find common cause with other women of color—neither with her South Asian clique nor with their replacement, her infinitely patient compatriot Perlene. While Rodgers and Lorde center on the Western gender dichotomy, Riley finds a greater obstacle: the gulf between Black men with strong cultural moorings and those Black women denied those moorings because "Our families have been fragmented, and many girls came here to fathers or stepfathers who were strangers."[41]

While her novel intersects with nearly all of the counterdiscourses featured in chapters 2 and 3, Riley's analysis differs from them, as she argues that elision performed in dominant discourse to produce the Black Other cannot be (re)negotiated to produce the Black subject. Her view of Black men is reminiscent of the anecdotes deployed by Du Bois, Césaire, and Fanon to theorize their status as Other, but here Riley goes one further by asserting that Black men can and will sacrifice Black women to enter the heteropatriarchal discourse of the (white) Western nation. While Riley's is perhaps the most pessimistic of all the counterdiscourses analyzed in this book, her focus on the particular struggle facing the Black woman seeking subject status provides a means of entry for the succeeding counterdiscourses on the Black female subject. These counterdiscourses, in turn, expand and ultimately overturn Riley's vision to usher in the diasporic space that, while offering subject status, does not entirely deny Riley's understanding of the nationalist discourse as a force with which all Black subjects must reckon.

Old White Men in the Countryside and Young Black Women from the City. Contemporary Black British literature has largely moved away from the narrow construction of London as the imperial center for the British nation, with its former Caribbean holdings on the margin, that one finds in earlier generations of writing from George Lamming, Grace Nichols, and Samuel Selvan. Naomi King's *O.P.P.* (1992), Jo Hodges's *The Girl with Brains in Her Feet* (1998), and Andrea Levy's *Fruit of the Lemon* (1999) further Riley's analysis of British racism, sexism, and the mechanism of dislocation, alongside considerations of class and diaspora. The novels differ from one another in significant ways (King's paperback, described as a "scorching bestseller" on its cover, is a canny potboiler, seeking to entertain while also offering some poignant commentary on gender, agency, and commodification in response to Victor Headley's intelligent and action-packed *Yardie*; Hodges's *Girl* is a coming-of-age story for a working-class biracial girl growing up in Leicester with her white mother; Levy's epiclike novel takes its protagonist to Jamaica and back, in the process underscoring the temporal and locational depth and breadth of the African Diaspora. Yet they share some striking commonalities. All three protagonists are young Black women trying to figure out what it means to be both Black and British; Levy and King return their characters to Jamaica after personal crises; all three authors have their young women fall in love with young white men who, they later realize, are unobtainable; Levy and Hodges pair their characters with best friends who are white and sexual rivals.

Whereas Riley posits white British men and women as united and opposed to Black women, these three novelists argue that gender differences extend beyond racial boundaries. Levy's Faith Jackson and Hodges's Jacqueline Jones ("Jack") are both weighted and buoyed by best friends who are willing to overlook racial difference or even serve as antiracist allies so long as they do not face sexual competition. In *Fruit of the Lemon*, Faith's best friend Marion, a young working-class woman, seeks acceptance through a series of sexual affairs with men. Both Faith and Marion, early-twenty-somethings, develop an interest in their housemate, whose status as a member of the upper class has unmistakable cachet and also holds out the possibility that were he to choose one of them as his lover, she would no longer be an outsider, no matter that she is Black or working class. In *Girl*, Jacqueline and her friend Maxine, both in their early teens, have crushes on Steve Green, whose status as the coolest and cutest boy in school confers the same possibility of social acceptance. Maxine, herself a member of the haute bourgeoisie (Steve's economic status is unclear, most likely middle class), does not seek social acceptance, but the idea that Jack—Black and working class—might be the object of Steve's affection is clearly anathema to her. Terrified of losing her only friend, Jack denies her attraction and instead falls for a mysterious farm boy named David Spencer, or "Spanner." In *O.P.P.*, one of King's quartet of protagonists, Maxine, a.k.a. Max, does not face a sexual adversary for Simon's affections but, as she discovers on her first and last visit to his family, she can never be anything other than his concubine.

In all three novels, the English countryside becomes the stage for heart-breaking but eye-opening encounters that baldly reveal to the Black female characters that, in the gendered discourse of the nation, the best they can aspire to is either asexual pal (Faith), sexual fling (Jack), or secret mistress (Max) vis-à-vis the white male subject. *O.P.P.* pulls the least punches in its rendering: Max, ambivalent in her feelings toward Andrew, decides that the two of them must visit his family in order for Andrew to prove that he does not simply view Max as his "bit on the side." From the moment of her arrival, Andrew's family displays its intense displeasure:

> Max stood in the gigantic room, feeling very uncomfortable. None of its occupants looked up to acknowledge the newly arrived couple. Lucinda sat motionless with her legs flopped over an armchair, pretending to read a book. Max noticed that the book was upside down. Abigail stood by a window peering out disinterestedly. Andrew could feel the tension in the air. His mother, Hannah, observed Max silently. Max got the message, she was unwelcome and wasn't sure how to deal with it. What she was sure of was that the next couple of days would be hell if this treatment continued.[42]

Fruit's Faith Jackson goes away with Simon, to his family's estate, albeit at his invitation and with the expectation that his parents will not be at home that weekend. In contrast to the chilly scene above, Simon's mother Margaret welcomes Faith, mistakenly assumes they are a couple, and in one of the final scenes of the visit vaguely suggests that she and Faith, as women, have both been victims of the dominant discourse and its constant erasure of marginalized histories and truths. Margaret is not fully enlightened: after learning that Faith's parents are from Jamaica, she is eager to know when her parents will return.

As they traverse the muddy countryside with Faith, Margaret and Simon are (metaphorically and literally) breezily unaware of her difficulties in keeping up with them. Their Wellington boots serve them well but Faith's, a borrowed and ill-fitting pair, inevitably become mired in the English muck. Faith is forced to leave one Wellington in the mud and proceed in her muddy stockinged feet into the village, where Simon suggests they stop in at the pub:

> There was a notice outside the pub. "Please remove muddy boots before entering." "Bloody hell," Simon laughed when he saw my foot which was so caked in mud that it looked like I still had a boot on.
>
> "Would you like to take your socks off as well, Faith?" Simon's mother asked. I said no. I already felt absurd walking in a pub without my shoes.
>
> As I opened the door and stood in the doorway my eyes caught the eyes of a man sitting at the bar. He had on a tweed jacket and he watched me with an expressionless face as I moved into the pub. I felt other eyes looking at me but I could not see them. And I thought the place hushed. I looked down and tried to hide my muddy foot from the clean one.[43]

Faith then encounters Andrew Bunyan, a lawyer of some note and respect, who greets her by demanding to know where she is from, rejects the answer of "London" with a laugh, and on discovering that her parents are from Jamaica recounts an encounter he once had there with a fisherman who shares his last name, a commonalty Andrew Bunyan finds hilarious given that Winston Bunyan wears dreadlocks and was "Black . . . Black!"[44] Faith responds by arguing that what Andrew takes for some wild coincidence is little more than an obvious history: "Your family probably owned his family once," which elicits giggles from Simon and wordless outrage from Bunyan.

Both *O.P.P.* and *Fruit* use the countryside as the embodiment of Britain's dominant discourse on race, the ultimate site of resistance to the Black, and the conscious home of the mythic Englishness in its worst forms: atavistic, xenophobic, sexist, and, it is important to note, increasingly decrepit. Both novels produce young white male characters whose charm and sensitivity belie their stake in the status quo and willingness to uphold it when the chips are down. Both novels also produce impotent and ailing fathers for these young men, and the fathers are heads of the households in name only; their wives hold the true reins of power. In *O.P.P.*, King argues that it is the women of the elite families who are the true arbiters of power, the inheritors of a decaying patriarchal regime who show little sign of introducing progressive (for example, feminist) change. *Fruit of the Lemon* suggests that, with the decline of the old regime, there is progressive thought but it, in the form of Margaret, still has a long way to go in moving from a passive to proactive stance. The decline of the fathers is mirrored in the urban setting, where both Faith and Max mistake weakness and confusion for changing values and attitudes. Both learn, through their countryside encounters, that the belief in the Black Other and white subject is not only alive and well but still the foundation for the country's racial behavior. In *Girl*, set in Leicester, an industrial town whose wealth and importance has since long passed, the countryside conflates with the urban but offers Jack a refuge from her irascible, struggling mother, demanding track coach, and the confusing, chilly climate of school. Effectively barred by Maxine from responding to Steve Green's tentative wooing, and having summarily rejected two friendly young Black men, Jack encounters Spanner, who responds to her specific desire for acceptance from a white male and vaguer sexual desire by getting her high and bedding her in the bucolic surroundings. Like Max and Faith, Jack mistakes these encounters for something far more substantial, and in seeking Spanner out again she discovers that he is only an itinerant worker at the farm he claimed was home and so she, too, is only temporary in his life.

In *O.P.P.* and *Girl*, the discovery that their white lovers will not or cannot accept them as mates plays a climactic moment: Andrew severs all ties with Max, becomes an earl and plans to marry an heiress, leaving Max devastated in the final scene: "It took a while for the full impact of her situation to sink in but, when it did, Max couldn't contain herself. She broke down sobbing. She had lost her friend, her lover and her financial security and she was strapped on her own with a baby. Everything she had planned for her future was now lost."[45] Jack is left equally devastated, the way only a thirteen-year-old can be, when she discovers from the woman at the farm that Spanner has left: "I don't know what I must have looked like, but the next thing I knew was she had me in her kitchen and was making me a nice cup of tea. Really worried about me she said she was. Should she fetch a doctor? But I thanked her for the cup of tea and told her I'd be all right, there'd be no need."[46] While *O.P.P.* closes its chapter on Max with her suffering from hubris (salvation is reserved for her three girlfriends) and an ambivalent lesson on interracial relationships (except neither too much nor too little from racial difference), Jack's heartbreak is repaired through the mending of all her other woes, suggesting that the acceptance she sought through Spanner is best obtained through those she knows and/or loves. Jack loses an important regional track meet, thinking of Spanner in the last few seconds, but this frees her from her coach's obsessive dream of nurturing a Black sprinter into superstardom. In addition, her mother reconciles with her boyfriend and agrees to marry him and, finally, tells Jack about her biological father, an African American serviceman. Although the novel ends with the announcement of the mother's marriage, the narrative suggests that all three events bear equal importance for Jack.

Girl, O.P.P., and *Fruit* all use the extended metaphor of the single white male and the countryside to examine the racialized and gendered discourse of nationhood and belonging vis-à-vis the Black female. However, unlike the shared anecdote of the Black male rejected by the white female that Du Bois, Fanon, and Césaire use to analyze their status as Other to the white Western nation, Hodges, King, and Levy produce very different analyses as to the meaning of those failed romantic encounters. Hodges's *Girl* and King's *O.P.P.* are the most starkly contrasted: in the latter, Max's failed romance ends her story, but in *Girl*, Spanner is the third young white male for whom Jack develops a romantic interest and, although all three white men represent the possibility of acceptance and belonging for Jack, unlike King and Levy, Hodges does not directly associate them with the landed gentry or the symbol of "true" Englishness. *Girl* even suggests that Jack's search for a white boyfriend is a misguided search for her Black father: her obsession with Spanner abruptly ends once she learns about her father. At the same time, the Black father remains a specular presence with certain contingencies: it is only when Jack's mother becomes engaged to her white fiancée that she is willing to acknowledge the daughter's father, now safely ensconced in her past. Although *Girl*'s major characters are almost all female (Jack, her mother, Soft Aunt Margaret, Maxine), the novel cannot close until certain actions have been taken by the supposedly secondary male characters (Spanner disappears; Coach Longborough relinquishes his track fantasy about Jack; Vic, the mother's boyfriend, reconciles with her and proposes), suggesting that while white British males can and will heavily influence the Black female subject, that influence need not necessarily be wholly romantic nor wholly negative. Both *Girl* and *O.P.P.* foreshadow the realization on the part of their protagonists that they need not seek masculine signifiers outside themselves by giving them full names that are feminine and nicknames that are masculine. While *Fruit*'s Faith does not follow this pattern in name, the uplifting tenor of her own appellation also points to these "boy problems" being met and overcome.

The roles that whites and Blacks play for these Black female protagonists partially hinge on the racial makeup of their environment. The characters in *O.P.P.*, while struggling and troubled, are nonetheless members of the Brixton community, one of the most famous Black British enclaves, and all possess strong cultural and familial ties to Jamaica. Like the characters in Victor Headley's *Yardie*, King's Black Britons are binational, simultaneously Jamaican and British, living in a world in which whiteness appears in the form of institutions: law enforcement, the courts, or landed gentry. Whites are vague, inhuman shapes, who, Headley and King seem to agree, belie the depth and breadth of their power. Both King's Max and Headley's protagonist D. forget this and pay the price (D. goes to jail). By contrast, *Girl*'s and *Fruit*'s protagonists are largely removed from a Black community. While Faith's family is Black, she, like Jack, avoids developing ties with other Blacks. Other than her parents and brother Carl, Faith's world is entirely white. As a result, greater emphasis and focus is placed on white Britons and their internal differences (such as class, sexuality, and gender) that the Black female must successfully negotiate in her quest for subject status.

Unlike *O.P.P.* and *The Unbelonging*, where Max and Hyacinth's confidantes are either of West Indian or South Asian descent, *Girl* and *Fruit* depict Maxine and Marion as white female "best friends" to explore issues of class and heterosexuality on a community level for Jack and Faith respectively.[47] Like *Girl*'s Spanner and *Fruit*'s Simon, Maxine and Marion seem to symbolize social acceptance and belonging for Jack and Faith but translate friendship into rivalry once the two protagonists attract the attention of desirable white men. In this, they are not unlike the more grotesque figures of Hannah, Lucinda, and Abigail in *O.P.P.*, who understand themselves as the regulators of heterosexual unions for their white men. In staging the question of national belonging through heterosexual, interracial relationships, and demonstrating that the Black female will not be allowed to "supplant" the white female in the nation's heterosexual union between the (white) female country and the (white) male citizen, all three texts agree that the answer lies not in seeking to play a role in this union, but elsewhere. It is in the "elsewhere" that we see differences develop.

Because *O.P.P.* casts a wider net in its themes than either *Girl* or *Fruit* (the final scene with Max is still several pages from the end of the novel, where the other plot points—romance and finance—are concluded), it is difficult to claim that King is arguing that the Black female is always already Other in Britain. Yet while all three novels posit that Englishness remains the exclusive province of white Britons, they also suggest that the Black female subject is defined through the diaspora rather than the nation. Following their romantic disappointments, *O.P.P.*'s Max and *Fruit*'s Faith go to Jamaica. Max's sister Merlene, who also decamps, writes a letter to her friend Andrea exclaiming over the change the move has wrought in her, now surrounded by "just plain good and decent people"; "in London," she writes, "I was lying, cheating and stealing, all kinds of rubbish. Not any more."[48] The novel concludes quickly after that. One third of the way through *Fruit*, Faith's parents insist she go to Jamaica after a nervous breakdown because, as Mrs. Jackson puts it, "everyone should know where they come from."[49]

Although *O.P.P.* produces Jamaica in the manner of a deux ex machina to solve the problems of Max and Merlene, Levy uses Jamaica to introduce the complexity and ambiguity of one's racial and ethnic roots. The bulk of Faith's visit is composed of oral histories told to her by friends and family, and as the story progresses, so does the sketch of the Jackson family tree, which begins with a nuclear family at the novel's outset and develops into a sprawling centuries-long diasporic history of immigrancy, war, marriage, death—as well as deceit, rape, exploitation, hatred, racism, self-loathing, not to mention branches of the family marked only with question marks, disputed arenas where a curtain has silently been drawn. Jamaica, Levy argues, is multiracial and multiethnic but also impoverished, provincial, and reactionary. While Faith Jackson returns with a more complete understanding of herself and her roots—which spread from Jamaica to West Africa to the United States to South America—the novel ends heavy with ambiguity. Faith, like her parents decades earlier, arrives in England during Guy Fawkes and like them first mistakes the fireworks of the ambivalent celebration as acknowledgment of her own return:[50]

> At first I thought it may be a welcome home for me. The distant horizon briefly lit gold by a shower of sparks like an electric dandelion. I thought it may be a welcome for me for having traveled so far and England needing me. A fluorescent green spiral that whizzed upwards and was gone. But I knew I couldn't be right. A crack and three red sparks floated slowly down and out. I knew I couldn't be right and wasn't. A brief fizzing green arc that turned gradually to silver-blue. No, I knew this was England, November the fifth. There are always fireworks on November the fifth. It was Guy Fawkes' night and I was coming home. I was coming home to tell everyone . . . My mum and dad came to England on a banana boat.[51]

The final line of this final paragraph roughly reproduces the opening line and dominant theme of *Fruit* in which Faith recalls being taunted by her schoolmates ("'Your mum and dad came on a banana boat,' that was what the bully boys at my primary school used to say"), suggesting that Faith's shame is the conflation of ancestors and commodities but she now has reclaimed this past and turned objects into subjects—or at least she knows the difference.[52] Yet the arrival on Guy Fawkes night, the ambiguous description of the fireworks—at once dazzling but violent, brilliant but ephemeral—and the slow realization that England is unmindful of her return cast a different light on this conclusion. This ending is hardly devastating, but it is ambiguous. The specific cause of Faith's visit to Jamaica was a nervous breakdown in which she could not even bear to look at her own reflection. The two events leading up to this breakdown were the visit to Simon's family estate and the aftermath of a racist attack on a multiracial gay bookstore in which Simon, the police, and Faith's housemates insistently reinscribe the event as a heroic event for Simon (who called the police on discovering a Black female employee injured), diligently erasing the racist motivation of the attackers (the initials of the National Front are spray painted on the walls of the bookstore, along with racial and sexual epithets). This event magnifies several smaller ones that precede it, in which Faith, her brother, her parents, or a Black person she encounters are the victims of racist behavior the whites around them refuse to acknowledge.[53]

The Unbelonging, O.P.P., and *Fruit of the Lemon* share similar concerns about racism in Britain, yet they differ markedly in their portrayal of Jamaica. Riley sees Jamaica as a land to which the immigrant cannot return despite a desperate need for refuge, whereas *O.P.P.* offers the island as a welcome refuge from the destructive temptations of material gain one finds in Britain. As such, King's figuration of Jamaica as a locational deus ex machina, appearing when all hope is lost, is largely figured within an idealist construct of a homogeneous, welcoming, and morally uplifting Black collective, an interesting contrast to the variegated Black subjects she portrays within the Brixton scene. While King's novel is the only one to fully explore the relationship between commodification and agency through Max's sexual and commercial forays, her unrealistic portrayal (where Jamaica is described only in the elaborate praise of a letter) offers little in the way of information on the diasporic or binational subject. While *Girl*'s Jack Brown has no ties to Jamaica, the novel does advocate the recuperation of one's Black ancestry, albeit in the form of knowledge rather than return. By implying that Jack does not require the physical presence of her father so much as his signification within her own discourse of identity, Hodges suggests that the act of retrieval for the diasporic subject can be accomplished through a signifying chain as opposed to actual travel. Jack does not need her father to be with her, but she does need him named in order to recognize herself as a subject. *Fruit of the Lemon* offers the most sustained and complex view of the diasporic subject, especially in its production of Jamaica as both a place of origin and the embodiment of diaspora, rich with a variety of racial, ethnic, commercial, and political ties to the Western Hemisphere and beyond.

All three novels clearly share a diasporic sensibility in the construction of the Black female subject in that neither Jamaica nor England can or will operate as a home space in the most traditional sense. Instead, subjects move toward belonging in the in-between that Riley designates as unbelonging. In the manner of the anecdotes constructed by Du Bois, Césaire, and Fanon, King, Levy, and Hodges have protagonists who are forced to confront their designation as the English Other once they are rejected as romantic partners. There is an interesting difference, however: they are first wooed and then rejected once the romance begins to take on an air of permanency, which creates a striking metaphor for the way in which Britain first fought to gain and establish colonial holdings through a discourse of belonging and inclusion, then attempted to reject or at the very least discourage colonized peoples from "returning" to the heart of the empire that claimed them.

In their counterdiscourses, Rodgers and Lorde suggest that, through the trope of the Black mother, the dialogic subject is produced by recognizing the fallacy of the binary that orders racial, gender, class, and subject discourses. By contrast, King, Rodgers, and Levy all deploy some version of diaspora as their trope for the dialogic subject. In both cases, subjects come to recognize themselves through other subjects, but in the case of the latter three authors it is more an internal rather than external process of retrieval. The primary reason for this difference may be located in the material: while Black British communities continue to expand, only King offers a world in which the Black subject can exist almost wholly among Blacks, although, like Lorde and Rodgers, she argues that these communities are still interpellated in many ways through (white) dominant discourse. For Hodges's and Levy's protagonists, their existence in a world that is largely white—native to the former, sought after by the latter—means that they will be rendered Other in this discourse unless they anchor themselves to a nonwhite chain of signification.

"England in Reverse." The concept of "reverse colonization" is the focus of Simon Gikandi's exceptional *Maps of Englishness*, an analysis of the ways in which England has been shaped by its former colonial members. Yet as early as 1966 one finds Louise Bennett opening her poem "Colonisation in Reverse" by wryly remarking

> What a joyful news, Miss Mattie;
> Ah feel like me heart gwine burs—
> Jamaica people colonizin
> Englan in reverse.

The stanzas that follow elaborate the great numbers of Jamaicans who are doing their patriotic duty by immigrating, as well as the "joys" of the dole, then closes:

What a devilment a Englan!
Dem face war an brave de worse;
But ah wonderin how dem gwine stan
Colonizin in reverse.[54]

What Gikandi's book and Bennett's poem offer is a reformulation of the dynamics of colonization that rejects Hegel's and Gobineau's dialectic structures where the colonizer assumes control of the colonized, a fallacy that nonetheless enjoys great currency even among those who term themselves antiracist. Gilroy's *The Black Atlantic* has been criticized for such a view. Joan Dayan asserts that "there is a problem of agency here. Gilroy grants 'art'—or 'culture,' his most privileged term—to the slave population . . . but only as an *offering* from master to subordinate."[55] Robert Miles goes even further, arguing that "those racialized Others in Europe who can successfully imagine another, non-African tradition or origin may find little that is meaningful in the celebration of the history of slavery, albeit a celebration that highlights the resistance to it."[56] By reformulating the terms of exchange as dialogic rather than dialectic, discourses that uphold "reverse colonization" force us to see subjects where once there were simply Others. Drawing on this discourse, King, Levy, and Hodges offer us a construction of the Black female subject that, although in some degree a function of the same type of gendered nationalist discourse Du Bois, Césaire, and Fanon highlight, is not wholly contingent on it. While the latter posit the nation in the form of vibrant, adamant young women, King and Levy offer sickly, ineffectual old white men and their indecisive sons, signaling that the power of the nation is decentered and in transition. Furthermore, the young women in the equation are our Black protagonists, whereas the white women are older, sometimes friendly or even maternal. Even in King's scenario, where we encounter openly hostile white women, Jamaica nonetheless remains an option.

While none of the Black female protagonists in these novels ends up as Other to the white Western nation, the narratives do not conclude with a fully (re)established subjectivity. Instead, all three—Max, Faith, and Jack—leave as subjects in the making, aware of the negotiation their identities require if they want to escape being wholly Other. The lack of a concrete subject status is hardly surprising, given the rupture each text enacts with nationalist and dialectic models. Because diaspora is inherently unstable—a nonlinear construct produced by fluid dynamics such as travel, discovery, conflict, and negotiation—one would be hard put to produce a subject who is mobile and multifaceted and yet concretely defined and wholly achieved. For Max and Faith, the dynamic of reverse colonization is a process by which the Black female confronts her status as Other, physically retreats by reenacting the colonization process, and moves from Britain to Jamaica to retrieve and recuperate her colonial roots. Jack also retreats (although more in mind than in body) from white British society and then emerges after retrieving knowledge about her father. In one final defiance of the dialectic, none of these protagonists then "merges" with English society—in fact, all three texts suggest that the next step is still rather vague and unknown. Max's recovery is narrated in a letter that is read aloud in Britain, Faith gazes at fireworks, and Jack is ready to move forward, though she is unsure toward what. Is it reasonable to expect more? We are, after all, still in the process of retrieval and recuperation. That next step, it seems likely, is for the next generation.

BEYOND NEGRITUDE? CONTEMPORARY BLACK FRENCH LITERATURE AND THE AFRO-PARISIAN NOVEL

Even relative to the United States, Britain, and Germany, where one will find great diversity within the Black literary communities, the Black arts scene in Paris likely most reflects the category of African diaspora—and its deconstruction. Alec Hargreaves and Mark McKinney write:

> At a first level of analysis, at least three different types of cultural space are open to France's post-colonial minorities: the dominant norms of the majority population, Diasporic spaces associated with the country of origin and with other minority groups in France and elsewhere, and separatist enclaves detached from both of those fields. In practice, each of these seemingly distinct and internally unified spaces—the potential or actual coexistence of which is itself a challenge to the traditional concepts of the nation state—is far less clearly bounded than it may appear at first sight.[57]

The concept of a postcolonial literature is not unlike a Venn diagram, where novels exploring North African, West African, East African, Guadeloupian, and Martinican identities are not mutually exclusive from one another nor from subjects who identify as Arab. Most books and articles focusing on postcolonial literatures in France examine the writings of *beur* authors (the term "beur" is derived from a backslang of the same name in which "Arabe" is phonetically inverted) and North African writers who identify as Maghrebi, Berber, or even Harki (the latter term denotes Algerians who allied themselves with France during the Franco-Algerian War and were forced to flee with the occupying force upon defeat).

Even if one were to focus exclusively on those writers who identify wholly as Black and come from former French colonies in West Africa or the Caribbean, one is forced to negotiate a series of overlapping categories and subcategories, from nationality to language, culture, politics, and personal history. Although French dominant discourse often conflates these distinct peoples, they do not conflate themselves—although all, to some degree or another, engage with the legacy of Negritude. In *Black Paris*, Bennetta Jules-Rosette asserts that "Négritude, an integral part of the African writers' landscape, is one of the most important French-African identity discourses emerging during the mid-twentieth century."[58] While this statement is hardly in dispute among Francophone scholars and writers, Jules-Rosette goes one step further by locating many contemporary postcolonial Francophone works as a counterdiscourse to Negritude. One finds a loose and tentative agreement with this among other writers. As early as 1972, Stanislas Adotevi, a prominent figure on the French African landscape and former professor at Université Paris Sept, deconstructed Senghor's concept of authenticity and a Black soul, echoing Wole Soyinka's comment that "a tiger does not display its tigritude" by proclaiming "La négritude est morte. Il faut lâcher le Nègre" ("Negritude is dead. We must release the Negro").[59] Although he is more circumspect, Michel Laronde offers the term "littérature décentrée," or decentered literature (a concept that he notes can also be found in Roland Barthes, Mireille Rosello, and Marc Sourdot), to describe minority immigrant literatures. In the introduction to his anthology *L'écriture décentrée*, Laronde explains that "decentered literature takes into account developments in literature from France that are marked by linguistic and cultural differences anchored in part to the foreign origin of the writers").[60] By way of example, Laronde points to works by both West African and *beur* authors but locates the concept of "décentrilisation" in the work of Roland Barthes and his critique of essentialisms such as racial stereotypes both "positive" and negative.[61] In *Declining the Stereotype* Mireille Rosello argues that, in their use of the stereotype, some major texts defy the dialectic pro-African structure that forms the central tenets of Negritude.[62]

In *La littérature nègre*, Jacques Chevrier argues that one can find a rejection of Negritude that moves beyond an anti-Negritudist use of stereotype.[63] While Chevrier locates contemporary African literature as moving against Negritude, Jules-Rosette presents a more complex picture, in which many African writers adhere to some or all of the tenets of Negritude or bypass the question altogether by simply producing texts that are not in dialogue with European politics or traditions. In her interview with Bernard Dadié, a writer from the Ivory Coast whose 1959 novel *Un nègre à Paris* (Black Man in Paris) ranks alongside René Maran's *Batouala* and Yambo Ouologuem's *Le Devoir de violence* as a seminal text in postcolonial Francophone literature, she avows that "here in Africa we have our own frames of discourse and techniques of criticism."[64]

Confronting Dialectics in the Diaspora: the Afro-Parisian Novel. Indeed, Jules-Rosette argues that Senghor's theory of "universalism" has grown in popularity since Negritude's arrival in the 1930s, pointing to writers such as Baptiste Tiémelé, Edouard Manick, and Bolya Baenga as examples of artists who, like Dadié, vigorously promote a unique cultural and philosophical vision of Africa in the world. I would agree with Jules-Rosette against Chevrier (as well as Laronde and Rosello, albeit in a lesser, more specific degree) that one will not find a unanimous rejection of Negritudist principles among African, DOM-TOM (*Département Outre-Mer et Territoires Outre-Mer*, or France's overseas departments and territories), and immigrant writers. Jules-Rosette argues that the specific and explicit rejection of Negritude is found within a relatively new literary movement she calls "parisianism," also referred to by some writers and publishers as "afro-parisian" literature.

One can find rough parallels between parisianism's critique of Negritude and the Black feminist critique of Black nationalism in that both reject the idea of an authentic and/or homogeneous Blackness as well as inviolable racial and national borders by producing the reality of the Black diaspora in all of its diversity and conflated categories. At the same time, the inherently feminist, dialogic stance one finds in writers such as

Audre Lorde and Carolyn Rodgers is not shared by all afro-parisian authors. One can also find rough parallels between the afro-parisian emphasis on the urban as an exemplum of the diaspora and that same emphasis in Afro-German and Black British literature; again, however, the feminist stances advocated by Ika Hügel-Marshall, May Ayim, Andrea Levy, Jo Hodges, and Naomi King are not a given with the afro-parisian. What afro-parisian novels do share is the production of "parisian" identity as one that does not exclude other identities (most specifically non-European nationalities) and, as Jules-Rosette puts it, "[parisianism] . . . questions old narratives of African belonging, turns away from pure orality, undermines African cultural specificity, and reconfigures point of view and characterization in writing."[65]

Because afro-parisian literature was only identified as such in the late 1980s, there are very few authors who can be placed in its canon; nonetheless, some of them, such as Calixthe Beyala and Simon Njami, are quite well known. *Black Paris* focuses on novels by Beyala and Simon (who are both Cameroonian) and Yodi Karone. Because this chapter is exclusively concerned with novels that examine the problem of Black subjectivity within Europe, I do not take up Karone, whose novel *A la recherche du cannibale amour* (In Search of Cannibal Love) frames the question of identity within the immigrant experience, and I avoid the works of Beyala, which have become increasingly controversial.[66] Instead, I discuss two novels, *African Gigolo* by Simon Njami and *Agonies* by Congolese author Daniel Biyaoula, which focus on the dilemma of Black subjectivity in France, albeit through different approaches: one engages a Black feminist consciousness, the other does not.

At the very beginning of *African Gigolo*, we are introduced to the protagonist, Moïse, and his female problem, or, rather, his lack of one. Moïse operates as a successful gigolo who specializes in white French women. This is part of a larger pattern of self-isolation: Moïse is estranged from his parents, has one platonic female friend, Mireille, and one Black African friend, Étienne. Aside from his mother, who appears only in the form of fearful missives reminding him of his familial duties, Black women appear only much later in the novel, serving as sexual breakthroughs. Moïse's desire to remain largely unattached extends into more abstract habits: only Mireille and Étienne know his real birthday, for he lies to everyone else, which, along with his refusal to maintain contact with his parents, effectively precludes his having any sort of spatial or temporal definition. The cause of Moïse's preference for an unsignified identity and individual existence are not specified, but early on Njami presents an intriguing conversation between Moïse and Étienne on the cultural and political identity—or, rather, lack thereof—of the African diaspora:

> Moïse closed the door without responding. On beautiful days, one of his favorite pastimes was to stretch out on the grass in Monceau Park, reading the poems of Guillaume Apollinaire. Étienne had taken up the habit of responding, engaging him in conversation once again on a discourse on the Surrealist recognition of Black art. He followed this with a good scolding on the concepts of the Dionysian and the Apollonian. Everything would unfold according to a carefully established ritual. Étienne began with a critique of poetic structure, which he then stretched out to encompass the Surrealists and contemporary French art. Moïse invariably responded that if only blacks had been more cunning, rather than crying about being robbed, they would have invented their own independent theories, rather than ones simply oppositional to their Western counterparts. Or, there were those who believed themselves exceptionally sly and had brandished the specter they then baptised Negritude.—Do you see, he concluded at last, that words such as Negritude are not very scientific. Not so much as Zulu-esque, or Pulidian. Those are words that ring true![67]

Despite this anti-Negritude stance, Moïse nonetheless profits from its essentialist notions of Blackness through the women he seduces. Early in the novel, we learn that his current female client "aimait la musique africaine et étudiait les civilisations précolumbiens" (loved African music and studied Precolumbian civilizations, 12); Étienne writes him a "manuel d'utilisation du mâle nègre à l'usage des femme occidentales" (user's manual for the Black male on Western women, 36); and he seduces one particularly resistant virgin by promising her marriage and a life in Africa, "où on fêtait Noël sous le soleil, et où des enfants couraient vers vous avec des brassées de fleurs" (where one celebrates Christmas under the sun and children run toward you with garlands of flowers, 56). The narrative leaves no doubt that Moïse is a gigolo not so much because he offers his body for sale but because he offers readily consumable African cultural identities to white women. It is not that Moïse wholly loathes his Cameroonian origins: "Il se sentit africain, se vécut africain dans toute sa chair, hors de toute volonté de chantage moral" (He felt himself to be African, lived in all of his flesh as an African, completely independent of any sort of desire born of moral blackmail, 87). Moïse's behavior, then, is less a reaction to Negritude than to the lack of philosophies or ideologies available for the Black Parisian with which he could negotiate an identity.

In line with Moïse's love for nineteenth-century French literature and theory (to which the texts makes many references) is a teasing parallel between his lack of direction and that of a famous antihero of the French Romantic tradition, Julien Sorel from Stendhal's *Le rouge et le noir* (The Red and the Black), who, as a well-educated son of a carpenter in the days of the Bourbon recapture of the monarchy, seeks a position befitting his skills rather than his class. Moïse meets Mathilde, a woman who bears the same name, roughly the same physical features, social position, influence—and the same haughty, seductive, and demanding personality as Julien's paramour. Like Stendhal's heroine, Njami's Mathilde uses her influence to secure a position for her lover/protégé. Moïse starts work for the unethical (and highly successful) art dealer Durand, traveling to Italy and then to Holland on business (and in the process seducing various women along the way). After receiving a letter from his mother begging him to return home and help his father and the family, Moïse retreats to his new life as Mathilde's lover and Durand's assistant, ashamed and unable to face the possibility of returning home with nothing to show beyond a slew of sexual conquests.

Escape is not so easily achieved, however, as these two new characters enter into the dialogues with Moïse on Africa's political and economic future and the role of the postcolonial African at home and abroad. Despite this range of topics, the conclusions Moïse draws are all the same: there is no known category for the particular type of African that he is. With Étienne he debates the pros and cons of Senghor's universalist theory of Black art and Black identity; with Mathilde he spars over the sexual and racial politics that must come into play between a Black man and white woman; with Durand, a gay man, he discusses masculine identity in relationship to women. In each of these discussions, Moïse finds himself constantly confounded by an unrelenting binary structure that further underscores his inability to fit in anywhere. Étienne chides him for rejecting "African" cultural values and mores; Mathilde, observing that her lover studiously avoids befriending other Africans and in fact ends up in heated, violent disputes when forced to socialize with them, questions whether or not he is still "African" and teasingly conflates this "African" identity with the heteronormative: "dans quelques années, vous ressemblerez à Durand comme deux gouttes d'eau" (in a few years, you and Durand will resemble each other like two drops of water, 99). Finally, Moïse is asked if he is willing to accept his similarity to Durand in being a "mysogine sans être phallocrate" (misogynist without being a phallocrat, 96), in which men either understand women as instruments to be played or else allow themselves to be castrated by them.

Moïse's inability to embrace definitions of the African male proffered by these three interlocutors comes to a head when he has sexual encounters with two women who also symbolize the illegitimacy of binary structures. The first is Sarah, Mathilde's "protégé," a young biracial woman from the Ivory Coast. On first seeing Sarah, Moïse attempts to categorize her as a self-hating Black ("Il lui parut évident qu'elle ne l'aimait pas. Qu'elle détestait, négresse, rencontrer un nègre dans ce milieu-là" (It was clear to him that she didn't like him. That she, a Negress, detested meeting a Negro in this milieu, 136). Sarah's friendliness, and then her mocking observation that he has been away from Africa cause him to project his own insecurities onto her:

> This girl had this obsolete patriotism of the dismantled and lost in her blood, those who fantasized about their continent rather than live there. At least, he thought to himself comfortingly, I escaped from those affectations. He had baptized this species of illness the "half breed complex."[68]

Try as he might, however, Moïse cannot resist a sexual invitation from Sarah, even as he claims that the impetus is less desire than anthropological curiosity (she echoes him). The encounter leaves Moïse wanting more of Sarah despite the impotence he now experiences with other women and his fears of what he finds so irresistible: the "paradoxe de ses yeux gris-vert" (paradox of her grey-green eyes), which he decides symbolize the "detonator" that Sarah has become for his life (148). Not unlike Riley's protagonist in *The Unbelonging*, Moïse and Sarah both seek subject status by trying to posit the other as a sexual object rather than as a subject, yet in each attempt they find themselves unable to negate their obvious conflation as Others in dominant discourse. Unable to realize his subjectivity through Sarah's objecthood, Moïse flees to Amsterdam.

The second "detonator" for Moïse is an Antillean prostitute he encounters in Holland, to whom he speaks in French, and she replies in Dutch, perhaps symbolizing the material realities that beset such a multilingual and multicultural African diaspora. In their first encounter, Moïse is not only impotent but brutally beaten up by a mugger. A few days later, Moïse spots his attacker, quietly pursues him, and then kills him, all the while dispassionately observing the (white) man's "sexe inerte qui pendouillait lamentablement entre ses jambes" (inert sex that swung sadly between his legs, 207). No longer filled with the unnamed fear and suicidal desires that have plagued him throughout the narrative, and having discovered that the vaunted Western phallus is just a penis, Moïse finds the Antillean and his sexual potency, which leads to the recuperation of a childhood memory: losing his virginity at the age of twelve to an enormous Black prostitute his father had procured for him.

Through these experiences—his desire for Sarah, his bilingual encounters with the Antillean, and the murder of the mugger—Moïse comes to realize that "Black" and "white" are ultimately empty categories, and that sex, death, and consciousness are not defined against one another but are in fact all part of life as a whole. Having realized the fallacy of binary definitions and that it is Étienne and Mathilde who are ill, not he, Moïse decides that his status as an "apatride" (stateless person) is not without meaning, that the binaries he so feared simply do not exist. Yet, not fitting into the prescribed category of an African does not mean that he lacks "les êtres, des visages, des mots. Il y avait son père et sa mère" (beings, faces, words. He had his father and his mother, 211). Acting on this epiphany, Moïse has one final sexual encounter with Mathilde, in which they are now no longer lovers but "deux ennemis, deux étrangers, deux adversaires" (two enemies, two strangers, two adversaries), then leaves his white female mentor to return to his Black mother—and by extension his father, Cameroon, and the whole of Africa.

Daniel Biyaoula's novel *Agonies*, written almost a decade after *African Gigolo* (and the Mitterand era), takes a very different approach to the question of the afro-parisian identity, albeit through the same lens of sexual and romantic liaisons. *Agonies* follows two romantic narratives. The main story belongs to Gislaine, a Black African woman, and her struggle to find an egalitarian relationship with an African man in an immigrant community steeped in patriarchal practices and misogynist behavior. However, gender inequities are not the only category of inquiry: the subplot follows the controversial romance between Gislaine's niece Maud and her boyfriend who, although also a denizen of Parqueville (a suburban ghetto of Paris), is forbidden to her by her father for being white. While the actions and reactions of Gislaine drive the plot, she serves as a nodal point for all the other major characters, to whom she is either aunt, sister, sister-in-law, neighbor, friend, or lover. She is not, it is interesting to note, a mother, either biologically or within a surrogate role. She is also a controversial figure for her community, simply for being a single Black woman who has very little to say about marriage (positively or negatively). Whereas *African Gigolo* begins with Moïse admiring his latest conquest and then being looked at while walking the streets of white Paris, *Agonies* begins in the second person (rather than the more remote third), opening with a discourse in pain and self-alienation, then follows the radioactive wake Gislaine leaves in her (mainly African) neighborhood of Parqueville.

In *Black Paris*, Bennetta Jules-Rosette identifies some traits of parisianism that are poststructuralist (subversion of traditional notions of time and space), modernist (antiheroes who offer little inspiration), and specifically anti-Senghorian (atonal, arrhythmic, antiprotest). In terms of how these novels represent large questions such as nationalism and subjectivity, *Agonies* addresses the complexities of these issues far more acutely than Njami's novel. The latter often collapses Cameroon with Africa as a whole and operates on a rigidly gendered discourse of the nation. *Black Paris* points out how Moïse's mother is a metaphor for the African nation, and the novel itself explains that Moïse seeks to master Paris by mastering white women's bodies.[69] *Agonies* uses terms such as "nouvelle tradition africaine" (to describe the defensive hypocrisy of Gislaine's brother Gabriel), "noir modern" (as Gislaine's lovestruck suitor Nsamu first describes her to a confidante), "inafricaine" and "inafricanité" (Nsamu's new definition for Gislaine when it is clear she does not return his affections), not only to deconstruct the notion of a homogeneous Africa or Black race but to encapsulate the ways in which concepts of national and racial belonging are used as bywords to oppress, restrict, and denigrate all sorts of marginalized people—and to demonstrate that even those themselves marginalized can be prone to using this vocabulary. Although *Agonies*, like *African Gigolo*, avoids moral centers and simplistic villains, Gabriel and Nsamu are the architects of the terms listed above and the culprits behind the majority of misogynist, homophobic, xenophobic, and chauvinist pronouncements that come from the Parqueville residents. Moreover, specific African nations are never mentioned; we are simply informed that some characters are from N'djamabidja, some from Kinshaduala, some from Ntchiyafua, and that Nsamu and Gabriel—and eventually the pacific Bernard—believe that the enmity these groups share back home should also be sustained abroad.

African Gigolo follows a strict dialectic of the subject, from self-love to self-hatred to self-realization, with women's bodies operating as metaphors for belonging and Black and white men as the phallic powers Moïse must confront. Desire is expressed only in sexual terms, as an analogy for either the male drive for agency or the female drive to dominate and/or destroy. Although *Agonies* also centers on desire it is almost anything but sexual. Nsamu desires Gislaine because she is impervious to his charms. Gislaine pursues Camille because she represents freedom from Nsamu's attentions and, Gislaine mistakenly believes, freedom in general. Camille comes to desire Gislaine as a prize that the great seducer Nsamu cannot have. And, although Maud and Guy are madly desirous of one another, their romantic infatuation supersedes sexual desire. *African Gigolo*'s staging of Moïse's desire focuses on overcoming and possessing it. Even while it acknowledges this desire is not moral or admirable, it is nonetheless portrayed as impressive in its naked strength. In both novels, desire signals the idealized drive of impossibilities we seek to make possible, our destructive aims that we pretend possess positive consequences. Rather than operate as the transcendent signifier for the subject, here desire signals the subject's inability to understand or at least acknowledge that all subjects are necessarily intersubjective. The most obvious case of this is Nsamu, who refuses to see Gislaine as anything but an object his manhood now desires. Gislaine, in turn, understands Camille as simply a desirable buffer between herself and Nsamu and then uses a willing Nsamu to block Camille. Nsamu and Gabriel act only to tear people apart, erecting or recalling separatist sentiments along gender, class, racial, and nationalist lines in order to assert their masculine privilege. In an ironic twist, Biyaoula points to the young interracial lovers, Maud and Guy, as the only ones who truly understand their intersubjective nature, their obligations to and their need for other people. As in King's, Lorde's, and Rodgers's theorizations of the Black subject located in the Black community, the failure to recognize *all* Blacks—including women—as subjects spells doom not only for those located as Other but for those who attempted to Other them in the first place.

Yet this does not mean that interracial romance is the key to our destructive desires: Bernard, happily married to a white French woman, Josiane, and the most virulent resister of the factionalism between the different Africans in Parqueville, becomes upset when that resistance is challenged by the romance between Gislaine and Camille and ungraciously harasses his old friend from his home. Nor do Guy and Maud provide an answer: in the final paragraph of the novel, right after Nsamu is stabbed and Gislaine is strangled by a jealous Camille, Maud, wondering when she will once again be with Guy, is on a plane heading home, Gabriel having made good on his threat to separate the two no matter what.

METROPOLIS, MODERNITY, AND THE
BLACK DIASPORIC SUBJECT

This focus on the metropolis as a site that, while not necessarily belonging to the diasporic Black, is nonetheless his/her home is shared by the majority of Afro-German and Black British novels (not to mention a majority of novels that deal with immigration). In the Afro-German text, the metropolis (usually but not exclusively Berlin) serves as a refuge from the reactionary and oppressive attitudes that pervade the rural space, although the Afro-German eventually realizes that the same vicious atavistic set of beliefs pervades both locations. In her essay "Das Jahr 1990" ("The Year 1990"), May Ayim goes one step further by paralleling the unification of Berlin with the rise of a racist nationalism. Although the realization is the same, the direction is reversed in *O.P.P.*, *Fruit of the Lemon*, and *The Girl with Brains in Her Feet*, where the city achieves its role as home of the diasporic Black through a striking contrast with the rural, the latter revealed as mired in a mythic past of patriarchal rule, racial homogeneity, and an almost feudal social organization. In all cases, Blacks align themselves with some version of the diaspora, which in turn is signified as synonymous with diversity, progress, and a more sophisticated understanding of the world. By pointing to their material existence within the metropolis (or, in the case of Afro-Germans, their preference for the city over the country), these counter-discourses highlight the elisions that produce them as Other in the first place. Whereas Du Bois, Césaire, and Fanon point to the fallacy that posits them as Other yet nonetheless renders them Other within that context, these later counterdiscourses are less convinced of the power of this fallacy. None of these texts dismisses this fallacy as an impotent wish, and in fact many agree that, in the wrong setting, the Black can become Other. Yet in locating the Black in the urban, they simultaneously move the white who speaks them as Other to the margins, whether that be the colonialist fantasy, the English countryside, or Mathilde's empty Paris mansion, splendid but lacking in meaning and humanity. Unlike the afro-parisian novel, the Black British and Afro-German texts featured in this chapter construct a world that is physically mixed but ideologically and economically segregated, and the enforcement of that segregation is laid squarely at the door of white patriarchy, including those who preach integration but practice something quite different. In *African Gigolo* and *Agonies* (and to a lesser degree in Calixthe Beyala's novels *Le petit prince de Belleville* and *Maman a un amant*), racist whites share the blame with equally resistant and reactive Blacks.

In marked contrast to the ambivalent portrayal of modernity that we find in Du Bois, Fanon, and the Negritudists (where sexual and racial relations are starkly aligned, usually within phallic machines of prog-ress—trains, subways, or in Du Bois's exception, the feminine enclave of the schoolroom), Black British and Afro-German texts align them-selves with technological progress by presenting racist, rural whites as technologically—and hence intellectually—backward, removed from the metropolis and stuck in time, a reversal of Hegel's, Gobineau's, and Jefferson's determinations of the *Black* as inherently primitive. The afro-parisian novel more closely resembles the critique of technology—pro-duced as nothing more than a servant of capitalism—that we find in the Black Arts movement and in the poetry of Audre Lorde and Carolyn Rodgers. The narratives are set in the ghetto, with their inhabitants daily enduring, battling, or resigning themselves to the role of exploited worker and consumer, central to capitalism's addiction to cheap labor and cap-tive consumers but deliberately marginalized from a central, controlling power. While Lorde, Rodgers, and other Black Arts artists decry the ways in which Blacks are forced to buy goods produced from outside their neighborhoods, Njami, Biyaoula, and Beyala point to the ways in which Africa and, by extension, the African immigrant's body are exploited for European profit.

In the Black British and Afro-German texts analyzed in this chapter, subjectivity is clearly intertwined with intersubjectivity. Afro-Germans are able to achieve a coherent, faithful, and positive understanding of themselves through their participation in Black, interracial, and/or feminist collectives at home and abroad. White German discourse, still reliant on colonialist paradigms, is unable to explain them; the diasporic discourse, however, appearing in the form of the collectives described, can both explain and inspire them. The heroines from *O.P.P.* realize too late that in attempting to destroy one another they destroy themselves, a critique also lodged at the men. *Fruit of the Lemon*'s Faith Jackson moves to develop her identity by fleshing out her family tree, which stretches across the globe through national, class, ethnic, and religious boundaries, and Jacqueline Brown from *The Girl with Brains in her Feet* achieves some sort of prepubescent closure by learning about her African American father and having her mother marry—an Englishman.

All these novels draw on and deploy the now unmistakable presence of the African diaspora in the West to confront the elision in Western discourse that locates them as always already outside Western history, culture, and civilization. In interrogating the racist discourses that confront their Black characters, these novels usefully remind us that this discourse is not, as it claims, informed by objective observation or scientific research; it is rather composed of the same provincial beliefs that operated in the West two hundred years earlier. Although most likely not deliberate, this argument is a wonderful response to the observation by Hegel and others that the Black stands outside history: it points to cosmopolitan Blacks in the Western urban center, then to the anti-Black discourse that fears and hates the African savage and asks which one truly stands outside the progress narrative.

These diasporic discourses also elaborate on the more textured view of Black and white communities first offered in Lorde and Rodgers. By engaging with the issue of race, as King, Hodges, and Levy do, they remind us that many of the same forces that locate the Black as Other also locate the white working class as Other. In making this observation, however, none of these authors suggests that the white working class and

Blacks of all classes can always already find common cause. The desire for subject status means many will try to take a shortcut by aligning themselves with dominant discourse in its production of poor and/or Black Others. In like kind, by subverting the myth of a homogeneous Blackness, these texts show us that heterogeneity, like the dialogic, must come with a cost: differing and oppositional views can and will confront all subjects at all times.

Yet if these counterdiscursive narratives seem to lack closure or gesture more vaguely than their predecessors to the nature of this new, diasporic subject, it is worth remembering that the diaspora is still in formation, and other voices have yet to be heard from. Denmark, Sweden, Finland, Italy, Spain, and Portugal can all point to growing Black communities and the possibility of an ever-expanding African diasporic tradition of counterdiscourses. Yet even as these diasporic subjects rise in number so does, it seems, the virulence and aggression of the racist discourse that angrily rejects them as subjects and, through physical, political, and social forces, brutally attempts to render them as others. Only time will tell if the Black subject is indeed more at the mercy of racist fallacy and force—as Du Bois, Césaire, and Fanon warned—or if, as these counterdiscourses assert, the virulence of this fallacy belies its inability to overthrow the new diasporic collective.

EPILOGUE

If the Black Is a Subject,

Can the Subaltern Speak?

I have tried here to show how, at least since the twentieth century, African diasporic thinkers have engaged with the racist discourse that produced them as Other and have responded with sophisticated critiques underscoring the combination of malevolent fantasy and brutal practice that attended the original construction of their alterity. At the same time, as I have traced both the ideal and material changes in these counterdiscourses over the generations, I have tried to show how attempts to impose a homogeneous and/or heteropatriarchal norm onto Black subjectivity returns us to the same unyielding and theoretically suspect discourses that first produced Black Others. More specifically, I have argued that race cannot operate in a vacuum, divorced from those other subject categories—gender, sexuality, and class—that are always already part and parcel of any subject status but especially that of the subaltern, who is often implicitly asked to hide or ignore those aspects of identity that do not conform to the heteronormative.

On the whole, the tradition that this book maps moves from less inclusive to more inclusive models of the subject, but these increasingly complex models do not—at least not now—reflect the textual politics of most African diasporic fiction today. Like their white counterparts, many Blacks in the diaspora prefer formations that, whether explicitly enunciating "nation" or "diaspora," implicitly embrace nationalist discourse's call for an enforced heteropatriarchal homogeneity through which "authentic" Blackness comes into being.

White communities have also passively supported these heteropatriarchal norms. The representation and rights of Black queers remains an unspoken issue in Black American politics, and gay rights organizations often elide or divide Blackness from queerness to argue that all Blacks have been "given" rights denied to some whites. This in turn recalls nineteenth-century white American feminists who explicitly appealed to the white majority against the Black minority.

Since the beginning of the nineteenth century, Black American feminists have successfully struggled to introduce a far more complex, textured, and inclusive notion of Black identity both within the United States and the diaspora as a whole. The results of these efforts—politically, socially, and culturally—are evident and thriving: more subalterns are speaking. Yet both within and outside the academy, those Blacks who speak without sympathy for heteropatriarchal formations are often ignored or condemned as perverse, emasculating, or "inauthentic," reminding us that not all Black subjects would like to hear all subalterns speak.

I would argue that Black feminist and queer discourses are intimately bound up in producing an African diasporic discourse that seeks to answer in the affirmative the question posed in the title of this epilogue. With the exception of the afro-parisian novels, the diasporic novels featured in chapter 5 that directly engage with Black subjectivity in the West are overwhelmingly written by women. In addition, the majority of these novels offer critiques of both white and Black nationalism. Other than Simon Njami's *African Gigolo*, the texts in this chapter are partially or wholly dialogic in their sensibility, but they all also make clear that dialectic models must nonetheless be grappled with. In other words, these texts warn that one should not confuse nationalism's atavistic and idealist tendencies with a waning influence or power. Yet this warning also reveals the inability of these books to imagine other types of relationships outside the heteronormative. Even as they challenge and critique the dialectic, these texts also reinscribe it through a strict rendering of gendered nationalist discourse, where heterosexual alliances serve as the standard model for belonging. This does not mean, however, that the queer Black subaltern cannot speak. There are contemporary novels that complicate this notion of belonging by giving us protagonists (or other central characters) who come into being outside or between discrete categories of race, sexuality, and gender. In Danzy Senna's *Caucasia*, the heroine Birdie is a biracial girl who looks "white" and is on the run with her white mother (who believes herself pursued by COINTELPRO). In Black Scottish poet Jackie Kay's first novel, *Trumpet*, a white widow and her adopted Black son must come together to negotiate the death of Joss Moody, a Black jazz trumpeter who is revealed as biologically female at the autopsy. Finally, there is Zadie Smith's *White Teeth*, a novel with a panoply of characters whose lives are so intertwined that their half-hearted attempts to construct or resurrect discretely bounded ethnic, cultural, or nationalist identities are always already doomed to comic failure. Such protagonists who defy easy categorization intensify the trend already extant in Afro-German, Black French, and Black British texts, namely, deconstructing, complicating, or, at their most extreme, exploding the heteronormative boundaries of the nation that threaten to produce them as Other. I believe that the current decade will see this trend continue, with Black European literary productions increasingly orienting and defining themselves in relationship to other Black communities in the diaspora rather than to white Western nations.

This is a trend that African American fiction—which has always boasted a strong literary tradition by and about African Americans in Europe—has yet to fully explore. Despite our international celebrity and a history of both forced and voluntary travel, African American discourses on other Blacks are most often defined against national, rather than diasporic, references. Given our relatively large role and resources, continuing to challenge this insularity and the oppressively homogeneous models for Blackness it inevitably produces would go a long way toward establishing even deeper and more meaningful ties in the diaspora. Above all else, this study emphasizes that, until *all* Black peoples in the diaspora, regardless of their marginalized status, can find representation within a theory of the subject, we cannot attach too much importance to Black subject formations that rely on and/or ignore the exclusions they perform. After all, the analysis of the African diasporic tradition in this text is far from exhaustive, and, one might paraphrase, it won't be over (or ovah) until the subaltern speaks.

NOTES

INTRODUCTION

1 Pp. 46–47.
2 Gates, *Figures in Black*, xx.
3 Gilroy, *The Black Atlantic*, 2.
4 By contrast, early white settlers in the New World did claim that space as their new home.
5 As I later argue, Jefferson's veil is most likely the inspiration for W. E. B. Du Bois's famous formulation in *Souls of Black Folk*.
6 Most postcolonial and poststructural theorists only refer to Hegel's master/slave dialectic when examining his analysis of slavery. I would argue that it is absolutely crucial to note the vastly different conclusions at which Hegel arrives when he analyzes the slave as an abstraction and when he is writing specifically on Black Africans.
7 The first Africans arrived in the New World only a few months after the first white settlers.

1. THE EUROPEAN AND AMERICAN INVENTION OF THE BLACK OTHER

1 Or, more specifically, only the European was considered an actual "man" in terms of subjectivity.
2 It is odd to speak of an American colonialism alongside Enlightenment Europe because it confuses the fact that the United States was itself "postcolonial." Recognizing this, I nonetheless want to underscore the close relationship and mind-set between European colonialists and these former American colonialists. Both were moving across the North American continent to claim lands and raw materials, and both were deeply engaged in capturing and exporting African slaves. Europeans and Americans shared a general sentiment of superiority, both intellectual and moral, over nonwhite peoples.
3 While many scholars tend to reference Hegel's theory of the master/slave dialectic to examine his views on the Negro and the slave trade, his reading of the "abstract" slave and the Black slave are radically different. In the former, Hegel

argues (with perfect dialectical reasoning) that the master is reliant on the slave for his identity. In the latter, the relationship between the white Western master and the Negro slave is a binary—the master does not rely on the slave for anything.

4   I say "him," as most of these discourses used the singular masculine in their discussion of the modern white subject and primitive Black Other.

5   Estimates on the number of Blacks in France in the eighteenth and nineteenth centuries run anywhere from the hundreds into the thousands. See Ivan Van Sertima's anthology *The African Presence in Early Europe* and Sue Peabody's *There Are No Slaves in France* for different (but not oppositional) accounts of Black life in France at the time.

6   Here I am specifically referring to Jefferson's attempt to introduce legislation that would banish any white woman found to have consorted with a Black man, an act even the Virginia legislature found too harsh. See Paul Finkelman's *Slavery and the Founders: Race and Liberty in the Age of Jefferson* for an extensive discussion on the myth of Jefferson's lifelong stance against slavery.

7   Balibar and Wallerstein, *Race, Nation, Class: Ambiguous Identities*, 38–39.

8   As later chapters will show, these variations are also varied within themselves.

9   Early in his introduction, Hegel allows that the Orient has displayed certain tenets that reflect the guiding principle of reason, but only partially because "the Orientals have not attained the knowledge—Man *as such*—is free; and because they do not know this, they are not free" (translation by J. Sibree).

10   " . . . der subjektive Wille hat auch ein substantielles Leben, eine Wirklichkeit, in der er sich im wesentlichen bewegt und das Wesentliche selbst zum Zwecke seines Daseins hat. Dieses Wesentliche ist selbst die Vereinigung des subjektiven und das vernünftigen Willens: es ist das sittliche Ganze—*der Staat*, welcher die Wirklichkeit ist, worin das Individuum seine Freiheit hat und genießt, aber indem es das Wissen, Glauben und Wollen des Allgemeinen ist." Hegel, *Vorlesungen über die Philosophie der Geschichte*, Werke 12, 55. Unless otherwise noted, all translations are my own.

11   Hegel, *Philosophy of History*, 40–41.

12   Hegel, *Philosophie*, 128.

13   "Was wir eigentlich unter Afrika verstehen, das ist das Geschichtslose und Unaufgeschlossene, das noch ganz im natürlichen Geiste befangen ist und das hier bloß an der Schwelle der Weltgeschichte vorgeführt werden mußte." Ibid., 129.

14   Forster, "Hegel's Dialectic Method," 133.

15   Hegel, *Philosophie*, 128–29.

16   The majority of Williams's readings of Hegel are drawn from the *Phänomenologie des Geistes* (Phenomenology of the Spirit).

17   "Genuine reciprocal recognition requires a renunciation of seizing upon the other, stripping him of his possibilities and reducing him to my own possibilities. This renunciation means granting the other freedom to recognize, or to withhold recognition. Not only is the other allowed to be, but the other's free, uncoerced recognition is crucial to the self. The recognition that really counts is

the recognition from the other that is not at the disposal of the self. Recognition (*Anerkennung*), unlike desire, does not essentially involve a reduction of the other to the same. *Anerkennung* involves a search for satisfaction in the *uncoerced* recognition of the other. Although recognition includes self-coincidence or satisfaction, this does not occur through the elimination of the other, but through membership or partnership with Other." Robert R. Williams, *Recognition: Fichte and Hegel on the Other*, 155.

18 Serequeberhan, "The Idea of Colonialism in Hegel's Philosophy of Right," 1. See also Gates's introduction to *Figures in Black*, in which he discusses Hegel's introduction to the *Philosophy of History*.

19 The European is not only under the moral imperative of reason to expand beyond his borders, his geography is also urging him on: "The sea gives us the idea of the indefinite, the unlimited and infinite; and in *feeling his own infinite* in that Infinite, man is stimulated and emboldened to stretch beyond the limited: the sea invites man to conquest, and to piratical plunder, but also to honest gain and commerce." Ibid., 90.

20 "The only essential connection that has existed and continued between the Negroes and the Europeans is that of slavery. In this the Negroes see nothing unbecoming to them, and the English, who have done most for abolishing the slave trade and slavery, are treated by the Negroes themselves as enemies. . . . We may conclude *slavery* to have been the occasion of the increase of human feeling among the Negroes. . . . but this existing in a State, slavery is itself a phase of advance from the merely isolated sensuous existence—a phase of education, a mode of becoming a participant in a higher morality and the culture connected with it. Slavery is in and for itself *injustice*, for the essence of humanity is *Freedom*; but for this man must be matured. The gradual abolition of slavery is therefore wiser and more equitable than its sudden removal." Ibid., 98–99.

21 Hegel, *The Philosophy of Right*.

22 Shlomo Avineri, *Hegel's Theory of the Modern State*.

23 Allen W. Wood, ed., *Hegel's Philosophy of Right*, 44. Of course, Hegel did not mean all human beings in that he barred nonwhites, women, and the poor from such considerations.

24 "It is a solution, furthermore, that does not violate the internal principles of this sphere. Given the structural contradictions inherent in civil society, colonialism becomes a very attractive, indeed a necessary option. Thus, non-European territories which do not share the peculiar European idea of property and society and thus do not have the strange problem of 'overproduction' are labeled 'generally backward industry' and thereby become the legitimate prey of colonialist expansion." Serequeberhan, "The Idea of Colonialism," 311.

25 Shohat and Stam, introduction, *Unthinking Eurocentrism: Multiculturalism and the Media*.

26 Bhabha, "Anxious Nations, Nervous States," 204.

27 See Gerard Delanty's *Inventing Europe*, and Lewis and Wigen's *The Myth of Continents* for a sustained discussion and analysis, respectively, of the con-

struction of Europe as a homogeneous entity in relationship to the "non-Western" world.

28 According to Louis Thomas's *Arthur de Gobineau: Inventeur de Racisme*, this quote is from a comment made by Prosper Merimée about Gobineau's *Essai*.

29 "Le mot *dégénéré*, s' appliquant à un peuple, doit signifier et signifie que ce peuple n' a plus la valeur intrinsèque qu' autrefois il possédait, parce qu' il n' a plus dans ses veines le même sang . . . il n' a pas conservé la même race que ses fondateurs . . . Il mourra définitivement, et sa civilisation avec lui." Gobineau, *Essai sur l'inégalité des races humaines*, 34–35.

30 "[Gobineau] never thought of applying his principles to a reconstruction or revolution of the political and social order." Cassirer, *The Myth of the Modern State*, 224.

31 Gobineau, *Essai*, 208.

32 Unable to reconcile the civilizations of China and Japan with his Aryan theory, Gobineau concludes that the Aryans must have settled China and Japan two millennia previously. And "other peoples" includes other whites—his definition of the Aryan does not include all white peoples, nor is his definition of Caucasoid peoples particularly uniform.

33 Cassirer, *The Myth of the Modern State*, 981.

34 "L'Arian est donc superieur aux autres hommes, principalment dans la mesure de son intelligence et de son énergie; et c'est par ce deux facultés que lorsqu'il parvient à vaincre ses passions et ses besoins matériels, il lui est également donné d'arriver à une moralité infinitivement plus haute, bien que, dans le cours ordinaire des choses, on puisse relever chez lui tout autant d'actes répréhensibles que chez les individus des deux autres espèces inférieur." Gobineau, *Essai*, 982.

35 "Ainsi placé sur une sorte de piédestal, et se dégageant du fond sur lequel il agit, l'Arian-Germain est une créature puissante. . . . Tout ce que cet homme croit, tout ce qu'il dit, tout ce qu'il fait, acquiert de la sorte une importance majeure." Ibid., 982.

36 Within his own small circle of friends and fans, Gobineau was known as an expert on oriental culture, especially in literature and the fine arts. His frequent references to "Oriental myths" are echoed in his rhetoric on the Aryan.

37 Hegel, *Philosophie*, 104.

38 "Les maîtres rencontrent aussi mille motifs de tolérer et quelquefois de servir cette tendance [de mélanger], le mélange du sang finit par s'opérer, et les hommes de deux origines, cessant de se rattacher à des tribus distinctes, se confondent de plus en plus." Gobineau, *Essai*, 981.

39 "C'est quand les éléments regulateurs des sociétés et les éléments developpés par les faits ethniques en arrivent à ce point de multiplicité qu'il leur devient impossible de s'harmoniser, de tendre, d'une manière sensible, vers une homogénéité nécessaire, et, par conséquent, d'obtenir, avec une logique commune, ces instincts et ces interêts communs, seules et uniques raisons d'être d'un lien sociale. Pas de plus grand fléau que cet désordre, car, si mauvais qu'il puisse rendre le temps présent, il prépare un avenir pire encore." Ibid., 345–46.

40 As the succeeding argument will show, Gobineau's definition of the Other is not stabilized within one racial category; for the sake of clarity, I will focus on his theory of the Negro and its relation to alterity, although it must be noted that at times the "Oriental" is designated as Other par excellence.

41 "[Le noir] est la plus humble et gît au bas de l'échelle. Le caractère d'animalité empreint dans la forme de son bassin lui impose sa destinée, dés l'instant de la conception. Elle ne sortira jamais du cercle intellectuel le plus restreint. Ce n'est cependant pas une brute pure et simple, que ce nègre a front étroit et fuyant, qui porte, dans la moyenne de son crâne, les indices de certaines énergies grossièrement puissantes. Si ces facultés pensantes sont médiocres ou même nulles, il possède dans le désir, et par suite dans la volonté, une intensité souvent terrible. Plusieurs de ses sens sont développés avec une vigueur inconnue aux deux autre races: le goût et l'odorat principalement. . . . À ces principaux traits de caractère il joint une instabilité d'humeur, une variabilité des sentiments que ne rien peut fixer, et qui annule, pour lui, la vertu comme la vice. On dirait que l'emportement même avec lequel il poursuit l'objet qui à mis sa sensitivité en vibration et enflammé sa convoitise, est un gage du prompt apaisement de l'une et du rapide oubli de l'autre. Enfin, il tient également peu à sa vie et à celle d'un autre; il tue volontiers pour tuer, et cette machine humaine, si facile à émouvoir est, devant la souffrance, ou d'une lâcheté qui se réfugie volontiers dans la mort, ou d'une impassibilité monstrueuse." Gobineau, *Essai*, 339–40.

42 See *Philosophie der Geschichte*, in which Hegel described Africa as no more than a barren wasteland wherein the African, cognitively unable to differentiate himself from others—in short, incapable of the intellectual capacity required to achieve subjectivity—exists in a savage, stagnant state "forever cloaked in darkness."

43 Both writers indulge themselves with tales of cannibalism, complete with the now-familiar tropes of fire, drums, gnashing teeth, and women and children with especially savage and voracious appetites.

44 See pp. 23–25 of *Philosophie* regarding Hegel's comments on the enslavement of Africans.

45 Leon-François Hoffman, *Le Nègre Romantique: Personnage littéraire et obsession collective*.

46 The African, of course, was not the sole recipient of this honor: the Native American was equally, if not more so, the unfortunate repository for these fantasies of conquest and heroism. We also find this discourse deployed against a range of other peoples including, at times, Jewish, Mediterranean, and Eastern European peoples.

47 In *The Myth of the Modern State*, William Cassirer argues that Gobineau's theory signals "a new step, and a step of the greatest consequence, when hero worship lost its original meaning and was blended with race worship and when both of them became integral parts of the same political program" (224). According to Cassirer, Hegel's metaphysical explanations were no longer in vogue at the time of Gobineau's *Essai*; Gobineau's generation "[was] in need of something more

palpable: of something 'that our eyes are able to see, our ears to hear, our hands to touch.' The new theory seemed to satisfy all these conditions" (230).

48 In *They Came Before Columbus*, Ivan Van Sertima marshals convincing evidence that African explorers predated Columbus's "discovery" of the Americas. For this argument, however, I will confine myself to the first Blacks who arrived just after the settlement of Jamestown. See *When and Where I Enter: A History of Black Women in America* by Paula Giddings for a fascinating discussion of the earliest Black settlers in Jamestown and seventeenth-century British attitudes toward Africans.

49 I use "predate" to make a distinction between those African Americans who are descended from the first Black slaves in America and those African Americans who are more recent arrivals, i.e., post-1865 African immigrants and immigrants of African descent.

50 In "Nigger Peasants from France," I discuss this translation and the conflation of the French peasant with the American "Negro" in detail.

51 Cassirer, *The Myth of the Modern State*, 232.

52 One must first take issue with Cassirer's reading of Gobineau's popularity among his contemporaries. As Louis Thomas, Tzvetan Todorov, Michael Biddiss, and others have noted, Gobineau's *Essai* was in fact quite unpopular at the time of its publication. Although some German theorists would use the theory of racial inequity to promote German unification and Aryan superiority, Gobineau himself noted with some despair the reaction of his peers. In a letter to Alexis de Tocqueville, who also took issue with Gobineau's claims, Gobineau writes "Merimée m'écrit que l'on voudrait me manger et qu'on parle de me brûler . . . Maury, votre bibliothécaire, m'assure qu'il m'a très maltraité dans un article dans l'Athenaeum." (Merimée writes that there is talk of eating me and burning me alive . . . Maury, your librarian, assures me that I come off very badly in his article in the *Athenaeum*.) Thomas, *Arthur de Gobineau*, 14. Further, the "glorification of race," as Cassirer terms it, is either operating on a definition of race that defies nineteenth- and twentieth-century norms, and so cannot be determined before the Enlightenment and the European colonization, or it must be viewed as concurrent with it, given that it was not until this time that "race" achieved a definition that incorporated all peoples Europeans had since encountered—or imagined. See Miller, *Blank Darkness: Africanist Discourse in French*.

53 Michael Biddiss, *Father of Racist Ideology: The Social and Political Thought of Count Gobineau*. Gobineau was an avid traveler and wrote a series of travelogues detailing his journeys through every inhabited continent except the Americas.

54 "J'admets, oui, j'admets, avant qu'on me le prouve, tout ce qu'on pourra raconter de merveilleux, dans ce genre, de la part des sauvages les plus abrutis. J'ai nié l'excessive stupidité, l'ineptie chronique, même chez les tribus les plus bas ravalées. Je vais même plus loin que mes adversaires, puisque je ne révoque pas en doute qu'un bon nombre des chefs nègres dépassent, par la force et abondance de leurs idées, par la puissance de combinaison de leur esprit, par l'intensité de

leurs facultés actives, le niveau commun auquel nos paysans, voire même nos bourgeois convenablement instruits et doués, peuvent atteindre. Encore une fois, et cent fois, ce n'est pas sur le terrain étroit des individualités que je me place. . . . Laissons donc ces puérilités, et comparons, non pas les hommes, mais les groupes." Gobineau, *Essai*, 313.

55 Simply as an aside, it is also interesting to pause at the defensiveness of his tone, which suggests he has encountered a frustrating amount of opposition from his fellow intellectuals. Most certainly, Alexis de Tocqueville and Prosper Merimée made clear their objection. Even further, the fact that Gobineau would insist that one couldn't compare individuals, only groups, points to an agenda that cannot easily include an apology for racist action. Within Gobineau's distinction, groups are the subject of theory, individuals the bases for praxis, especially if one considers the legacy of Enlightenment humanism.

56 It is possible that Hegel's Negro serves as the blueprint for Gobineau's French peasant.

57 "Certainement l'élément noir est indispensable pour développer la génie artistique dans une race, parce que nous avons vue quelle profusion de feu, des flammes, d'étincelles, d'entraînement, d'irréflexion réside dans son essence, et combien l'imagination, ce reflet de la sensualité, et toutes les appétitions vers la matière le rendent propre à subir les impressions que produisent les arts, dans un degré d'intensité tout à fait inconnu aux autres familles humaines. C'est mon point de départ, et s'il n'y avait rien à ajouter, certainement le nègre apparaît comme le poète lyrique, le musicien, le sculpteur par excellence. . . . Oui, encore, le nègre est la créature humaine la plus énergiquement saisie par l'émotion artistique, mais à cette condition indispensable que son intelligence en aura pénétré le sens et compris la portée." Gobineau, *Essai*, 473–74.

58 Yet Gobineau's disclaimer with regard to individuals who may display intellectual or moral acuity above or below their race simultaneously allows him to insist on the accuracy of his racial stereotypes and dismiss evidence to the contrary, which at that time typically came in the form of the individual achievements of certain Blacks.

59 Aryan tribes must have started traveling not long after prehistoric times in order to have founded all the oldest civilizations known to the nineteenth-century historian—if one is to believe the discourse of Gobineau.

60 One can argue that this does not excuse Gobineau from the ways in which his theories were then harnessed to American chattel slavery (or later, even the Holocaust), despite his refusal to acknowledge culpability.

61 One might argue that recontextualizing this particular structure of subjectivity with regard to the social identity produces an agenda that parallels the American civil rights movement of the 1960s and 70s and its call for complete racial integration.

62 "L'État est partagé en deux fractions, que ne séparent pas des incompabilités de doctrines, mais de peaux: les mulâtres se tiennent d'un côté, les nègres de l'autre. Aux mulâtres appartient, sans aucun doute, plus d'intelligence, un esprit plus

ouvert à la conception. Je l'ai déjà fait remarquer pour les Dominicains: le sang européen a modifié la nature africaine, et ces hommes pourraient, fondus dans une masse blanche, et avec de bons modèles constamment sous les yeux devenir ailleurs citoyens utiles." Gobineau, *Essai*, 186.

63 Gobineau's opinion on this matter is a mixture of relief and disdain: on one hand, he is glad that such stock are not polluting superior breeds, yet he considers this refusal to intermix a great affront.

64 "Dopo tanti anatemi, Gobineau torna dunque a sottolineare che il *mélange* ha anche un valore positivo, quando poche gocce del sangue di una varietà inferiore trasmettono al popolo eletto quel che in essa c'è di valido, e cioè, in questo caso, la creatività artistica." (After so many things that are an anathema, Gobineau then turns to underscore that those of mixed blood also have a positive quality, when just a few drops of an inferior variety of blood that possess something of value are transmitted to the chosen people—in this case, artistic creativity.) Castradori, *Le radici dell'odio*, 109.

65 "Les mulâtres auraient habité les bords de la mer, afin de se tenir toujours avec les Européens dans des rapports qu'ils recherchent. Sous la direction de ceux-ci, on les aurait vus marchands, courtiers surtout, avocats, medecins, reserrer des liens qui les flattent, se mélanger de plus en plus s'améliorer graduellement, perdre, dans des proportions données, le caractère avec le sang africain." Gobineau, *Essai*, 187.

66 This notion of whitening the Negro and placing the offspring within positions of limited authority was in fact practiced in the French, Spanish, and Portuguese colonies wherein those of mixed race were encouraged to view themselves as superior, to celebrate their white ancestry and disdain their African and other nonwhite ancestors. Although the American South also practiced the placement of lighter-skinned Blacks in domestic or even secretarial positions in the house, the act of miscegenation, although just as frequent as in the European colonies, was nonetheless an absolutely taboo subject; a master's illegitimate "mulatto" offspring were rarely recognized, whereas European colonizers, when removed from their white families and European society, took less trouble in disguising, and sometimes even informally recognizing, these children. The American translation of the *Essai* does not include these passages.

67 My thanks to Simon Gikandi for pointing this out.

68 Hegel, of course, did not mean that participation in the state was the only determinant of subjectivity; women, nonwhites, recent immigrants, and the poor were persona non grata and therefore not included on the roster of potential citizens. At the same time, Hegel's failure to state this explicitly in his discourse resulted in later figures (as the third chapter will reveal) deploying this discourse as a democratic imperative.

69 This should not be confused with a belief in racial equality, an idea Washington and Franklin could not yet grasp but one argued by Hamilton (himself a product of the West Indies and an extramarital coupling).

70 Those apologists for Jefferson who turn to the "Manners" section of *Notes*

on the State of Virginia often fail to notice that Jefferson is not protesting slavery as an abomination against the slave but as an industry and practice with a disturbingly negative effect on the white slaveholders.

71 Jefferson was known as an avid student of the classics and also an Enlightenment thinker, the latter deriving its idea of logos from the ancient Greek philosophers. It is not surprising then that he would approach the law as a means of "being."

72 See Henry Louis Gates's *The Trials of Phillis Wheatley* for a fascinating narration of Phillis Wheatley's "trial of authorship."

73 For very different reasons, both Rousseau and Voltaire enjoyed remarking on the static quality of nature as opposed to the dynamic quality of man.

74 Although animals were credited as making noises in order to indicate something specific, such as hunger, it was not considered "language" per se, in that animals were not considered capable of reflection. The speaking animal characters in La Fontaine were of course meant to add a certain humor to the lesson, but also to suggest that at times human beings were capable of sensations and actions that fell below behavior unfit for animals, in spite of the human ability to speak.

75 *The Portable Thomas Jefferson*, 193.

76 Ibid.

77 Many conservative scholars and critics have argued that earlier drafts of the Declaration, in which slavery is discussed (but not revoked), overrides Jefferson's racist musings in the *Notes*. I fail to be convinced by this argument and would in fact argue that the failure of the Declaration's final draft to right such a gross wrong further confirms Jefferson's antipathy toward emancipation.

78 In his letter to Edward Coles, Jefferson urges his young follower against leaving Virginia (where those such as Jefferson had instituted legislation disallowing a slave owner to free his bondsmen) to manumit his slaves, arguing that a more gradual plan is needed because "men . . . of this color we know, brought from their infancy without necessity for thought or forecast, are by their habits rendered as incapable as children of taking care of themselves, and are extinguished promptly wherever industry is necessary for raising young . . . I hope then, my dear sir, you will reconcile yourself to your country and its unfortunate condition; that you will not lessen its stock of sound disposition by withdrawing your portion from the mass" (*The Portable Thomas Jefferson*, 546–47). Coles ignored this advice, left Virginia, and manumitted all of his slaves anyway.

79 *The Portable Thomas Jefferson*, 190–91. As Paul Finkelman has pointed out, Jefferson fails to note that the ancient Greeks (who comprise his three examples and in fact comprised the majority of slaves who later came to distinguish themselves in science or the arts) were already considered by the Romans to be a people gifted in knowledge and the arts—Romans based their pantheon, their literature, much of their political system, and even their manners on the "Greek" model—hardly prefiguring European attitudes and relations toward Blacks. Jefferson also fails to notice that his argument is tautological: he bases his claim of Negro inferiority on the fact that Negroes are not white and thus must be inferior.

80 And, as will be discussed later, it was Jefferson's belief that this intermixture would ultimately harm whites.

81 Without doubt, nineteenth-century chattel slavery was one of the most brutal systems of enslavement known to Western history, if not the overall worst. Finkelman questions whether Jefferson is deliberately being disingenuous, surrounded as he was by a slaveholding economy, and certainly witness to, if not aware of, the conditions of American Blacks in bondage.

82 Given that slaves were usually forbidden to learn how to read, often on pain of death for both the tutor and tutee, not to mention kept in degraded conditions, one wonders again if Jefferson is playing ignorant in order to make this argument.

83 *The Portable Thomas Jefferson*, 191.

84 See introduction to Finkelman, *Slavery and the Founders*.

85 *The Portable Thomas Jefferson*, 186.

86 And is therefore unchanging, possessing a relatively inert quality that should not be tampered with.

87 Therefore, those who blame white slaveholders for the prolongation of slavery are in fact blaming the wrong party.

88 *The Portable Thomas Jefferson*, 186; my emphasis.

89 *The Portable Thomas Jefferson*, 186–87.

90 Jefferson made many statements advocating intermixture between whites and American Indians. Although he believed that American Indians lacked many of the accomplishments of whites, he nonetheless held that they were not only capable but naturally inclined to progress and would most likely achieve parity with whites should they choose to become citizens of the union.

91 Indeed, Jefferson's prescription for miscegenation and integration recalls Gobineau's discourse on the mulatto. See Anthony F. C. Wallace's *Jefferson and the Indians* for a fascinating analysis of the rather bizarre and unique way Jefferson envisioned the incorporation of certain American Indian nations into the new republic.

92 *The Portable Thomas Jefferson*, 188.

93 One wonders if Jefferson ever considered repatriation seriously, given the impracticality of shipping millions "back" to Africa and the rather vague outlines he gives for such a plan. In addition, Jefferson, who inherited one of the largest American fortunes for that time, was a spendthrift who relied on slave labor to settle his debts and maintain his luxurious lifestyle after his inheritance had been spent.

2. THE TROPE OF MASKING IN THE WORKS OF W. E. B. DU BOIS, LÉOPOLD SÉDAR SENGHOR, AND AIMÉ CÉSAIRE

1 See chapter 5's section on the legacy of Negritude in the Francophone literary diaspora.

2 Depending on which school one subscribes to, this "step" can be understood as anything from a significant change to a small transition.

3 Du Bois, *The Souls of Black Folk*, 5.

4 I say "attempts" because these two possibilities of merger between a social minority and a dominant majority are hardly equivalent, especially when one considers the means by which the Black was brought to and forced to remain in North America. My thanks to Marlon Ross for pointing this out to me.

5 Despite the boldness of Du Bois's analyses, we must question how we are to read his statement that the white world has much to actively *teach* the Negro, whereas the Negro has a passive "message" for the white world.

6 In fact, one of the more misleading aspects of Hegel occurs in his master-slave dialectic in the *Phenomenology*, where, utterly unlike his reading of African slaves, he accords the slave the power of recognition. I discuss this in detail in the first chapter. For a thorough discussion on the intersection between Du Bois and Hegel, see Shamoon Zamir's *Dark Voices*.

7 The production of the citizen as representative of the nation is in fact related to the production of the American nation but will only be invoked here with regard to the production of the (white) American subject and his relation to the nation-as-logos as a logocentric subject.

8 I would argue that, based on their approach and rhetoric, the majority of Du Bois's works are geared toward, but not exclusive to, a white audience. Rather than move into the confusing question of audience in the arena of counter-discourse, I will work on the premise that, as counterdiscourse to Jefferson's *Notes*, Du Bois is addressing all those, Black or white, who are familiar with the American discourse on the Negro.

9 Du Bois, *The Souls of Black Folk*, 3–4.

10 Ibid., 4.

11 Du Bois, *An ABC of Color*, 129. This collection includes selections chosen by Du Bois from over a half century of his writings, introduction by John Oliver Killens.

12 Ibid., 128.

13 We are also shown how the white subject fears the inevitable: the revelation that the Black is in fact equal to the white.

14 Of course, one should not assume that marriage and lasciviousness are mutually exclusive, but the narrator's assumption immediately marks him as monogamous or disingenuous—or both.

15 It is unclear whether or not the narrator would reproduce this bias with a working-class Black, but the question is probably moot. The narrator, after having been insulted by ignorant and dull whites, is no doubt overjoyed to outwit and further frustrate a white person whom *society* would recognize as ignorant and dull—possibly in the narrator's favor.

16 It should be noted that at the beginning of his encounter, the narrator does in fact suggest that the wayfarer and southern Blacks should unite forces and vote against those who continue to impoverish them. But this suggestion is quickly rejected by the wayfarer and not pursued by the narrator, who is first befuddled, then frustrated and sarcastic.

17   Rees, *The Algebra of Revolution*, 105.

18   As we will see in the next chapter, Frantz Fanon also draws on this famous philosophical example but reads it toward slightly different ends.

19   This is not unlike Hegel's contradictory consideration of the African as both Other and extra-dialectical.

20   *The Souls of Black Folk*, 202.

21   And, it should be underscored, to many other writers.

22   Rees, *The Algebra of Revolution*, 68.

23   Although *Souls* is not concerned with fully exploring the intersection of class and race, it, "On Being Crazy," and other articles from the *Crisis* in this era indicate an underlying theme that the Black is not the only one who suffers disenfranchisement, nor the only one who stands to gain should this American hypocrisy be challenged.

24   "Mais de toutes les influences, la plus déterminante semble avoir été celle des ethnologues et de leurs prédécesseurs: Gobineau, Lévy-Bruhl, Delavignette, G. Hardy, et surtout celle du romantisme de Leo Frobenius. Dans les analyses précédentes, nous avons souligné l'ambiguïté de l'adhésion aux thèses de ces savants. Oui, declare Césaire, nous avons lu Gobineau, Senghor et moi. C'était surtout pour le refuser, puisque c'était le grand théoricien français du racisme. Mais en même temps, je dois le reconnaître, Senghor l'aimait beaucoup. Il l'aimait, cela se comprend: il lui savait gré d'avoir dit: "l'art est nègre." Le Nègre est artiste. Si dans la civilisation occidentale il y a quand même quelques gouttes de sang noir en eux. Par conséquente, l'attitude à l'égard de Gobineau était fort ambivalente." Mbwil a Mpaang N'gal, *Aimé Césaire*, 186.

25   See the introduction and first chapter of Christopher Miller, *Blank Darkness: Africanist Discourse in Seventeenth-Century France*.

26   For a detailed description and analysis of the discourse on the French colonizer, see Frantz Fanon, *Peau noire, masques blancs*.

27   This is an important distinction: to say that the Aryan *does not* possess artistic talent renders the statement too ambiguous, suggesting that the Aryan *could* come to possess this talent and/or that the Aryan *chooses* to forgo this talent. Gobineau is much more specific: the Aryan, by virtue of his utterly rational mind, *is incapable* of possessing a quality that is natural to the Negro. Again, this is not to say that Gobineau is a champion of the Negro, merely that his statements prove useful in certain contexts.

28   Despite the atavistic attitude of this particular racist discourse, it is far from defunct: debates in 1999 on the preamble to the Australian constitution regarding the Aboriginal reveal an unconsciously ironic determination to fit history into racist propaganda; that is, official channels are still debating whether or not to acknowledge that the Aboriginal preceded the white (by some 120,000 years).

29   Although Jefferson described the Negro as possessing rhythm, his rhetoric does not extend to a means of expression that might be conflated with linguistic capability.

30   "J'aurais dû, si j'étais resté logique à l'albo-europèene, intituler ce troisième

chapitre "La Parole, la Poésie et l'Art africains." Si je ne l'ai pas fait, c'est pour rester fidèle à ma pensée: pour mettre l'accent sur la Négritude, qui sous-tend toute la civilisation africaine, même sous son aspect arabo-berbère. Mais l'accent doit être mis aussi sur la Parole, qui est, en même temps, poésie et art, c'est-à-dire Création." Senghor, *Fondements de l'africanité ou Négritude et arabité*, 34–35.

31 Of course Africa is an enormous continent with a wide diversity of cultures, peoples, and languages, obviously calling Senghor's rather sweeping generalization into question. Given the alternative, that is, pointing either only to Senegal (his birthplace) or enumerating every African nation in his description, his choice of terms is understandable but not wholly justified. As counterdiscourse to the sweeping pronouncements Hegel and Gobineau made with regard to Africa and the Negro, Senghor's terminology fulfills a rhetorical requirement. All the same, it is a significant aporia in an argument notable for its creative and intelligent strategies.

32 As opposed to reason, Senghor's creation bespeaks a far more inclusive mission, barring only those who have not been created. In "Prière aux Masques," which I analyze later in this chapter, we see how Senghor creates reason and creation not necessarily as binary oppositions but links the former to European colonization and posits the latter as its solution. I say "necessarily" because there are moments where the two seem opposed, but creation is posited as that which envelops all other terms, one of course being reason, suggesting creation as the synthesis and reason as antithesis.

33 See Sartre's introduction to *Les damnés de la terre*, in which he praises Fanon for deploying Negritude as the stage of antithesis reacting against colonialism.

34 This argument has, of course, been challenged by those both inside and outside anthropology. Nevertheless, this view is still held by many leading figures in the field, not to mention the mainstream public.

35 "Nous commencerons donc, nous avons commencé par la parole, par la Poésie, qui, dans presque toutes les civilisations, est l'art majeur. Majeur surtout en Afrique parce que, dans la poésie, la parole est proférée, agie, sous la forme qui charme le plus parce que c'est la plus active." Senghor, *Ce Que Je Crois*, 119.

36 As the recent furor over Ebonics has indicated, the West is yet unable to credit Blacks with possessing a language. Outraged that Ebonics receives serious consideration, popular discourse thus asserts that Blacks possess no language. Contrary to the claims of the Linguistic Society of America, the American public considers Ebonics nothing more than a series of mispronounced mimicries, i.e., "bad English."

37 Echoes of this idea can be found in the European discourses that compare and contrast "Northerners" and "Southerners." The latter are stereotyped as a people who communicate through physical gestures and lively and loud sounds, supposedly an indication of a lesser intellect. With the occasional exception of England, this idea can be found in every major Western European country.

38 More on this at the end of the chapter.

39 By invoking the trope of the speech act and claiming Africa as the place where it is fully realized, Senghor is indirectly pointing to a schism in European cultural values. On one hand, European discourse promotes itself as a highly intellectual (i.e., "abstract") culture; on the other hand, it defines Aryan superiority through the will to power.

40 Diana Fuss and other noted theorists have written excellent critiques of the sexism and misogyny within the Negritude discourse of Fanon, Césaire, and Senghor. In *Aimé Césaire*, Janis L. Pallister suggests that the tendency to see as misogynist Césaire's failure to locate women outside domestic roles such as nurturing and childbirth is a misreading of his essentialism.

41 Although Senghor's direct references to Hegel are few, his role as the theorist of Negritude makes it difficult to believe that he ignored perhaps the largest figure in the Western canon, especially one who made extensive comments on the Negro, slavery, and the need to colonize.

42 However, Africans did in fact possess several different forms of writing. In *They Came Before Columbus*, Ivan Van Sertima argues that it is ridiculous for Europeans to claim a superior civilization because of writing when they possess only one alphabet—and African civilizations have produced several.

43 I consider Senghor's description of "Africa" problematic for obvious reasons and of course must note a contradiction in his invocation of African unity, considering his later political actions, in which, as president of Senegal, he undertook political and military actions against neighboring African countries.

44 Although terrifying, these portrayals simultaneously suggest something of the outrageous. Because the African is a primitive, his use of masks is also considered funny and anachronistic in the modern European world.

45 A preponderance of Western cartoons, movies, television shows, and other promotional images depict Africans wearing masks or at least some sort of face painting, which comes to the same thing; it is often the primary signifier of difference.

46 Picasso's revolutionary use of the African mask, often celebrated as the necessary shot in the arm needed by modern art, both reifies and subverts this concept. On one hand, Picasso points to the mask as an abstraction, not a face in and of itself. At the same time, his deployment of the mask underneath the rubric of the "primitive," in tandem with his failure to strictly delineate the "African" mask from the "African" face, suggests that the mask is in fact the face of the primitive art, and hence of the primitive him- or herself.

47 "Masques! O Masques!
Masque noir masque rouge, vous masques blanc-et-noir
Masques aux quatre point d'où souffle l'Esprit
Je vois salue dans le silence!
Et pas toi le dernier, Ancêtre à tête de lion.
Vous gardez ce lieu forclos à tout rire de femme, à tout sourire qui se fane
Vous distillez cet air d'éternité où je respire l'air de mes
Pères.

Masques aux visages sans masque, dépouillés de toute fossette comme de toute
ride.
Qui avez composé ce portrait, ce visage mien penché sur l'autel de papier blanc
A votre image, écoutez moi!
Voici que meurt l'Afrique des empires—c'est l'agonie d'une princesse pitoyable
Et aussi l'Europe à qui nous sommes liés par le nombril.
Fixez vos yeux immuables sur vos enfants que l'on commande
Qui donnent leur vie comme le pauvre son dernier vêtement.
Que nous répondions présents à la renaissance du Monde
Ainsi le levain qui est nécessaire à la farine blanche.
Car qui apprendrait le rythme au monde défunt des machines et des canons?
Qui pousserait le cri de joie pour réveiller morts et orphelins à l'aurore?
Dites, qui rendrait la mémoire de vie à l'homme aux espoirs éventrés?
Ils nous disent les hommes du coton du café de l'huile
Ils nous disent les hommes de la mort.
Nous sommes les hommes de la dance, dont les pieds
reprennent vigueur en frappant le sol dur."
Senghor, *The Collected Poetry*, 277–78.

48   If not synonymous with that signifier!

49   Aimé Césaire, interview by René Depestre at the Cultural Congress of Havana in
1967, translated from the Spanish by Maro Riofrancos, in *Discourse on Colonialism*, 67.

50   "Au bout de petit matin, sur cette plus fragile épaisseur de terre que dépasse de
façon humiliante son grandiose avenir—les volcans éclateront, l'eau nue empor-
tera les taches mûres du soleil et il ne restera plus qu'un bouillonnement tiède
picoré d'oiseaux marins—la plage des songes et l'insensé réveil." *The Collected
Poetry*, 35.

51   In context, "alexins" appears to be a form of "elixirs." I would read "hypoglosse,"
translated as "hypoglossal," as a brilliantly performative counterdiscourse to
(and ironic commentary on) the European characterization of the Black as
deficient in language—"glossal," of course, referring to the act of explanation or
interpretation. "Poussis surnuméraires" translates as "supernumerary." "Tera-
tique" is from "teratical," meaning "monstrous."

52   *The Collected Poetry*, 35.

53   "Je ne suis d'aucune nationalité prévue par les chancelleries./Je défie le cra-
niomètre. Homo sum etc./Et qu'ils servent et trahissent et meurent./Ainsi soit-
il. Ainsi soit-il. C'était écrit dans la forme de leur bassin." Ibid., 62–63.

54   "Il faut savoir jusqu' où je poussai la lâcheté. Un soir, dans un tramway en face de
moi, un nègre.
       C'était un nègre grand comme un pongo qui essayait de se faire tout petit sur
un banc de tramway. Il essayait d'abandonner sur ce banc crasseux de tramway
ses jambes gigantesques et ses mains tremblantes de boxeur affamé. Et tout
l'avait laissé, le laissait. Son nez qui semblait une péninsule en dérade et sa
négritude même qui se décolorait sous l'action d'une inlassable mégie. Et le

mégissier était la Misère. Un gros oreillard subit dont les coups de griffes sur ce visage s'étaient cicatrisés en îlots scabieux. Ou plutôt, c'était un ouvrier infatigable, la Misère, travaillant à quelque cartouche hideux. On voyait très bien comment le pouce industrieux et malveillant avait modelé le front en bosse, percé le nez de deux tunnels parallèls et inquiétants, allongé la démesure de la lippe, et par un chef-d'oeuvre caricatural, raboté, poli, verni la plus miniscule mignonne petite oreille de la création.

. . . Un nègre comique et laid et des femmes derrière moi ricanaient en le regardant.

Il était COMIQUE ET LAID,

COMIQUE ET LAID pour sûr.

J'arborai un grand sourire complice. . . .

Ma lâcheté retrouvée!" Ibid.

55   My own sense is that Césaire is invoking Africa and this man as an African. On a literal level, the massive body of the man seems deliberately drawn to recall the size and grandeur of the African continent, juxtaposed against the terrifying poverty of a large sector of the population. Both Césaire and Fanon have noted that the French fail to distinguish between Caribbeans and Africans anyway: both are black and therefore inferior. Regardless of this man's actual origin, therefore, he stands in for Africa in the eyes of the Western subject.

56   Of course, the trope of the mask is far more complex than I have rendered here. I do want to explain, however, that just as the "African mask" functions as a synecdoche for Africa in Western discourse, the discourse and counterdiscourse on the mask use it as a synecdoche for the whole Black body. That is to say, as Césaire's unsettling passage reveals, the whole body of the African is subject to a discourse on deformity and disproportionate members.

57   "ceux qui n'ont inventé ni la poudre ni la boussole
ceux qui n'ont jamais su dompter la vapeur ni l'électricité
ceux qui n'ont exploré ni les mers ni le ciel mais ceux
sans qui la terre ne serait pas la terre
. . . pour ceux qui n'ont jamais rien inventé
pour ceux qui n'ont jamais rien exploré
pour ceux qui n'ont jamais rien dompté
mais ils s'abandonnent, saisis à l'essence de toute chose
ignorants des surfaces mais saisis par le mouvement de toute chose
insoucieux de dompter, mais jouant le jeu du monde
véritablement les fils aînés du monde
poreux à tous les souffles du monde
aire fraternelle de tous les souffles du monde. . . ."
The Collected Poetry, 64–68.

58   At the same time, one might wonder why, in these lines of invocation, Césaire uses "Ceux qui n'ont," rather than "les noirs qui n'ont . . . "—in other words, his refusal to race his subjects offers up tantalizing ambiguities.

59   "Et à moi mes danses/mes danses de mauvais nègre/À moi mes danses/la danse

brise-carcan/la danse saute-prison/la danse il-est-beau-et-bon-et-légitime-
d'être-nègre/À moi mes danses et saute le soleil sur la raquette de mes mains."
Ibid., 82.

60 "je te livre ma conscience et son rythme de chair
je te livre les feux où brasille ma faiblesse
je te livre le chain-gang
je te livre le marais
je te livre l'intourist du circuit triangulaire
dévore vent
. . . mais alors embrasse
comme un champ de justes filaos
le soir
nos multicolores puretés
et lie, lie-moi sans remords
lie-moi de tes vastes bras à l'argile lumineuse
lie ma noire vibration au nombril même du monde
lie, lie-moi, fraternité âpre
puis, m'étranglant de son lasso d'étoiles
monte,
Colombe
monte
monte
monte
Je te suis, imprimée en mon ancestrale cornée blanche.
monte lécheur de ciel
et la grand trou noir où je voulais me noyer l'autre lune
c'est là que je veux
pêcher maintenant la langue
maléfique de la nuit en son immobile verrition!"
Ibid., 82–84.

61 Du Bois, *The Souls of Black Folk*, 215.

3. SOME WOMEN DISAPPEAR

1 The goals of this chapter are to show how Fanon's mask offers a critique of
idealist formations and a call to action and to analyze how Fanon's discourse
helped to perpetuate the exclusion of women from the counterdiscourse of
subjectivity (an exclusion derived in large part from Western discourses on the
nation).

2 "Nous attachons une importance fondamentale au phénomène du langage.
C'est pourquoi nous estimons nécessaire cette étude qui doit pouvoir nous livrer
un des éléments de compréhension de la dimension *pour-autrui* de l'homme de
couleur. Etant entendu que parler, c'est exister absolument pour l'autre. Le Noir
a deux dimensions. L'une avec son congénère, l'autre avec le Blanc. Un Noir se

comporte différément avec un Blanc et avec un autre Noir. Que cette scissiparité soit la conséquence directe de l'aventure colonialiste, nul doute. . . . Qu'elle nourisse sa veine principale au coeur des différentes théories qui ont voulu faire du Noir le lent acheminement du singe à l'homme, personne ne songe à le contester. Ce sont des évidences objectives, qui expriment la réalité." Fanon, *Peau noire*, 13.

3 Césaire also lived and studied in Paris, so their respective differences cannot be determined along the lines of colony and metropolis.

4 Fanon uses the word "congénère," which means both an animal who is a member of the same group or species or a type of muscle. I use the term "compatriot" to extend Fanon's literal meaning, but I wish to call attention to the exact term in French, particularly the first definition.

5 "L'affirmation théoretique et pratique de la suprématie du Blanc est la thèse: la position de la négritude comme valeur antithétique est le moment de la négativité." Fanon, *Peau noire*, 107.

6 Ibid., 14.

7 "On comprend que la première action du Noir soit une réaction, et puisque le Noir est apprecié en reference à son degré d'assimilation, on comprend aussi que le debarqué ne s'exprime qu'en français. C'est qu'il tend à souligner la rupture qui s'est désormais produite." Ibid., 75.

8 Of course, white Americans were also foreign to North America but, as my second chapter indicates, that is *not* how they viewed themselves. This idea of the white as native to North America is still in force today. By contrast, the majority of British and French colonizers in the Caribbean were loath to equate themselves with the islands, which they considered as fierce and as strange as the Black slaves they had brought with them. Both the space and the slaves were "exotics," Others-from-without.

9 Conniff and Davis, *Africans in the Americas*, 73.

10 Tellingly, the French language (like the German) has only one word for the English terms "Negro" and "nigger." I do not want to anticipate Fanon and use one term over the other. In any event, given the context, it makes little difference which word the little girl meant to use.

11 "J'existais en triple: j'occupais de la place. J'allais à l'autre . . . et l'autre évanescent, hostile mais non opaque, transparent, absent, disparaissait. J'étais tout à la fois responsable de mon corps, responsable de ma Race, de mes ancêtres. Je promenais sur moi un regard objectif, D'ecouvris ma noirceur, mes caractères ethniques." Fanon, *Peau noir*, 90.

12 It is worthwhile to point out the difference of alterity that Fanon perceives. As he becomes Other in this white company, he notes that, although he is hostile, at least he is not transparent, evanescent, absent. This might indicate the influence of the Hegelian discourse of the Other-as-void.

13 *Peau noire*, 6.

14 "Avant d'ouvrir le procès, nous tenons à dire certaines choses. L'analyse que nous

entreprenons est psychologique. Il demeure toutefois évident que pour nous la véritable désalienation du Noir implique une prise de conscience abrupte de réalités économiques et sociales. S'il y a complexe d'infériorité, c'est à la suite d'un double processus:

—économiques d'abord

—par intériorisation ou, mieux, épidermisation de cette infériorité, ensuite." Ibid., 8.

15 Diana Fuss, "Interior Colonies."

16 See her introduction to *Frantz Fanon*.

17 "Il l'entreprendra et la mènera non pas après une analyse marxiste ou idéaliste, mais parce que, tout simplement, il ne pourra concevoir son existence que sous les espèces d'une combat mené contre l'exploitation, la misére et la faim." *Peau noire*, 181–82.

18 "Parler une langue, c'est assumer un monde, une culture. L'Antillais qui veut être blanc le sera d'autant plus qu'il aura fait sien l'instrument culturel qu'est le langage."

19 As many postcolonial and minority scholars have pointed out, the West has yet to drop its centuries-old formula of justifying violent incursions into other nations by claiming to save the nonwhite woman from the nonwhite man.

20 Du Bois, *The Souls of Black Folk*, 4.

21 " 'Maman, regarde le nègre, j'ai peur!' Peur! Peur! Voilà qu' on se mettait à me craindre. Je voulus m'amuser jusqu'à m'étouffer, mais cela m'était devenu impossible. Je ne pouvais plus, car je savais déjà qu'existaient des légendes, des histoires, l'histoire, et surtout l'*historicité*, que m'avait enseignée Jaspers. Alors le schéma corporel, attaqué en plusieurs points, s'écroula, cédant la place à un schéma épidermique racial. Dans le train, il ne s'agissait plus d'une connaissance de mon corps en troisième person, mais en triple personne. Dans le train, au lieu d'une, on me laissait deux, trois places. Déjà je ne m'amusais plus. Je ne découvrais point de coordonnées fébriles du monde." Fanon, *Peau noire*, 90. See note 11.

22 See chapter 2 for the full text of the tramway scene.

23 McClintock, *Imperial Leather*, 31.

24 Harris, ed., *The LeRoi Jones/Amiri Baraka Reader*, 79–80.

25 Wallace, "Variations on Negation and the Heresy of Black Feminist Creativity," 124–38.

26 In part two of a two-part article from the January 1989 issue of the *Atlantic Monthly*, titled "The Unfinished War," Nicholas Lemann describes the reaction to the report as "bitterly, wildly, unreasoningly hostile," partly because "[Moynihan] had grown up partly in the slums himself, and was raised by a single mother. He knew what the world was like." Lemann asserts that the report was rejected because Moynihan "had come up against the black power movement, which did not like it when a white man described black society as being somehow ruined, and also against the white left, which was becoming less sympathetic to the idea that the values of middle-class America—the values that had

gotten us into Vietnam—were so noble that poor people ought to embrace them," 60.

27 Gray-White, *Too Heavy a Load*, 217.

28 Dubey, *Black Women Novelists and the Nationalist Aesthetic*, 17.

29 To be clear without leaving the reader catatonic, I will simply say that an "assumption of homogeneity" is not unlike strategic essentialism, but not wholly selfsame with it.

30 Condé, "Pan-Africanism, Feminism and Culture," 65.

31 Lorde, *Showing Our Colors*, xiii–xiv.

32 Gilroy, *The Black Atlantic*, 15.

33 See Gikandi's "Introduction: Africa, Diaspora, and the Discourse of Modernity" and Barnes's "Black Atlantic—Black America" in the "Black Atlantic" issue of *Research in African Literatures* (winter 1996).

4. *HOW I GOT OVAH*

1 Wallace, "Variations on Negation," 125.

2 Ibid. Obviously, I disagree with Wallace's claim that Black feminists tend to avoid theory, 132–33.

3 Bakhtin, "Forms of Time," in Holquist, ed., *The Dialogic Imagination: Four Essays by M. S. Bakhtin*, 91. My emphasis.

4 Neal, "The Black Arts Movement," 184–85.

5 Ibid., 186.

6 See Phillip Harper's *Are We Not Men?*, in which he discusses the deployment of this binary in Black Arts poetry.

7 This patriarchal narrative also fails to take into account the many men who "stray" and produce children with women of a different race.

8 This is my theoretical conclusion, but it is hardly definitive, as of late there has been renewed interest in Hegel's master-slave dialectic and its implications vis-à-vis subjectivity and the subaltern.

9 *Black Women Novelists*, 7.

10 Rodgers does not specify denomination, nor does it seem important, as what is stressed is the history and connection the Black church has had with its Black community since the slave era.

11 "It is impossible to assess the actual merit of Carolyn Rodgers' achievements at this point. And it is difficult to see where she will go from here. She has changed from a rebel to a religious royalist, but a religious royalist of a peculiarly different state was present from the start. . . . Her frantic search for love, the constant battle with her mother, the ambiguity of religion, are factors that run wild in her soul." Parker-Smith, "Running Wild in Her Soul," 408.

12 See Phillip Bryan Harper's chapter on the Black Arts movement in *Are We Not Men?*

13 Carolyn M. Rodgers, *How I Got Ovah*, 1.

14 Of course, the ideal white woman had straight hair.

15 The resemblance of "ovah" to female eggs, ova, reveals the connection of the female gender with revolution, empowerment, and biological reproduction. My thanks to both Melissa Waldman and Anne Poduska for this observation.

16 In this particular case, the dialectic is powered by *Sehnsucht*, or yearning, rather than *Aufhebung*, or overcoming. In other words, the Black theorists discussed in chapter 2 do not understand the ideal and material as inherently opposed to one another but as seeking to unite with one another. By contrast, Rodgers and Lorde understand them as always already conflated and never separate.

17 As Michael Holquist puts it, the "Greenwich Mean Chronotope" is "a standard time for orienting other time/space relations that are appropriate to the discussion of a given text" (*Dialogism*, 121).

18 *How I Got Ovah*, 8.

19 This is likely a reference to Nikki Giovanni's observation in *Gemini* that white bank clerks like to deposit Black money, but it is quite a different story when the Black client attempts to withdraw his or her funds. In "A Revolutionary Tale" (also in *Gemini*), Giovanni comments sourly on the welfare office and its manifold attempts to withold funds from the rightful recipients, much in the way the mother in *How I Got Ovah* understands the social security board in the following stanza.

20 Rodgers, *How I Got Ovah*, 9–10.

21 Ibid., 21.

22 Ibid., 24–25.

23 Ibid., 56.

24 Ibid., 79.

25 Audre Lorde, *Coal*, 6.

26 Audre Lorde, *The Black Unicorn*, 3.

27 Ibid., 9.

28 In *Cables to Rage*, the original collection in which this poem appeared, the lightning presages the manifestation of feminine power within its latest, urban setting.

29 Lorde, *Coal*, 70.

30 See Gwendolyn Mikell, ed., *African Feminism*, for excellent essays on the patriarchal legacies of British colonial culture in sub-Saharan Africa.

31 Lorde, *Coal*, 13.

32 Ibid., 21.

33 Ibid., 27.

34 By "self-negating," I am referring to those extreme and yet not uncommon edges to the popular discourse on motherhood in which it is assumed a "good" mother would willingly sacrifice her own interests for that of the child. Too often, our discussion of fatherhood assumes that what is best for the father is also best for the child, or that it is natural for our papas to be rolling stones. We tend to be less forgiving of mothers who abandon their children.

35 Contrary to popular belief, a woman's reproductive organs play a much more active role: sperm does not select the egg, the egg selects which sperm it will

allow to penetrate its outer cell wall. The sperm does not then "fertilize" the egg, but, in breaking the cell wall, creates mitosis, or the splitting of cells, and imparts its DNA. While this may seem like a difference without a distinction, the truth is that mitosis can also be instigated through an electrical current, for example, and that the fetus does not require the DNA of the father to develop into a healthy, normal baby, only the DNA of its mother. This is not to darkly suggest that men can therefore be done away with, only that medical science has done little to dispel the popular myth that the female is the passive receptacle who can only conceive by being impregnated by a man, and that this myth has been deployed as the central basis for religious, political, and social discourses seeking to limit the freedoms of women. Like the race science of the nineteenth century, these discourses attempt to claim that they are only obeying the biological imperative, or the will of the divine, as manifested by nature.

36 Lorde, *The Black Unicorn*, 6.

37 Ibid., 112–13.

38 Lorde, *The Black Unicorn*, 118.

39 Moglen, "Redeeming History," 204.

40 Homans, "'Racial Composition': Metaphor and the Body in the Writing of Race," 201.

41 Ibid., 205.

42 Holquist, *Dialogism*, 18.

43 At least, men cannot *yet* give birth.

44 *How I Got Ovah*, 54. The back slash between "me" and "i" is within the actual line of the poem.

45 Because most African Americans (including myself) have not done the research to determine from which African nations our ancestors arrived, we end up using the wholly white categories "African" and/or "West African" in place of actual names, dates, and places. Another question lingers: if it is our ancestry, rather than a shared ideology or racist experience, that makes us "Black," what about the roughly 40 to 60 percent of "white" Americans who, known or more likely unbeknownst to themselves, also have Black ancestors? How accurate is it to locate them as Black subjects? The fact that neither of these questions has become central (or even marginal, to be truthful) to discourses on the Black subject in the West allows us to leave them by the wayside until they do become concrete concerns to Black identity—when either we face an onslaught of white Americans clamoring to be recognized as Black or staunch opposition from West Africans to the acknowledgment that diasporic Blacks have African ancestry.

5. THE URBAN DIASPORA

1 *Notes of a Native Son*, 174. I must add here that the West except in an idealist sense (to which Baldwin may have been referring), was never "white" to begin with.

2 Many references to this essay often misquote its title, placing an impersonal

pronoun where one does not exist, often a signal that the essay has been misinterpreted. In this essay, Baldwin argues (as he does in the other essays in this collection) that the Black in the West is a signifier for Western modernity, progress, and change. Many misinterpret this essay as a Baldwinian lament on the way in which he is read as a savage in a Swiss village.

3 It is important to note that, in the French countryside, "newly arrived" can mean within the last few centuries.

4 This lack of distinction may soon be a thing of the past. With the rise of Eastern European immigration following the destruction of the Berlin Wall, one can see an explicit return to a system in which those designated as "Slav," or Eastern European, are considered inferior to Western, or Aryan, "whites."

5 Katharina Oguntoye, May Ayim, and Dagmar Schultz, eds., *Farbe bekennen*, 9.

6 There are many terms currently circulating to describe Germans of African descent, rivaling even the multitude of terms we find in the United States: African-German (with or without the hyphen), Afro-German, Black German, Germans of color, or even simply German. The last three terms include all nonwhite Germans, while the first two generally refer only to those of African descent; here I will use the term "Afro-German," as it is this term, rather than the first, that I find used in the anthologies, autobiographies, and literature written by Germans of African descent.

7 Blackshire-Belay, ed., *The African-German Experience*, ix.

8 Lester, "Blacks in Germany and German Blacks," 114.

9 Oguntoye et al., *Farbe bekennen*, 51.

10 The passage continues, "This process did not begin with the Nazis or Hitler, but as early as the Weimar Republic. In addition to the barely acceptable names 'half-breed' and 'mulatto,' the pejorative label 'bastard' was used unreservedly to describe Afro-German children. In 1927, the Society for Racial Hygiene even began discussing the possibility of sterilizing such children for 'eugenic reasons.' It is impossible to determine how many Afro-German children were sterilized at this time. It is known, however, that by the mid-1920s the Imperial Ministry had already considered handing over Afro-German children to mission societies, with enough financial support to send them abroad" (181).

11 Robert W. Kesting, "Forgotten Victims," 33.

12 The German title, "daheim unterwegs," most likely a reference to a line in the poem "entfernte verbindungen" (distanced ties) by the poet May Ayim, is a deliberate oxymoron, in that "daheim" means "at home" while "unterwegs" means "on the way" or "in transit." I have chosen the second definition for "unterwegs" in order to underscore what I believe both the author and the poet are suggesting: that they are seeking a home in their very own country. "On the way home," of course, does not highlight this ironic paradox. The English translation of this autobiography is titled *Invisible Woman*.

13 I have not discussed Massaquoi's autobiography in this section, as its focus is largely on his survival during the war years rather than questions of race and nationality.

14 In the English translation of *Showing Our Colors*, Helga Emde writes, "As a child I saw only Black soldiers, and I ran away from them in fear and terror. This fear clearly shows that I must have internalized the prejudices and racism of my surroundings at a very early stage" (101–02). Not all Afro-Germans have white mothers and Black fathers; many, such as Julia Berger and Katharine Oguntoye, had West African or Afro-German mothers and fathers.

15 In " 'German Brown Babies Must Be Helped' " Yara-Colette Lemke Muniz de Faria writes about the hundreds of World War II *Besatzungskinder* who were almost immediately put up for adoption by their white German mothers. Interestingly, African American families adopted many of these children.

16 "In den ersten Tagen nach dem 9. November 1989 bermerkte ich, daß kaum Immigrantinnen und Schwarze Deutsche im Stadtbild zu sehen waren, zumindest nur selten solche mit dunkler Hautfarbe. Ich fragte mich, wie viele Jüdinnen (nicht) auf der Straße waren. Ein paar Afro-Deutsche, die ich im Jahr zuvor in Ostberlin kennengelernt hatte, liefen mir zufällig über den weg, und wir freuten uns, nun mehr Begegnungsmoglichkeiten zu haben. Ich war allein unterwegs, wollte ein bißchen von der allgemeinen Begeisterung einatmen, den historischen Moment spüren und meine zurückhaltende Freude teilen. Zurückhaltend deshalb, weil ich von den bevorstehenden Verschärfungen in der Gesetzgebung für ImmigrantInnen und Zufluchtsuchende gehört hatte. Ebenso wie andere Schwarze Deutsche und ImmigrantInnen wußte ich, daß selbst ein deutscher Paß keine Einlandungskarte zu den Ost-West-Feierlichkeiten darstellte. Wir spürten, daß mit der bevorherstehenden innerdeutschen Vereinigung eine zunehmende Abgrenzung nach außen einhergehen würde—ein Außen, das uns einschließen würde. Unsere Beteiligung am Fest war nicht gefragt.

Das neue "Wir" in—wie es Kanzler Kohl zu formulieren beliebt—"diesem unserem Lande" hatte und hat keinen Platz für alle.

"Hau ab du Neger, hast du kein Zuhause?"

Zum ersten Mal, seit ich in Berlin Lebte, mußte ich mich nun beinahe täglich gegen unverblümte Beleidigungen, feindliche Blicke und/oder offen rassistische Diffamierungen zur Wehr setzen." Ayim, *Grenzenlos und unverschämt*, 90–91.

17 Oguntoye et al., *Farbe bekennen*, 181, 165.

18 I have often traded anecdotes with other African Americans about conversations with white Germans in which they jokingly suggest our nonwhite coloring is due to eating too much chocolate or drinking too much Coca-Cola.

19 As the succeeding sections of this chapter will show, France and Britain are not entirely homologous in their racial discourse, either to one another or to the United States.

20 Oguntoye et al., *Farbe bekennen*, 150, 151.

21 That is to say, I do not think that the wholesale rejection of a Black citizenry is natural to any Northern European nation. Despite the much smaller presence of Black Swedes and Black Danes (the majority of whom, like Afro-Germans, are biracial), metropolitan Danes and Swedes tend to assume that those Blacks who are obviously biracial are in fact Danish and Swedish and will speak to them in

their native language. To my knowledge, the only other Western European nation that conceives its citizenry as wholly antithetical (perhaps even more so than Germany) to Blackness is Austria, which of course has a long and overlapping history with Germany.

22 Indeed, many German academics working on African American and/or African diasporic culture and history complain about the hostility of their colleagues in acknowledging Afro-Germans as a "legitimate" minority, much less an actual and productive presence within German borders. The categories of Others-from-within and Others-from-without achieve a different resonance when applied to those whites who are enthusiastic supporters and/or students of antiracism, African and/or African diasporic literatures, histories, and cultures *outside* their nation but remain traditionally hostile and derogatory of "*their* niggers."

23 "The self-portraits and the poetry presented by the women [in *Farbe bekennen*] reveal that a braiding of the plural selves has occurred in varying degrees—in some cases still rather tenuously—but the fact that it has begun to take place within this marginalized group and the manner in which it is expressed call attention to issues of racism and sexism which parallel those raised elsewhere in feminist literature and in African-American Studies." Hodges, "The Private/Plural Selves of Afro-German Women and the Search for a Public Voice," 222.

24 As I was writing this book, only two had been published, although readers now have Tina Campt's new book on the discourse of Afro-German identity through World War II, *Other Germans*.

25 I am assuming the interlocutor is a man because in "Afro-Deutsch II," which seems to continue the one-sided conversation, the speaker makes a sexist comment.

26 May Ayim, *Blues in Schwarz weiss* (Blues in Black and White), 18, although Ayim has a triple word play here through homonyms. In German, "white" is "Weiß," and the first-person conjugation of "to know" in the present tense is weiß, offering the (loosely translated) alternative title of *Blues in Black Knowing*.

27 Ibid, 19. German grammar makes it impossible to honor the line break without rendering the lines unreadable in English.

28 The practice of training light-skinned Blacks to work as administrators, missionaries, and educators—representatives of white civilization to their darker (and therefore less civilized) fellow colonials—was undertaken in French, British, and German colonies in Africa, as well as in the United States.

29 Carl Peters is the German version of the Great White Hunter, famous in both literature and film.

30 One will also find the term "African German," although I have only heard it used by African Americans, not by Black Germans.

31 Transliterated "Initiative of Black Germans and Blacks in Germany."

32 "ADEFRA ist ein Forum in dem wir als Schwarze Frauen gemeinsam unsere Stärken entwickeln und unsere Identitäten entfalten können. Wesentliche Schwerpunkte sind daher die Auseinandersetzung mit Geschichte(n), Kulture(n) und Lebensrealitäten Schwarzen Frauen (in der BRD und weltweit) und

mit unseren Gemeinsamkeiten und Unterschieden (Alter, Sozialisten, Herkunft, Lebensform, etc.). Wichtig für uns ist dabei auch, die Perspektive Schwarzer Frauen in Bezug auf Politik und Geschichte öffentlich zu machen."

33 Maryse Condé has also been an active contact and supporter.

34 In fact, the majority of German and American scholarly engagements with contemporary Afro-German discourses focus on the interaction between minority, gender, and sexual identities, an intersection reflected in many of the autobiographical sketches from *Farbe bekennen* and Hügel-Marshall's personal narrative.

35 The term "Black British," while common to the scholarship in this field, is not used by very many Blacks in Britain.

36 Barnor Hesse, ed., *Un/settled Multiculturalisms*: 98–99.

37 Indeed, as Ivan Van Sertima's *The African Presence in Early Modern Europe* notes, there is evidence that West African travelers may have reached Northern England before Caesar.

38 It should be pointed out that the overwhelming majority of the *Windrush* immigrants were men.

39 These settings are also amenable to a more Foucauldian reading of institutional discourses and their deployment of power, although one would have to revise Foucault (like Ann Laura Stoler's *Race and the Education of Desire*) to include that one category he refuses to engage except superficially: race.

40 *The Unbelonging*, 84.

41 Quote by Joan Riley on the jacket cover of the 1985 edition.

42 Naomi King, *O.P.P.*, 147–48.

43 Andrea Levy, *Fruit of the Lemon*, 127–28.

44 Ibid., 130.

45 King, *O.P.P.*, 212.

46 Jo Hodges, *The Girl with Brains in Her Feet*, 195.

47 The difference between West Indian and South Asian identity, of course, conflates with the identities of those residents of Jamaica who can also claim South Asian ancestry.

48 King, *O.P.P.*, 216.

49 Levy, *Fruit*, 162.

50 Guy Fawkes was an antiroyalist revolutionary who is commemorated on the day his revolt against James I in 1605 was defeated and Fawkes was killed, November 5.

51 Levy, *Fruit*, 339.

52 Ibid., 3.

53 The one exception is Faith's gay boss in the costume department at the BBC. Although he is clearly able to locate and define racist discourse, his interest in contravening and/or condemning the discourse and/or practice is less clear.

54 Bennett's poem is anthologized in Proctor, ed., *Writing Black Britain, 1948–1998*, 16–17.

55 Dayan, "Paul Gilroy's Slaves, Ships, and Routes," 9.

56 Miles, "Explaining Racism in Contemporary Europe," 194–95.

57 Hargreaves and McKinney, eds., "The Post-Colonial Presence in France," 12.

58 Jules-Rosette, *Black Paris*, 2.

59 Adotevi, *Négritude et négrologues*, 216.

60 "L'Écriture décentrée rendrait compte de développements à l'intérieur de l'Hexagone d'une littérature marquée par des différences linguistique et culturelles ancrées en partie dans l'origine étrangère des écrivains." *L'écriture decentrée*, 7.

61 It is still a matter of some debate in the United States and Europe as to whether *any* stereotype, given its reductive logic, can be positive. While most Americans who identify as antiracist find little or no redeeming qualities in stereotypes, their political allies in Europe insist that the issue is more complicated, pointing to a more diverse set of origins and usages of the stereotype than one will find in the United States.

62 "At times, what is fixed and immobile is manipulated in an apparently apolitical moment of humorous transgression; at other times, the most basic level of originality is abandoned and replaced by sentences that even the most conventional author would probably refuse to take credit for. Throughout the texts, stereotypes stand out as though framed and displayed in a gallery, but they are never discussed, criticized, or denied. No attempt is ever made to substitute a racial slur with a (still racial) compliment. No book could be further from the reappropriative choices of some proponents of Negritude, for example. Whether the stereotype is flattering or insulting, the texts treat it in a similar manner." Rosello, *Declining the Stereotype*, 134.

63 "A peine les territoires d'outre-mer étaient-ils emancipé de l'ancienne métropole que cette vision unanimiste de la culture nègre allait voler en éclats, tandis qu'à la passion de la Négritude succédait l'ère des désillusions. Les années soixant-dix donnent en effet naissance à une nouvelle littérature qui prend ses distances vis-à-vis des idées et des positions défendues par Léopold Senghor et ses amis—cela est particulièrement visible dans le discours théorique des intellectuels, philosophes, historiens . . . tels Marcien Sowa, Stanislas Adotevi, Joseph Ki-Zerbo, Paulin Hountoundji . . .—et dans laquelle les thèmes du conflit des cultures et de la quête de l'identité perdue cèdent peu à peu la place à la satire sociale et politique et à l'analyse des mutations d'une monde en pleine crise." (Scarcely were the overseas territories emancipated from the old metropolis that the unanimous vision of Black culture flew into pieces, while Negritude's passion was succeeded by an era of disillusionment. The 1970s gave birth, in effect, to a new literature that distanced itself from the ideas and positions defended by Léopold Senghor and his friends—this is particularly visible in the theoretical discourses of intellectuals and historians such as Marcian Sowa, Stanislas Adotevi, Joseph Ki-Zerbo, Paulin Hountoundji—and where the themes of cultures conflict and the search for a lost identity give way more and more to social and political satire and to the analysis of the mutations of a world clearly in crisis.) Chevrier, *La littérature nègre*, 12.

64 Jules-Rosette, *Black Paris*, 145.

65 Ibid., 179.

66   For more details on Bayala and the controversy surrounding her works, see Nicki Hitchcott, "Calixthe Beyala and the Post-Colonial Woman."

67   "Moïse referma la porte sans répondre. L'une de ses occupations favorites était d'aller s'allonger pendant les beaux jours sur l'herbe du parc Monceau, à lire des poèmes de Guillaume Apollinaire. Étienne avait pris l'habitude de le rejoindre et entamait derechef un discours sur la reconnaissance de l'art nègre par les sur-réalistes. S'ensuivait une bonne engueulade sur les notions d'apollien et de dionysaque. Tout se déroulait selon un rituel soigneusement établi. Étienne commençait par une critique en règle du poète, qu'il étendait ensuite aux sur-réaliste et à tout l'art français contemporain. Moïse répondait invariablement que si les nègres avaient été plus futés, plutôt que de crier aux voleurs, ils auraient inventé eux-même leurs propres théories, qu'ils auraient opposées à celles des Occidentaux. Au lieu de cela, quelques-uns qui s'étaient crus les plus malins avaient brandi le spectre de ce qu'ils baptisèrent la négritude.
      —Vois-tu, concluait-il enfin, des mots comme négritude, ça fait pas assez scientifique. Pas assez vrai. Zoulouique ou peulidien. Voilà des mots qui sonnent juste." Simon Njami, *African Gigolo*, 30–31.

68   "Cette fille avait dans le sang ce patriotisme désuet des déclassés, des paumés, qui fantasmaient leur continent plutôt que de le vivre. Au moins, songeait-il avec soulagement, ai-je échappé à cette mièvrerie-là. Il avait baptisé cette espèce de maladie . . . le 'complexe du métis'." Ibid., 138.

69   Jules-Rosette, *Black Paris*, 166.

BIBLIOGRAPHY

Abel, Elizabeth, Barbara Christian, and Helene Moglen, eds. *Female Subjects in Black and White: Race, Psychoanalysis, Feminism*. Berkeley: University of California Press, 1997.

ADEFRA homepage: http://www.woman.de/adefra.html.

Adotevi, Stanislas. *Négritude et négrologues*. Paris: LeCastor Astral, 1998.

Apostolos-Cappadona, Diane, and Lucinda Ebersole, eds. *Women, Creativity, and the Arts: Critical and Autobiographical Perspectives*. New York: Continuum, 1997.

Ashcroft, Bill, Gareth Griffiths, Helen Tiffin and Sarah Menin. *The Empire Writes Back: Theory and Practice in Post-Colonial Literatures*. New York: Routledge, 1989.

Avineri, Shlomo. *Hegel's Theory of the Modern State*. London: Cambridge University Press, 1972.

Ayim, May. *Blues in Schwarz weiss*. Berlin: Orlanda Frauenverlag, 1995.

———. *Grenzenlos und unverschämt*. Berlin: Orlanda Frauenverlag, 1997.

Balibar, Etienne, and Immanuel Wallerstein. *Race, Nation, Class: Ambiguous Identities*. Translated by Chris Turner. New York: Verso, 1991.

Baraka, Imamu Amiri. *"Dutchman" and "The Slave": Two Plays*. New York: Morrow, 1964.

Barnes, Natasha. "Black Atlantic—Black America." In the "Black Atlantic" issue of *Research in African Literatures* 27, no. 4 (winter 1996): 106–7.

Bernal, Martin. *Black Athena: The Afroasiatic Roots of Classical Civilization*. New Brunswick: Rutgers University Press, 1987.

Beyala, Calixthe. *Le petit prince de Belleville*. Paris: A. Michel, 1992.

———. *Maman a un amant*. Paris: A. Michel, 1993.

Bhabha, Homi K. "Anxious Nations, Nervous States." *Critical Inquiry* 6 (winter 1991): 204.

Biddiss, Michael. *Father of Racist Ideology: The Social and Political Thought of Count Gobineau*. London: Weidenfeld and Nicholson, 1970.

Blackshire-Belay, Carol Aisha, ed. *The African-German Experience: Critical Essays*. Westport, Conn.: Praeger, 1996.

Brody, Jennifer DeVere. *Impossible Purities: Blackness, Femininity, and Victorian Culture*. Durham: Duke University Press, 1998.

Campt, Tina M. *Other Germans: Black Germans and the Politics of Race, Gender, and Memory in the Third Reich.* Ann Arbor: University of Michigan Press, 2003.

Carby, Hazel. *Race Men.* Cambridge: Harvard University Press, 1998.

Cassirer, William. *The Myth of the Modern State.* New Haven: Yale University Press, 1946.

Castradori, Francesca. *Le radici dell'odio: Il Conte de Gobineau e le origini del razzismo.* Milan: Xenia Edizioni, 1991.

Ceasar, James. *Reconstructing America: The Symbol of America in Modern Thought.* New Haven: Yale University Press, 1997.

Césaire, Aimé. *Aimé Césaire: The Collected Poetry.* Translated by Clayton Eshleman and Annette Smith. Berkeley: University of California Press, 1983.

———. *Cahier d'un retour au pays natal.* Paris: Hatier, 1978.

———. Interview by René Depestre at the Cultural Congress of Havana in 1967. Translated from the Spanish by Maro Riofrancos and translated by Joan Pinkham. *Discourse on Colonialism.* New York: Montly Review Press, 1972.

Chandler, Nahum Dimitri. "The Economy of Desedimentation: W. E. B. Du Bois and the Discourse of the Negro." *Callaloo* 19 no. 1 (1996): 78–93.

Chevrier, Jacques. *La littérature nègre.* 2d ed. Paris: Armand Colin, 1999.

Condé, Maryse. "Pan-Africanism, Feminism, and Culture." In *Imagining Home: Class, Culture, and Nationalism in the African Diaspora,* edited by S. Lemelle and R. D. G. Kelley. New York: Verso, 1994.

Conniff, Michael L., and Thomas J. Davis. *Africans in the Americas: A History of the Black Diaspora.* New York: St. Martin's, 1994.

Dayan, Joan. "Paul Gilroy's Slaves, Ships, and Routes: The Middle Passage as Metaphor." *Research in African Literatures. The Black Atlantic* 27, no. 4 (winter 1996): 9.

Delanty, Gerard. *Inventing Europe: Idea, Identity, Reality.* New York: St. Martin's, 1995.

de Gobineau, Comte Arthur. *Essai sur l'inegalité des races humaines.* Paris: Editions Gallimard, 1983.

———. *The Intellectual and Moral Diversity of Races.* Translated by Henry Hotz. Philadelphia: Lippincott, 1856.

Derrida, Jacques. *Positions.* Translated and annotated by Alan Bass. Chicago: University of Chicago Press, 1981.

Du Bois, W. E. B. *An ABC of Color.* New York: International Publishers, 1989.

———. *The Souls of Black Folk.* New York: Penguin, 1989.

Dubey, Madhu. *Black Women Novelists and the Nationalist Aesthetic.* Indianapolis: Indiana University Press, 1994.

Evans, Mari, ed. *Black Women Writers (1950–1980): A Critical Evaluation.* Garden City, N.Y.: Anchor/Doubleday, 1984.

Fanon, Frantz. *L'an de la révolution algérienne.* Paris: F. Maspero, 1966.

———. *Peau noire, masques blancs.* Paris: Éditions du Seuil, 1952.

———. *The Wretched of the Earth.* Translated by Constance Farrington. New York: Grove, 1965.

Finkelman, Paul. *Slavery and the Founders: Race and Liberty in the Age of Jefferson.* Armonk, N.Y.: M. E. Sharpe, 1996.

Forster, Michael. "Hegel's Dialectic Method." In *The Cambridge Companion to Hegel,* edited by Frederick C. Beiser. Cambridge: Cambridge University Press, 1993.

Frederickson, George M. *The Black Image in the White Mind: The Debate on the Afro-American Character and Destiny, 1817–1914.* Middletown, Conn.: Wesleyan University Press, 1971.

Friedman, Jonathan. "Nationalism in Theory and Reality." *Critical Review* 10, no. 2 (spring 1996): 155.

Fuss, Diana. "Interior Colonies: Frantz Fanon and the Politics of Identification." In *Identification Papers: Readings on Psychoanalysis, Sexuality, and Culture.* New York: Routledge, 1995.

Gasbarrone, Lisa. " 'The Locus for Other': Cixous, Bakhtin, and Women's Writing." In *A Dialogue of Voices: Feminist Literary Theory and Bakhtin,* edited by Karen Hohne and Helen Wussow. Minneapolis: University of Minnesota Press, 1994.

Gates, Henry Louis, Jr. *Figures in Black: Words, Signs, and the "Racial" Self.* New York: Oxford University Press, 1987.

——. *The Trials of Phillis Wheatley: America's First Black Poet and Encounters with the Founding Fathers.* New York: Basic Civitas Books, 2003.

Giddings, Paula. *When and Where I Enter: A History of Black Women in America.* New York: William Morrow, 1996.

Gikandi, Simon. "Introduction: Africa, Diaspora, and the Discourse of Modernity." In the "Black Atlantic" issue of *Research in African Literatures* 27, no. 4 (winter 1996): 1–6.

——. *Maps of Englishness: Writing Identity in the Culture of Colonialism.* New York: Columbia University Press, 1996.

Gilman, Sander L. *On Blackness Without Blacks: Essays on the Image of the Black in Germany.* Boston: G. K. Hall, 1982.

Gilroy, Paul. *The Black Atlantic: Modernity and Double Consciousness.* Cambridge: Harvard University Press, 1993.

Giovanni, Nikki. *Gemini: An Extended Autobiographical Statement on My First Twenty-Five Years of Being a Black Poet.* Indianapolis: Bobbs-Merrill, 1972.

Gray-White, Deborah. *Too Heavy a Load: Black Women in Defense of Themselves.* New York: Norton, 1999.

Grimm, Reinhold, and Jost Hermand, eds. *Blacks and German Culture.* Madison: University of Wisconsin Press, 1986.

Harper, Phillip Brian. *Are We Not Men?: Masculine Anxiety and the Problem of African-American Identity.* New York: Oxford University Press, 1996.

Harris, William J., ed. *The LeRoi Jones/Amiri Baraka Reader.* New York: Thunder's Mouth Press, 1993.

Hargreaves, Alec, and Mark McKinney, eds. "Introduction: The Post-Colonial Problematic in France." In *Post-Colonial Cultures in France.* New York: Routledge, 1997.

Headley, Victor. *Excess*. London: X Press, 1993.

——. *Fetish*. London: X Press, 1994.

——. *Yardie*. New York: Atlantic Monthly Press, 1993.

Hegel, Georg Wilhelm Friedrich. *Phänomenologie des Geistes*. Berlin: Akademie Verlag, 1998.

——. *Philosophy of History*. Translated by J. Sibree. New York: Dover, 1956.

——. *The Philosophy of Right*. Translated by T. M. Knox. Oxford: Oxford University Press, 1967.

——. *Vorlesungen über die Philosophie der Geschichte*, Werke 12. Frankfurt am Main: Suhrkamp Taschenbuch Verlag, 1970.

Henderson, Mae Gwendolyn. "Speaking in Tongues: Dialogics, Dialectics, and the Black Woman Writer's Literary Tradition." In *Changing Our Words: Essays on Criticism, Theory, and Writing by Black Women*, edited by Cheryl Wall. New Brunswick, N.J.: Rutgers University Press, 1989.

Hesse, Barnor, ed. *Un/settled Multiculturalisms: Diasporas, Entanglements, Transruptions*. London: Zed, 2000.

Hitchcott, Niki. "Calixthe Beyala and the Post-Colonial Woman." In *Post-Colonial Cultures in France*, edited by Alec Hargreaves and Mark McKinney. New York: Routledge, 1997.

Hodges, Carolyn. "The Private/Plural Selves of Afro-German Women and the Search for a Public Voice." Special issue, "The Image of Africa in German Society," of *Journal of Black Studies* 23, no. 2 (1992): 222.

Hodges, Jo. *The Girl with Brains in Her Feet*. London: Virago, 1998.

Hoffman, Leon-François. *Le Nègre Romantique: Personnage littéraire et obsession collective*. Paris: Payot, 1973.

Hohne, Karen, and Helen Wussov, eds. *A Dialogue of Voices: Feminist Literary Theory and Bakhtin*. Minneapolis: University of Minnesota Press, 1994.

Holquist, Michael, ed. *The Dialogic Imagination: Four Essays by M. S. Bakhtin*. Translated by Caryl Emerson and Michael Holquist. Austin: University of Texas Press, 1981.

——. *Dialogism: Bakhtin and His World*. New York: Routledge, 1990.

Homans, Margaret. " 'Racial Composition': Metaphor and the Body in the Writing of Race." In *Female Subjects in Black and White: Race, Psychoanalysis, Feminism*, edited by E. Abel et al. Berkeley: University of California Press, 1997.

Hügel-Marshall, Ika. *Invisible Woman: Growing Up Black in Germany*. Translated by Elizabeth Gaffney. New York: Continuum, 2001.

Jacobs, Harriet A. *Incidents in the Life of a Slave Girl*. Edited by Lydia Maria Child. New York: AMS Press, 1973.

James, Joy, and Tracey Denean Sharpley-Whiting, eds. *The Black Feminist Reader*. Malden, Mass.: Blackwell, 2000.

Jamison, Angelene. "Imagery in the Women Poems: The Art of Carolyn Rodgers." *Black Women Writers (1950–1980): A Critical Evaluation*, edited by Mari Evans. Garden City, N.Y.: Anchor Books, 1984.

Jefferson, Thomas. *Notes on the State of Virginia*. Trenton, N.J.: Wilson & Blackwell, 1803.

———. *The Portable Thomas Jefferson*. Edited by Merrill D. Peterson. New York: Viking Penguin, 1977.

Johnson, Linton Kwesi. *Tings an Times: Selected Poems*. Newcastle upon Tyne: Bloodaxe, 1991.

Jordan, Winthrop D. *The White Man's Burden: Historical Origins of Racism in the United States*. New York: Oxford University Press, 1974.

Jules-Rosette, Bennetta. *Black Paris: The African Writers' Landscape*. Chicago: University of Illinois Press, 1998.

Kay, Jackie. *The Adoption Papers*. Newcastle upon Tyne: Bloodaxe, 1991.

———. *Off Colour*. Newcastle upon Tyne: Bloodaxe, 1998.

———. *Other Lovers: Poems by Jackie Kay*. Newcastle upon Tyne: Bloodaxe, 1993.

———. *Trumpet*. New York: Pantheon, 1998.

Kesting, Robert W. "Forgotten Victims: Blacks in the Holocaust." *Journal of Negro History* 77, no. 1 (winter 1992): 30–36.

King, Naomi. *O.P.P.* London: X Press, 1992.

Lambert, Michael C. "From Citizenship to *Négritude*: 'Making a Difference' in Elite Ideologies in Francophone West Africa." *Comparative Studies in Society and History: An International Quarterly* 35, no. 2 (April 1993): 257–58.

Lamming, George. *The Emigrants*. Ann Arbor: University of Michigan Press, 1994.

———. *In the Castle of My Skin*. New York: Schocken, 1983.

Laronde, Michel. *L'écriture decentrée: Sous la langue de l'Autre dans le roman contemporain*. Paris: L'Harmattan, 1996.

Lefkowitz, Mary. *Not Out of Africa*. New York: Basic, 1997.

Lemann, Nicholas. "The Unfinished War." *Atlantic Monthly* (January 1989): 52–74.

Lester, Rosemary. "Blacks in Germany and German Blacks: A Little-Known Aspect of Black History." In *Blacks and German Culture*, edited by Reinhold Grimm and Jost Hermand. Madison: University of Wisconsin Press, 1986.

Levy, Andrea. *Every Light in the House Burnin'*. London: Review Press, 1994.

———. *Fruit of the Lemon*. London: Headline Books, London, 1999.

———. *Never Far from Nowhere*. London: Review Press, 1996.

Lewis, Martin W., and Kären E. Wigen. *The Myth of Continents*. Berkeley: University of California Press, 1997.

Little, Monroe H. Jr. "The Black Military Experience in Germany: From the First World War to the Present." In *Crosscurrents: African Americans, Africa, and Germany in the Modern World*, edited by David McBride et al. Columbia, S.C.: Camden House, 1998.

Lorde, Audre. *The Black Unicorn: Poems*. New York: Norton, 1978.

———. *Cables to Rage*. London: Paul Breman, 1973.

———. *Coal*. New York: Norton, 1970.

Maran, René. *Batouala*. Translated by Alvah C. Bessie. New York: Limited
    Editions Club, 1932.
Marshall, Paule. *Praisesong for the Widow*. New York: Putnam's, 1983.
Marx, Karl. *The Eighteenth Brumaire of Louis Bonaparte*. Translated by Eden and
    Cedar Paul. London: G. Allen & Unwin, 1926.
Massaquoi, Hans J. *Destined to Witness: Growing Up Black in Nazi Germany*. New
    York: William Morrow, 1999.
McBride, David, Leroy Hopkins, and Carol Aisha Blackshire-Belay, eds.
    Crosscurrents: African Americans, Africa, and Germany in the Modern World.
    Columbia, S.C.: Camden House, 1998.
McClintock, Anne. *Imperial Leather: Race, Gender, and Sexuality in the Colonial
    Contest*. New York: Routledge, 1995.
Mikell, Gwendolyn, ed. *African Feminism: The Politics of Survival in Sub-Saharan
    Africa*. Philadelphia: University of Pennsylvania Press, 1997.
Miles, Robert. "Explaining Racism in Contemporary Europe." In *Racism,
    Modernity, and Identity on the Western Front*, edited by Ali Rattansi and Sallie
    Westwood. Westwood, Mass.: Polity, 1994.
Miller, Christopher L. *Blank Darkness: Africanist Discourse in French*. Chicago:
    University of Chicago Press, 1985.
Moglen, Helene. "Redeeming History." In *Female Subjects in Black and White:
    Race, PsychoAnalysis, Feminism*, edited by E. Abel et al. Berkeley: University of
    California Press, 1997.
Morrison, Toni. *Beloved*. New York: Penguin, 2000.
Muniz de Faria, Yara-Colette Lemke. "German Brown Babies Must Be Helped."
    Callaloo 26, no. 2 (spring 2003): 342–62.
Naylor, Gloria. *Mama Day*. Boston: G.K. Hall, 1989.
Neal, Larry. "The Black Arts Movement." In *Within the Circle: An Anthology of
    African American Literary Criticism from the Harlem Renaissance to the
    Present*, edited by Angeline Mitchell. Durham: Duke University Press, 1994.
N'gal, Mbwil a Mpaang. *Aimé Césaire: Un homme à la recherche d'une patrie*.
    Dakar: Les Nouvelles Editions Africaines, 1975.
Nichols, Grace. *The Fat Black Woman's Poems*. London: Virago, 1984.
——. *Lazy Thoughts of a Lazy Woman and Other Poems*. London: Virago, 1989.
Njami, Simon. *African Gigolo*. Paris: Éditions Seghers, 1989.
Oguntoye, Katharina. *Eine afro-deutsche Geschichte: Zur Lebenssituation von
    Afrikanern und Afro-Deutschen in Deutschland von 1884 bis 1950*. Berlin: Hoho
    Verlag Christine Hoffmann, 1997.
Oguntoye, Katharina, May Opitz, and Dagmar Schultz, eds. *Farbe bekennen:
    Afro-deutsche Frauen auf den Spuren ihrer Geschichte*. Berlin: Orlanda
    Frauenverlages, 1986.
Opasan, Ola. *Many Rivers to Cross*. London: X Press, 1998.
Opitz, May, Katharina Oguntoye, and Dagmar Schultz, eds. *Showing Our Colors:
    Afro-German Women Speak Out*. Translated by Anne V. Adams. Amherst:
    University of Massachusetts Press, 1992.

Ouologuem, Yambo. *Le Devoir de violence*. Paris: Éditions du Seuil, 1968.

Pallister, Janis. *Aimé Césaire*. New York: Twayne, 1991.

Parker-Smith, Bettye J. "Running Wild in her Soul: The Poetry of Carolyn Rodgers." In *Black Women Writers (1950–1980)*, edited by Mari Evans. Garden City, N.Y.: Doubleday/Anchor, 1984.

Peabody, Sue. *"There Are No Slaves in France": The Political Culture of Race and Slavery in the Ancien Régime*. New York: Oxford University Press, 1996.

Proctor, James, ed. *Writing Black Britain, 1948–1998: An Interdisciplinary Anthology*. Manchester: Manchester University Press, 2000.

Rees, John. *The Algebra of Revolution: The Dialectic and the Classical Marxist Tradition*. London: Routledge, 1998.

Riley, Joan. *A Kindness to the Children*. London: Women's Press, 1992.

———. *The Unbelonging*. London: Women's Press, 1985.

Rodgers, Carolyn M. *How I Got Ovah: New and Selected Poems*. Garden City, N.Y.: Anchor, 1975.

———. "The Literature of Black." *Black World* (June 1970): 5–13.

Rosello, Mireille. *Declining the Stereotype: Ethnicity and Representation in French Cultures*. Hanover: University Press of New England, 1998.

Schneiders, Werner. *Aufklärung und Vorurteilskritik: Studien der Vorurteilsgeschicht*. Stuttgart-Bad Cannstatt: Frommann-Holzboog, 1983.

Senghor, Léopold Sédar. *Anthologie de la nouvelle poésie nègre et malgache de langue française*. Paris: Presses Universitaires de France, 1977.

———. *Ce Que Je Crois: Negritude, Francite et Civilisation de L'universel*. Paris: B. Grasset, 1988.

———. *The Collected Poetry: Léopold Sédar Senghor*. Translation and introduction by Melvin Dixon. Charlottesville, Va.: Caraf, 1991.

———. *Fondements de l'africanité ou Négritude et arabité*. Paris: Présence Africaine, 1967.

Senna, Danzy. *Caucasia*. New York: Riverhead, 1998.

Serequeberhan, Tsenay. "The Idea of Colonialism in Hegel's Philosophy of Right." *International Philosophical Quarterly* 29, no. 3 (September 1989): 301–318.

Sharpley-Whiting, T. Denean. *Frantz Fanon: Conflicts and Feminisms*. New York: Rowman and Littlefield, 1998.

Shohat, Ella, and Robert Stam. *Unthinking Eurocentrism: Multiculturalism and the Media*. New York: Routledge, 1994.

Smith, Adam. *An Inquiry into the Nature and Causes of the Wealth of Nations*. New York: A. M. Kelley, 1966.

Smith, Sidonie, and Julia Watson, eds. *Women, Autobiography, Theory: A Reader*. Madison: University of Wisconsin Press, 1998.

Smith, Zadie. *White Teeth*. London: Hamish Hamilton, 2000.

Stendhal. *Le rouge et le noir: Chronique de 1830*. Paris: Hatier, 1968.

Stoler, Ann Laura. *Race and the Education of Desire*. Durham: Duke University Press, 1995.

Thomas, Louis. *Arthur de Gobineau: Inventeur du Racisme (1816–1882)*. Paris: Mercure de France, 1941.

Todorov, Tzvetan. *On Human Diversity: Nationalism, Racism, and Exoticism in French Thought*. Cambridge: Harvard University Press, 1993.

Van Sertima, Ivan. *They Came Before Columbus*. New York: Random House, 1976.

Van Sertima, Ivan, ed. *The African Presence in Early Europe*. New Brunswick, N.J.: Transaction Publishers, 1985.

Wallace, Anthony F. C. *Jefferson and the Indians: The Tragic Fate of the First Americans*. Cambridge: Harvard University Press, 2001.

Wallace, Michele. "Variations on Negation and the Heresy of Black Feminist Creativity." *Women, Creativity, and the Arts: Critical and Autobiographical Perspectives*. New York: Continuum, 1997.

Williams, Robert R. *Recognition: Fichte and Hegel on the Other*. Albany: SUNY Press, 1992.

Wood, Allen W., ed. *Hegel's Philosophy of Right*. Translated by H. B. Nisbet. Cambridge: Cambridge University Press, 1986.

Wright, Michelle. "Nigger Peasants from France." *Callaloo* 22, no. 4 (1999): 831–852.

Zamir, Shamoon. *Dark Voices: W. E. B. Du Bois and American Thought, 1888–1903*. Chicago: University of Chicago Press, 1995.

INDEX

Ayim, May (*continued*)
257 n.25, 257 n.27; "Afro-Deutsch II,"
192, 197, 257 n.25; *Blues in schwarz
weiss*, 257 n.26; feminism of, 217; ventriloquism used by, 197; "Das Yahr
1990," 224

Baenga, Bolya, 216
Bakhtin, Mikhail: dialogic discourse of,
141–42, 143, 167; laughter used by, 159;
simplest time chronotope of, 12, 137–
38, 139
Baldwin, James: "Stranger in the Vil-
lage," 183–84, 254–55 n.2
Balibar, Etienne: *Race, Class, and Nation*,
7–8, 31–32
Banneker, Benjamin, 56–57
Baraka, Amiri, 11, 132, 140, 146, 147, 163;
Dutchman, 130–31
Barnes, Natasha, 134
Barthes, Roland, 215–16
Batouala (Maran), 216
Baum, Laura, 188, 190
Beloved (Morrison), 178–79
Bennett, Louise, 199; "Colonisation in
Reverse," 212–13
Berber writers, 215
Berger, Astrid, 188
Berger, Julia, 256 n.14
Berlin unification, 224
Besatzungskinder (Occupation Babies),
187, 256 n.15
"Between Ourselves" (Lorde), 173–76
beur authors, 215–16
Beyala, Calixthe, 217; *Maman a un
amant*, 225; *Le petit prince de Bell-
eville*, 225
Bhabha, Homi, 26, 37–38
Biddiss, Michael, 15, 46–47, 238 n.52
binaries, 38
biracial children, 139, 140–41, 180, 186,
252 n.7
Biyaoula, Daniel: *Agonies*, 25, 217, 221–
24, 225

Black Arts movement, 11–12; and gender,
132–33; negation of the negation in,
139–40; and patriarchal construction
of the Black nation, 130, 131; poetry of,
143–44, 162–63; successes of, 181–82.
See also Black mothers; *The Black
Unicorn; Coal; How I Got Ovah*
The Black Atlantic (Gilroy), 4, 6–7, 13,
180, 213
Black British, 197–214, 225, 226, 258 n.35
Black communities, 134. *See also* urban
diaspora
Black Danes, 256–57 n.21
Black female subject, absence of, 124–31,
132
Black feminists, 11–12, 136, 141–42, 216–
17, 230
Black identity in the West, 1–26; and
Black women, 10–13; counterdiscourses on, generally, 3–7, 24 (*see
also* Black mothers; masking; *specific
writings*); creating identity, 13–25; and
dialectic, 8–10; Gates on, 4–6; Gilroy
on, 4, 6–7; harmful/healing potential
of, 1, 2; and heteropatriarchal norms,
10–13, 229–31 (see also *The Black Unicorn; Coal; The Unbelonging*); hypercollective vs. hyperindividual, 2;
Kincaid on, 1, 2; Others-from-within
vs. Others-from-without, 7–8, 31–32,
64, 86–87, 233 n.4 (see also *Essay on
the Inequality of the Human Races;
Notes on the State of Virginia; Philosophy of History; The Souls of Black
Folk*); postcolonial theory from the
African diaspora, 25–26; and race, 6–
7; and racism, 1–2; and shared historical moment/cultural trope, 2–3; as a
social category, 6–7
"Black Is Beautiful," 148–49
Black mothers, 5; agency of, 139–41; vs.
Black nationalist constructions, 142;
and consciousness, 179; and dialectics/
dialogics, 136–44, 179–80; and the na-

tionalist myth, 12. See also *The Black
Unicorn; Coal; How I Got Ovah*
Black nationalist movement, 11–12, 111–
35; and Black mothers, 142; and masculine power, 140–41, 144; misogyny/
sexism of, 132, 138, 168, 177, 181; and
racial homogeneity, 140–41; simplest
time chronotope of, 12, 23, 138; successes of, 181–82; and women's agency
as mothers, 139–41. See also *Black
Skin, White Masks*
"Blackness" (Kincaid), 1, 2
Black Other, European/American invention of, 27–42; by Jefferson (see *Notes
on the State of Virginia*); logical fallacies in dialectic of, 8–10, 16; and nationalist discourse, 27–32, 233 n.1; the
Negro and the dialectic of race, 42–52;
Other-from-within vs. Other-from-
without, 7–8, 31–42, 64, 86–87 (see
also *Essay on the Inequality of the Human Races; Notes on the State of Virginia; Philosophy of History; The Souls
of Black Folk*); persistence of the Black
Other, 27; sociohistorical/theoretical
analysis of, 28; subjective agendas of,
52–53. *See also* Black Others, generally
Black Others, generally: counterdiscourses on, 3–7, 24 (*see also* Black
mothers; masking; *specific writings*);
and dialogic structures, 4; differences
among, 4, 7–8, 13, 24, 31, 233 n.4;
Gobineau on, 43–46, 237 n.40, 237
n.43; Hegel on, 44–46; male vs. female, 4; vs. white subjects, 4, 9. *See
also* Black Other, European/American
invention of; Others; *Philosophy of
History*
Black Power, 177, 181–82
Blacks: ancestry of, 254–55 n.45; artistic
abilities of, 48, 69, 85, 86, 87, 88, 92, 244
n.27; linguistic ability of, 87, 89–91, 245
n.36; physicality of, 90; suffering/vio-
lence of, 147, 156. *See also* Negro

Blackshire-Belay, Carol Aisha, 185
Black Skin, White Masks (Fanon), 9, 10,
111–35, 250 n.10; on action vs. logos,
120–21, 122–23; Algerian woman in,
116, 125; on *Aufhebung* (upheaval), 111;
on collective identity, 115–16; on the
colonialist logos, 20, 111–13, 250 n.4;
critical reception of, 67; female subject's erasure in, 19–20; on idealist vs.
materialist dialectic, 20, 111–12, 116,
117–20; influence of, 20; on language,
112–13, 115, 121–22; Marxist dialectic
in, 120–21; masking in, 19, 67, 112, 113–
14, 116–17, 120, 122–24; master/slave
dialectic in, 119–20, 122; methodology
of, 118–19; and Other-as-void, 250
n.12; on self/Other, 113, 115; on white
female as rejecting Black male, 20–21,
128–29; women without agency in, 139
Black Swedes, 256–57 n.21
The Black Unicorn (Lorde): on the
American nation/African diaspora,
161–62; "Between Ourselves," 173–76;
Black lesbian in, 162, 164; Black
mother in, 22–23, 175, 176–77, 178,
179–81; "The Black Unicorn," 163–64;
"Coniagui Women," 167; "Dahomey,"
167–68; demonization of men in, 180–
81; dialogic reading of, 162–63; "From
the House of Yemanja," 167, 173; "Future Promise," 176; human desire in,
162; on idealist fallacy in heteropatriarchal discourse, 22–23; "Oaxaca," 164–67, 168–69, 171, 253 n.28;
"125th Street and Abomey," 167; on
race, 163–64; "Solstice," 176; "The
Trollop Maiden," 176; "The Woman
Thing," 164–65, 168–69, 171, 172; "The
Women Can Dance with Swords in
Their Hands," 167
Black women: and Black identity in the
West, 10–13; erasure of, 124–31, 132, 136;
hairstyles of, 147–49; heterogeneity of,
141–42. *See also* Black mothers

Fanon, Frantz (*continued*)
  influence/popularity of, 19, 123; on
  the nation, 183; Negritude deployed
  by, 245 n.33; on recognition, negative
  aspect of, 142. See also *Black Skin,
  White Masks*
Farbe bekennen, 185, 187, 188, 190–91, 257
  n.23, 258 n.34
Fawkes, Guy, 210, 258 n.50
Fichte, Johann Gottlieb, 178
Figures in Black (Gates), 4–6, 37
Finkelman, Paul, 241 n.79
*Fondements de l'africanité ou Négritude
  et arabité* (Senghor), 88–92, 245
  nn.31–32
"for muh' dear" (Rodgers), 145–51, 155
Forster, Michael, 34
Foucault, Michel, 199
founding fathers, 140, 141
France: Africa's colonization by, 45; Blacks
  in, 30, 214–24, 225, 234 n.5, 257 n.28;
  Black troops from, 186; racial discourse
  in, 256 n.19; whiteness in, 184
Franklin, Benjamin, 54, 240 n.69
"From the House of Yemanja" (Lorde),
  167, 173
Fruit of the Lemon (Levy), 25, 199, 203–
  12, 213–14, 224, 226, 258 n.53
Fuss, Diana, 118, 121
"Future Promise" (Lorde), 176

Gadamer, Hans-Georg, 141, 143, 151
Gasbarrone, Lisa, 159
Gates, Henry Louis, Jr., 35, 81; *Figures in
  Black*, 4–6, 37
gay rights, 230
gender: and Black Arts movement, 132–
  33; and Black-white encounters, 126–
  27; and colonial identity formation,
  125–26. See also Black women; women
"Generations" (Lorde), 169–70, 171
Germany: Africa's colonization by, 45;
  Blacks in, 257 n.28 (see also Afro-
  Germans); citizenship in, 184; Ger-

manness in, 185; occupation of, 185,
  187; racist stereotypes in, 189–90;
  whiteness in, 184
Gikandi, Simon, 134; *Maps of Englishness*, 212–13
Gilroy, Paul: *The Black Atlantic*, 4, 6–7,
  13, 180, 213; on diasporic understanding of the Black subject, 195; on diasporic unity, 133–34; on Hegel's
  dialectic, 35
Giovanni, Nikki, 144, 253 n.19
The Girl with Brains in Her Feet (J.
  Hodges), 25, 199, 203–4, 206–8, 211–
  14, 224, 226
Gobineau, Arthur, Count de, 9; Césaire
  as influenced by, 85; dialectic of, 11; on
  the Negro artistic drive, 18; on the
  Negro as crazed, 147; on Oriental
  myths, 42, 236 n.36; Senghor as influ-
  enced by, 85; travelogues of, 238 n.53;
  whiteness categories of, 184. See also
  *Essay on the Inequality of the Human
  Races*
Goldschmidt, Miriam, 188
Gray-White, Deborah, 132
Great Britain. *See* Britain
Greenwich Mean Chronotope, 180
Grier, William, 132

hairstyles, 147–49, 252 n.14
Hamilton, Alexander, 54, 240 n.69
Hargreaves, Alec, 214
Harki writers, 215
Harlem Renaissance, 87, 177
Harper, Phil, 163
Headley, Victor: *Yardie*, 203, 208
Hegel, G. W. F., 9; on African exploitation, 86; on Aryans, 90; dialectics of,
  11, 29–30, 79, 137, 233–34 n.3; on Europeans, 94; on Germany, 184; influence
  of, 29; master/slave dialectic of, 80,
  142, 233–34 n.3, 233 n.6, 243 n.6; on
  the negation of the negation, 80; on
  the Negro as crazed, 147; on the Negro

as lacking logos, 18; on Orientals as unfree, 234 n.9; *Phenomenology of the Spirit*, 68–69, 119–20, 243 n.6; *Philosophy of Right*, 8, 72, 86; on reason as the Absolute, 10, 18, 151; on recognition, 142, 178; Senghor as influenced by, 246 n.41; on slavery, 233–34 n.3. See also *Philosophy of History*

Henderson, Mae Gwendolyn, 12, 141–42, 143, 146, 161

Hernton, Calvin, 132

Hesse, Barnor, 198

heteropatriarchal norms, 10–13, 229–31. See also *The Black Unicorn; Coal; The Unbelonging*

Hitler, Adolf, 30

Hodges, Carolyn, 192, 257 n.23

Hodges, Jo, 217; *The Girl with Brains in Her Feet*, 25, 199, 203–4, 206–8, 211–14, 224, 226

Hoffman, Leon-François, 45–46

Holquist, Michael, 12, 138, 180

Homans, Margaret, 179, 180

Horkheimer, Max, 34

How I Got Ovah (Rodgers), 144–61; Black church in, 144, 145, 159, 252 n.10; "Breakthrough," 181; "The Children of Their Sin," 155–58; conflict/violence in, 157–58; consciousness in, 157–58; critical reception of, 144; demonization of men in, 180–81; dialectical reading of, 144, 252–53 n.11; dialogic reading of, 144–45, 146–48, 150–51, 153, 155, 160–61, 253 n.16; "for muh' dear," 145–51, 155; hair in, 147–49; "how i got ovah II/It Is Deep II," 158–59, 178; "IT IS DEEP," 152, 153–55; "JESUS WAS CRUCIFIED," 151–54, 155, 253 n.19; "Living Water," 160–61, 178; "Masquerade," 160, 181; mother/daughter subjectivities in, 22, 23, 144–47, 149–50, 151–55, 158–60, 172, 177, 179–81; "Poem for Brother/for the Nation," 174–75; "Portrait," 153;

thesis/antithesis in, 22; title of, 150, 253 n.15; "U Name This One," 158; vernacular used in, 166; woman as landscape in, 147

"how i got ovah II/It Is Deep II" (Rodgers), 158–59, 178

Hügel-Marshall, Ika, 188, 217; *Daheim unterwegs*, 187, 190, 255 n.12, 258 n.34

humanism, 28–29

identity, and the nation, 28–29

ISD (Initiativer Schwarze Deutsche und Schwarze in Deutschland, or Black German and Blacks in Germany Initiative), 195–96

"IT IS DEEP" (Rodgers), 152, 153–55

Jamaica/Jamaicans, 209–10, 211, 258 n.47

Jamison, Angeline, 144, 152

Jefferson, Thomas, 9; on Black suffering/violence, 147, 156; and the Declaration of Independence, role in, 54–55, 57; dialectic of, 11; on expatriation of Blacks, 64, 242 n.93; on intermixture of whites and American Indians, 242 n.90; on language, 56–57; on law, 55, 241 n.71; slavery stance of, 31, 54, 55–57, 234 n.6, 241 n.78. See also *Notes on the State of Virginia*

"JESUS WAS CRUCIFIED" (Rodgers), 151–54, 155, 253 n.19

Johnson, Barbara, 136

Jordan, Winthrop, 56

Jules-Rosette, Bennetta, 215, 216, 217, 222

Karone, Yodi: *A la recherche du cannibale amour*, 217

Kay, Jackie: *Trumpet*, 231

Kesting, Robert W., 186

Kincaid, Jamaica: "Blackness," 1, 2

King, Naomi, 217; *O.P.P.*, 25, 199, 203, 204–9, 211–14, 226

Kuo, Erika Ngambi Ul, 186

Index | 275

Tocqueville, Alexis de, 238 n.52, 239 n.55
Todorov, Tzvetan, 238 n.52
"The Trollop Maiden" (Lorde), 176
Trumpet (Kay), 231

"U Name This One" (Rodgers), 158
The Unbelonging (Riley): on Black collective identity, 199–201; Black female
as Other in, 24–25, 199–202; on Blackness as gendered, 200; influence of,
199; on nationalism, 202–3; on Pan-
Africanist discourse, 200–201; on racism, 211; on white women and Black
men, 202
unified plurality, 192
United States. *See* America
universalism, 216
urban diaspora, 12–13, 183–227; in Britain,
197–214, 225, 226, 258 nn.37–38; in
France, 214–24, 225; in Germany (*see*
Afro-Germans); growth of, 227; and
idealist discourse vs. diasporic reality,
23; and metropolis/modernity, 224–27;
and national myths, 183–84, 255 n.1

Van Sertima, Ivan, 238 n.48, 246 n.42
veil/mask trope. *See* masking
Voltaire, Jean François Marie Arouet, 29,
241 n.73

Walker, David: *Appeal,* 27
Wallace, Michele, 125, 136, 199

Wallerstein, Immanuel: *Race, Class, and
Nation,* 7–8, 31–32
Washington, George, 240 n.69
Wheatley, Phillis, 56–57
whiteness, 183–84, 255 n.1, 255 nn.3–4
White Teeth (Smith), 231
Wiedenroth, Ellen, 188, 189
Williams, Robert R., 35, 39, 234–35 n.17
Windrush narrative/generation, 197–98,
258 n.38
"The Woman Thing" (Lorde), 164–65,
168–69, 171, 172
women: Black vs. white, 129–30; erasure
of, and chronotopes, 138–39; erasure
of, and masking, 124–31, 132; saving
nonwhite women from nonwhite
men, 251 n.19; sexual reproduction by,
172, 253–54 n.35; white women and
Black men, 127–30, 186. *See also* Black
mothers; gender
"The Women Can Dance with Swords in
Their Hands" (Lorde), 167
writing, 91, 246 n.42

"Das Yahr 1990" (Ayim), 224
Yardie (Headley), 203, 208
Young Hegelians, 81

*Zami: Towards a New Spelling of My
Name* (Lorde), 172
Zamir, Shamoon, 68–69, 81

Michelle M. Wright was born in Rome, Italy, the daughter of an African American diplomat and Polish-Czech American schoolteacher. She was raised there as well as in Holland, Belgium, and Morocco. She is an associate professor of African American and African diasporic literature and theory at Macalester College.

Library of Congress Cataloging-in-Publication Data
Wright, Michelle M.
Becoming Black : creating identity in the African diaspora /
Michelle M. Wright.
p. cm.
Includes bibliographical references and index.
ISBN 0-8223-3211-6 (cloth : alk. paper)
ISBN 0-8223-3288-4 (pbk. : alk. paper)
1. Blacks—Race identity. 2. Identity (Psychology)
3. African diaspora. I. Title.
HT1581.W69 2003   305.896—dc21   2003012318